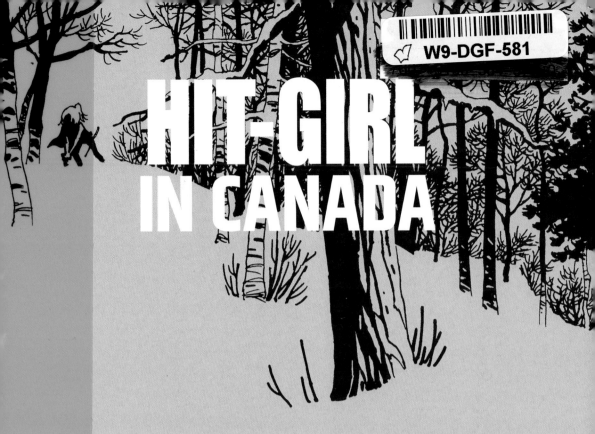

HIT-GIRL
IN CANADA

JEFF LEMIRE WRITER
EDUARDO RISSO ARTIST
PATRICIA MULVIHILL COLORIST
CLEM ROBINS LETTERER

MELINA MIKULIC DESIGN AND PRODUCTION
RACHAEL FULTON EDITOR

HIT-GIRL and **KICK-ASS** created by **MARK MILLAR** and **JOHN ROMITA JR.**

IMAGE COMICS, INC.

Robert Kirkman — Chief Operating Officer
Erik Larsen — Chief Financial Officer
Todd McFarlane — President
Marc Silvestri — Chief Executive Officer
Jim Valentino — Vice President

Eric Stephenson — Publisher / Chief Creative Officer
Corey Hart — Director of Sales
Jeff Boison — Director of Publishing Planning & Book Trade Sales
Chris Ross — Director of Digital Sales
Jeff Stang — Director of Specialty Sales
Kat Salazar — Director of PR & Marketing
Drew Gill — Art Director
Heather Doornink — Production Director
Nicole Lapalme — Controller

IMAGECOMICS.COM

W9-DGF-581

ONE

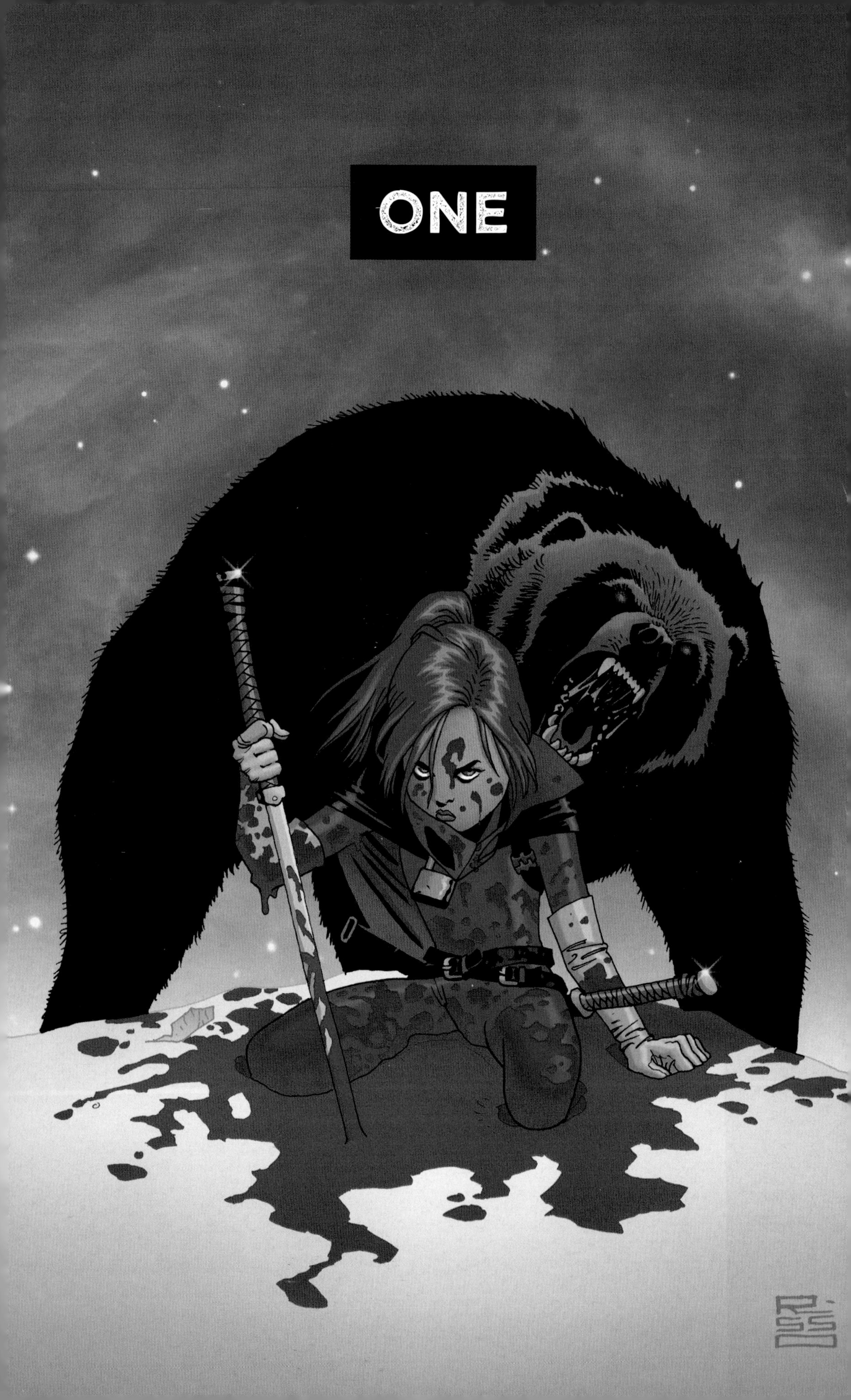

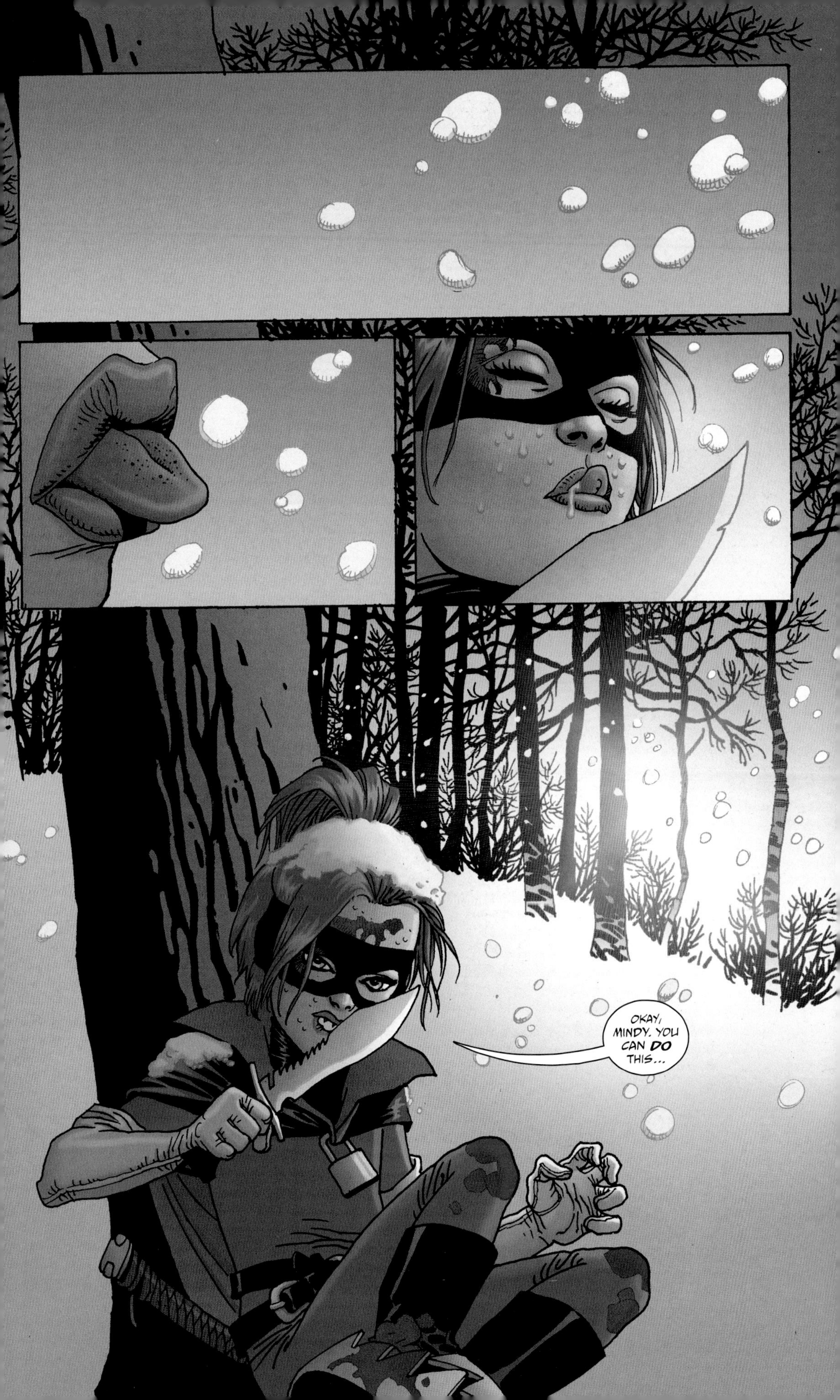
OKAY, MINDY. YOU CAN DO THIS...

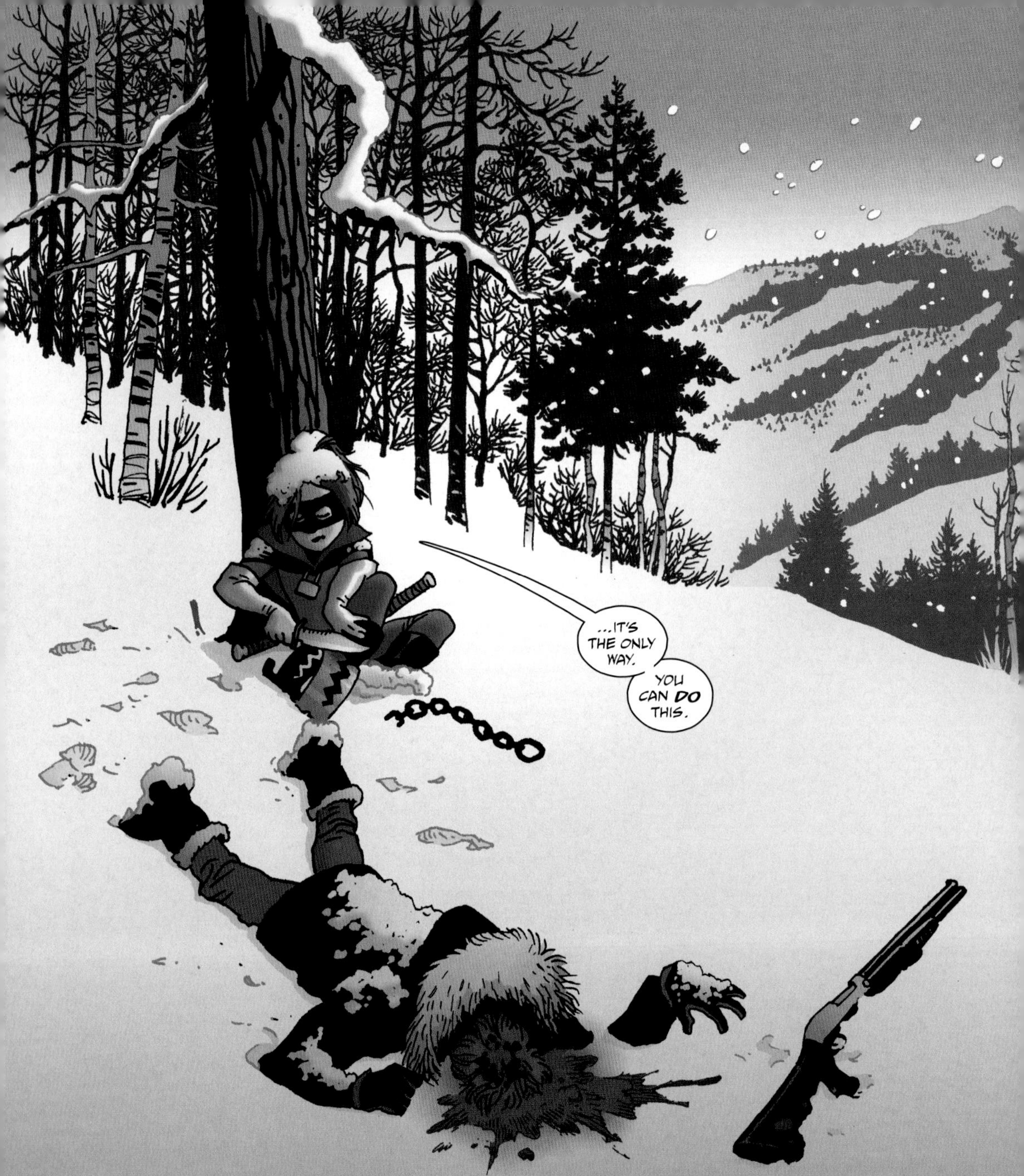
...IT'S THE ONLY WAY.
YOU CAN DO THIS.

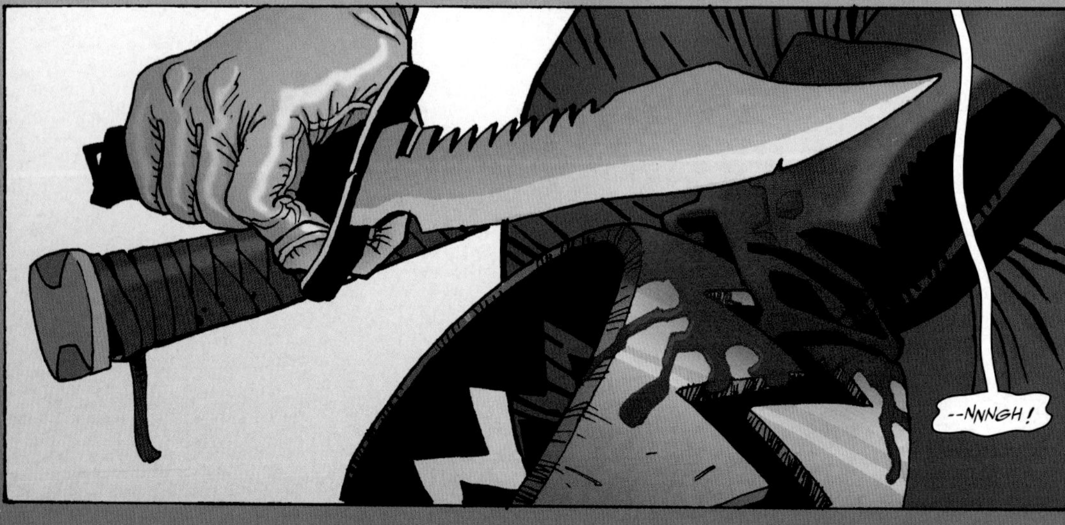
--NNNGH!

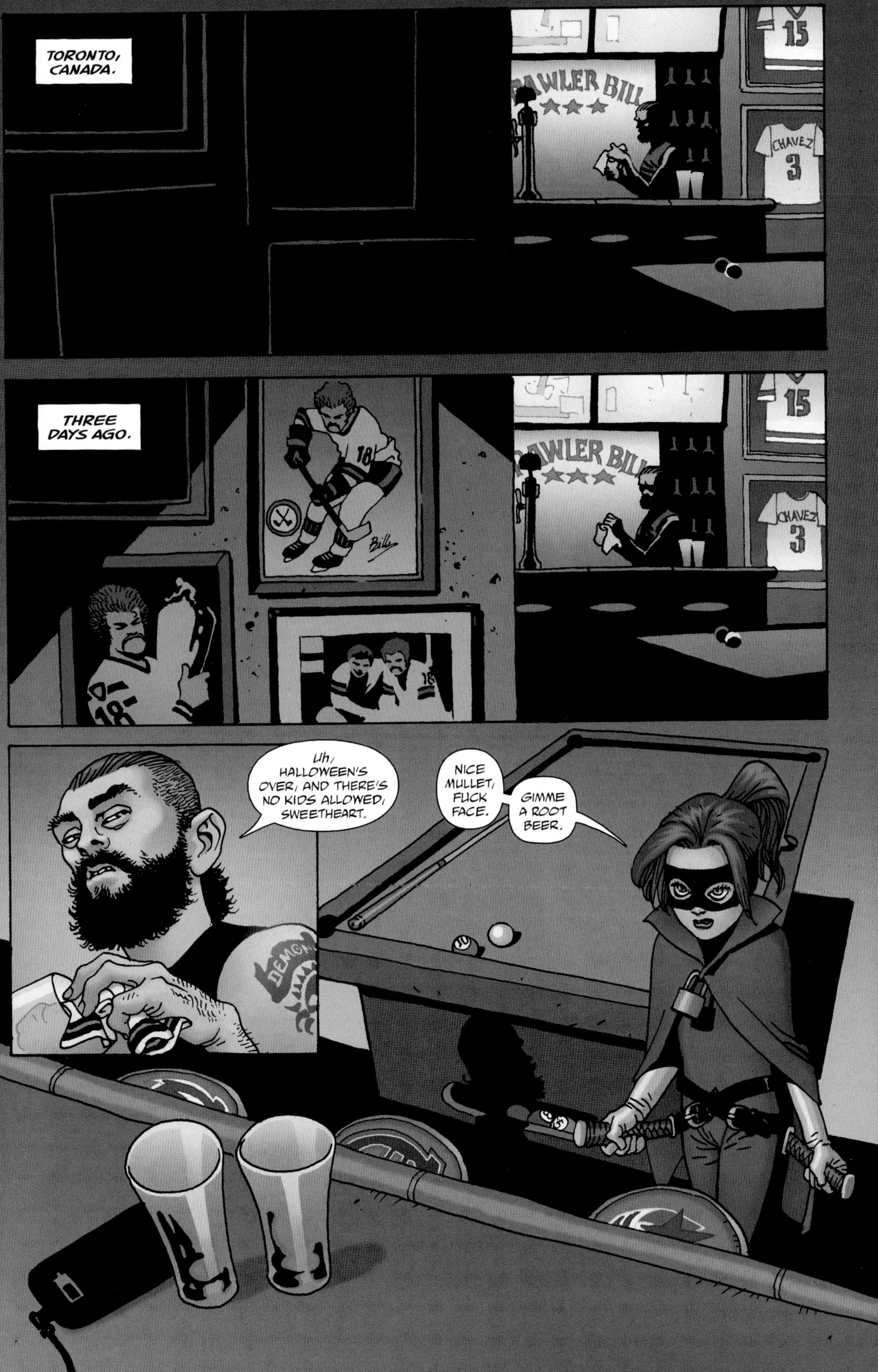
TORONTO, CANADA.
RAWLER BILL
15
CHAVEZ 3
THREE DAYS AGO.
18
Bill
UH, HALLOWEEN'S OVER, AND THERE'S NO KIDS ALLOWED, SWEETHEART.
NICE MULLET, FUCK FACE.
GIMME A ROOT BEER.

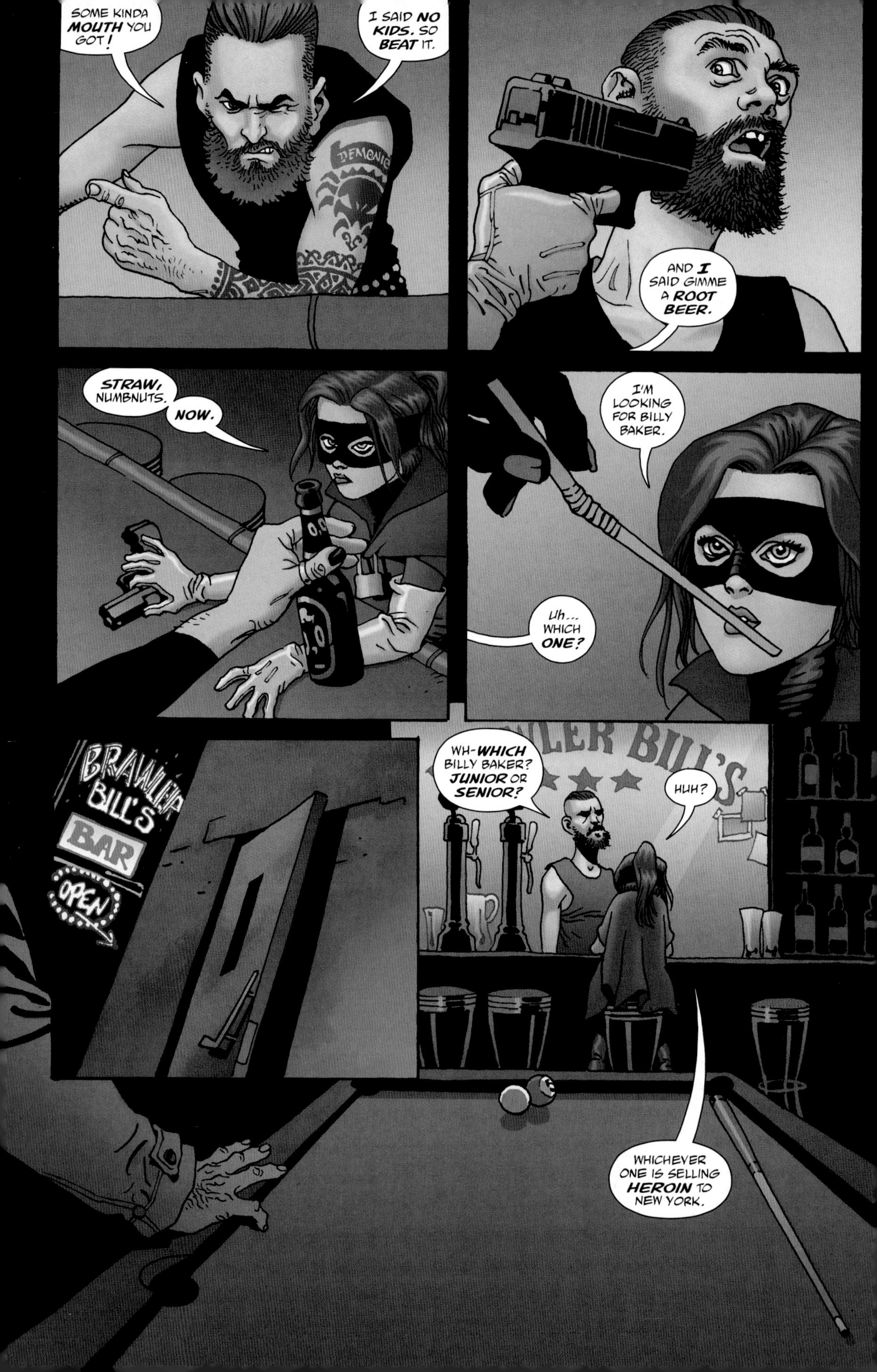

SOME KINDA MOUTH YOU GOT!
I SAID NO KIDS. SO BEAT IT.
AND I SAID GIMME A ROOT BEER.
STRAW, NUMBNUTS.
NOW.
I'M LOOKING FOR BILLY BAKER.
Uh... WHICH ONE?
BRAWLER BILL'S
BAR
OPEN
WH-WHICH BILLY BAKER? JUNIOR OR SENIOR?
HUH?
WHICHEVER ONE IS SELLING HEROIN TO NEW YORK.

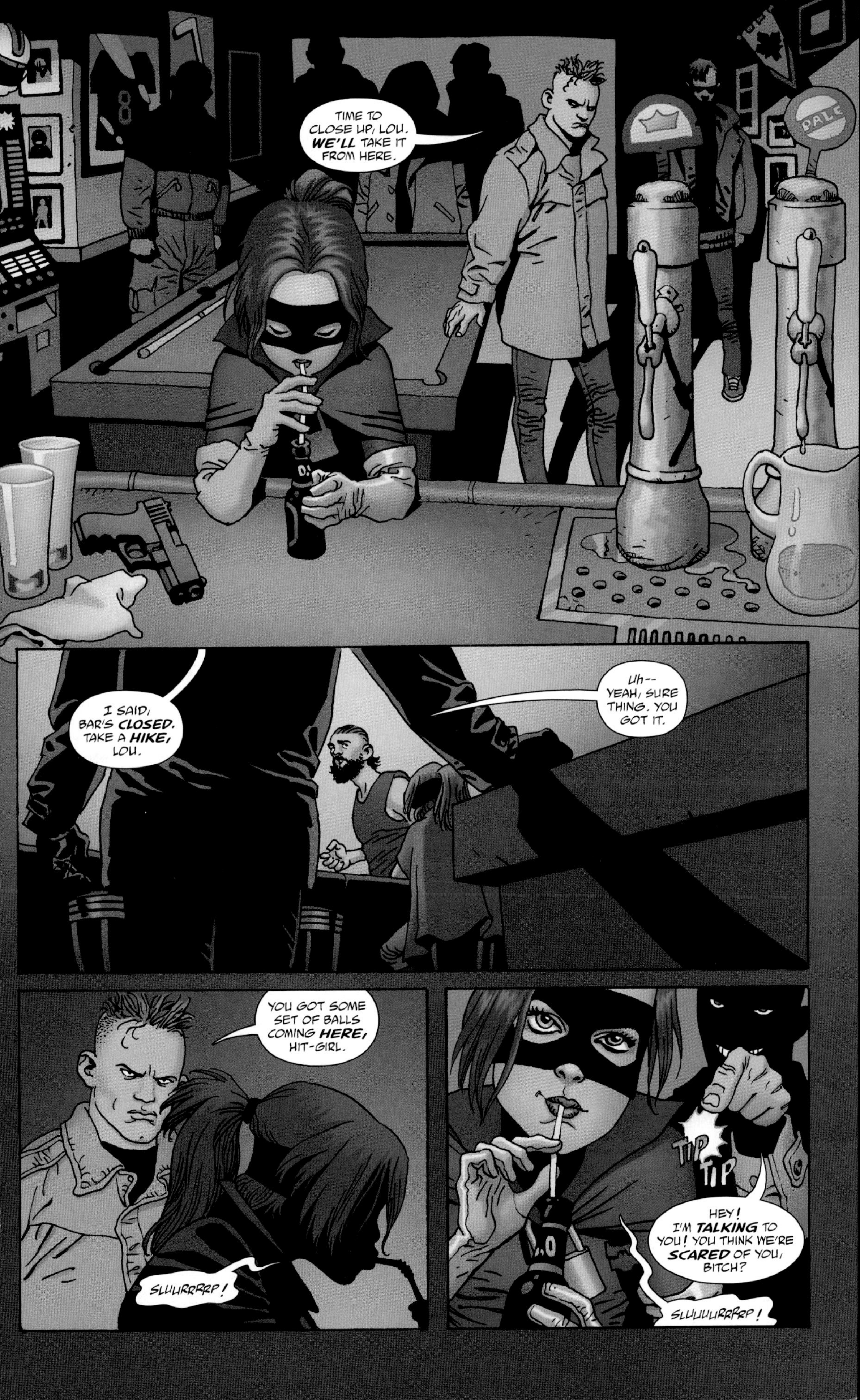
TIME TO CLOSE UP, LOU. WE'LL TAKE IT FROM HERE.
I SAID, BAR'S CLOSED. TAKE A HIKE, LOU.
UH-- YEAH, SURE THING. YOU GOT IT.
YOU GOT SOME SET OF BALLS COMING HERE, HIT-GIRL.
SLUURRRRP!
TIP
TIP
HEY! I'M TALKING TO YOU! YOU THINK WE'RE SCARED OF YOU, BITCH?
SLUUUURRRRP!

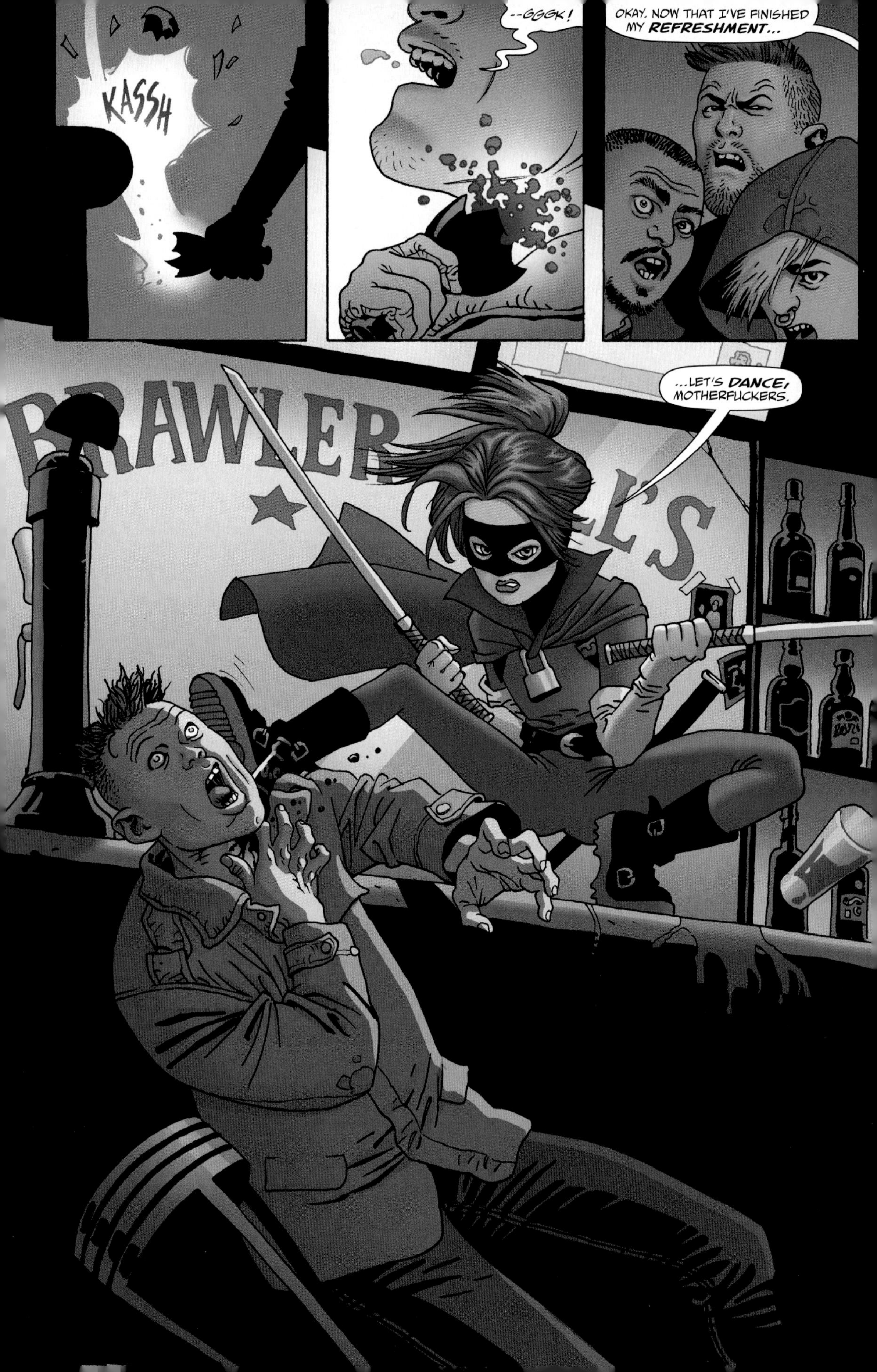
KASSH
--GGGK!
OKAY, NOW THAT I'VE FINISHED MY REFRESHMENT...
BRAWLER
...L'S
...LET'S DANCE, MOTHERFUCKERS.

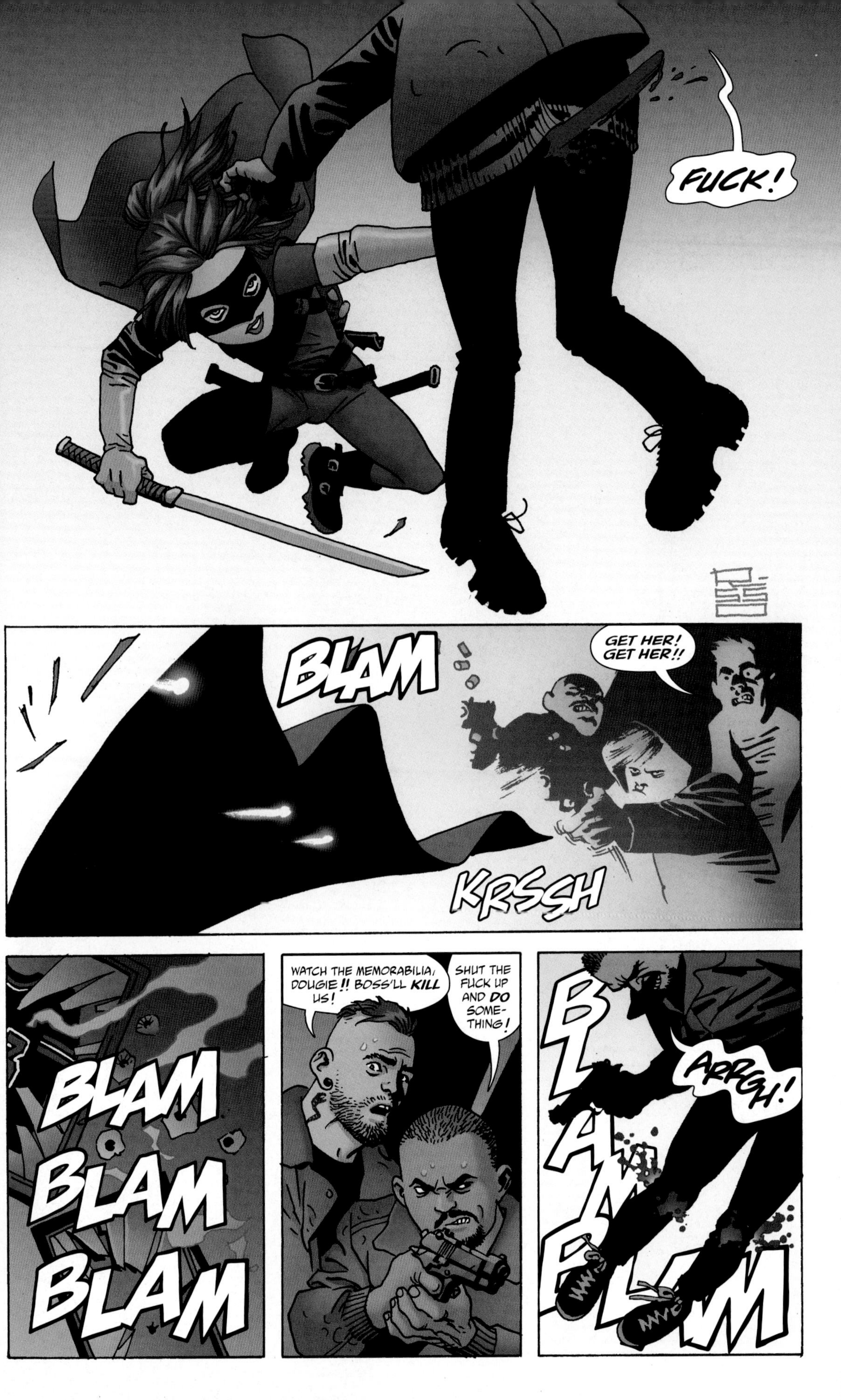
FUCK!
BLAM
GET HER! GET HER!!
KRSSH
BLAM
BLAM
BLAM
WATCH THE MEMORABILIA, DOUGIE!! BOSS'LL KILL US!
SHUT THE FUCK UP AND DO SOME-THING!
BLAM
ARRGH!
BLAM

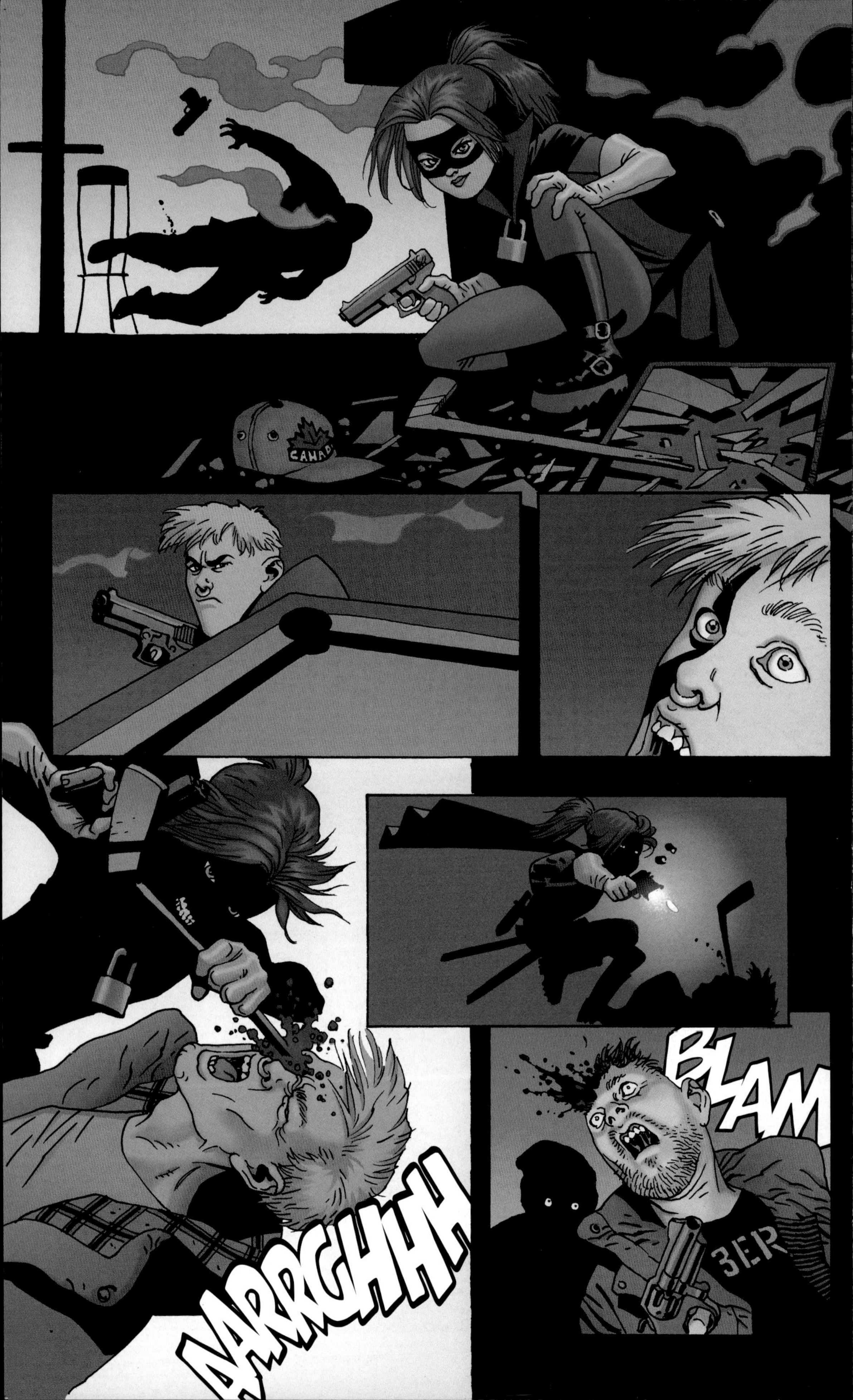

CANAD
AARRGHHH
BLAM
3ER

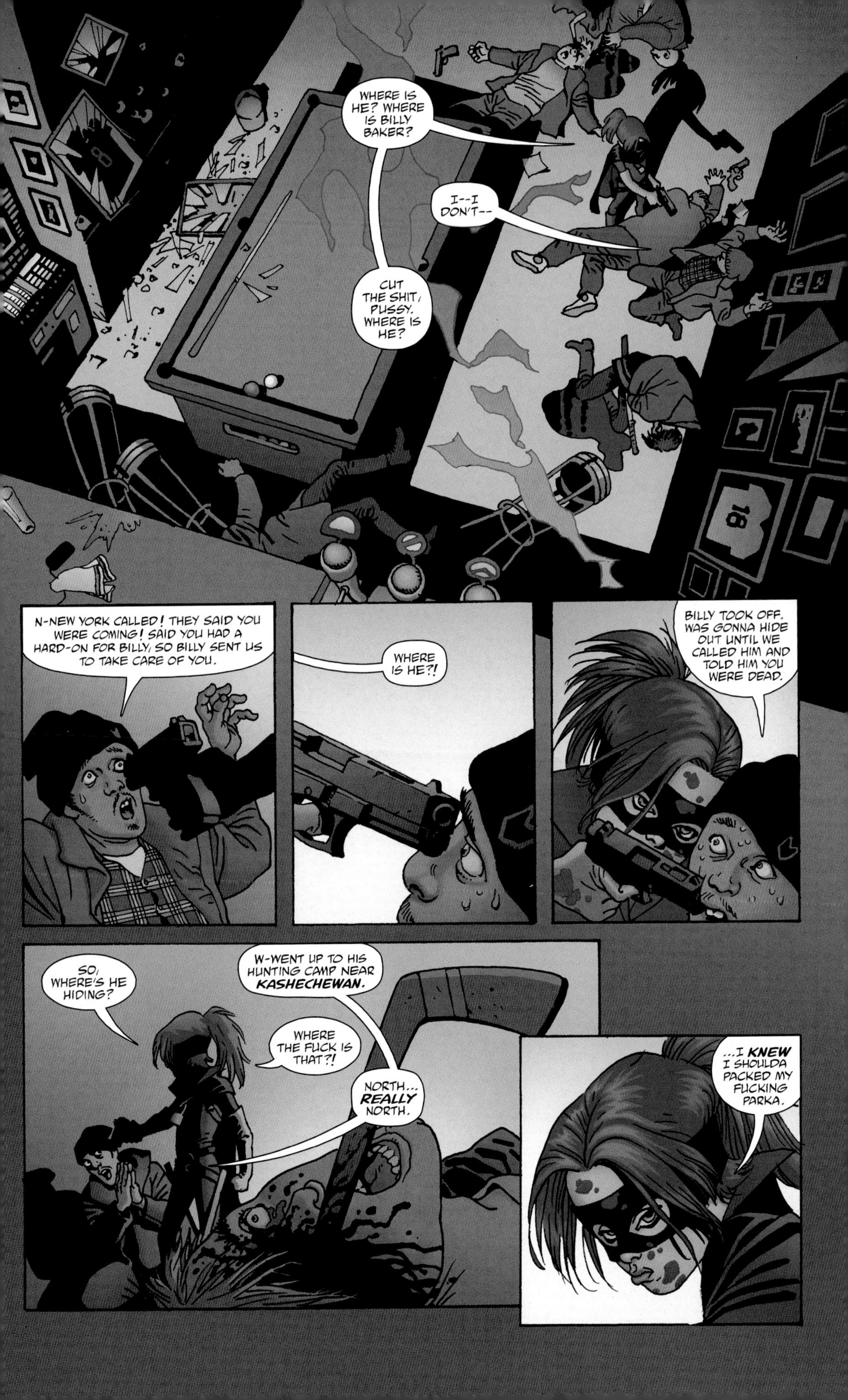
WHERE IS HE? WHERE IS BILLY BAKER?
I--I DON'T--
CUT THE SHIT, PUSSY. WHERE IS HE?
N-NEW YORK CALLED! THEY SAID YOU WERE COMING! SAID YOU HAD A HARD-ON FOR BILLY, SO BILLY SENT US TO TAKE CARE OF YOU.
WHERE IS HE?!
BILLY TOOK OFF. WAS GONNA HIDE OUT UNTIL WE CALLED HIM AND TOLD HIM YOU WERE DEAD.
SO, WHERE'S HE HIDING?
W-WENT UP TO HIS HUNTING CAMP NEAR **KASHECHEWAN.**
WHERE THE FUCK IS THAT?!
NORTH... **REALLY** NORTH.
...I **KNEW** I SHOULDA PACKED MY FUCKING PARKA.

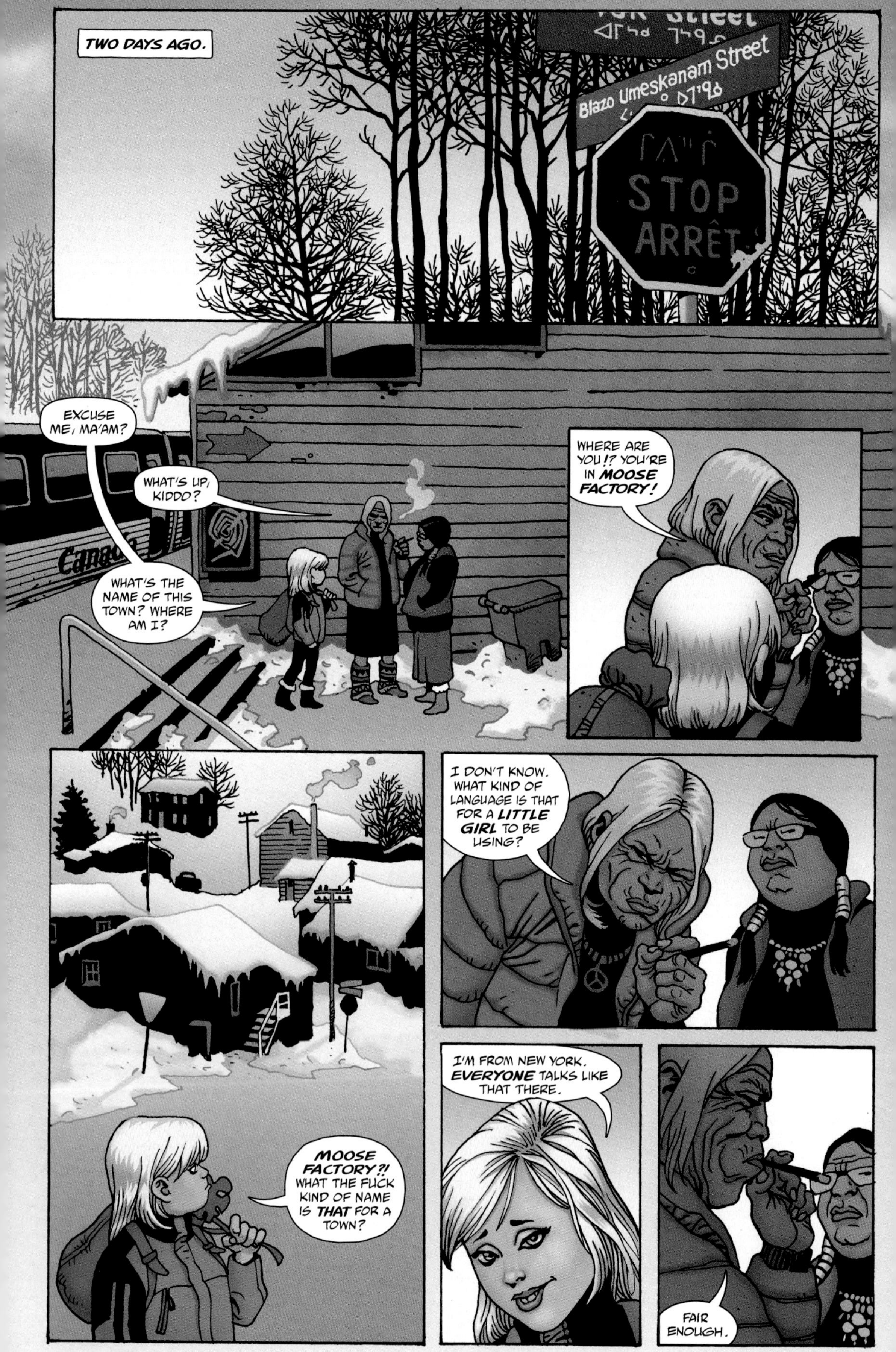
TWO DAYS AGO.
Blazo Umeskanam Street
STOP
ARRÊT
EXCUSE ME, MA'AM?
WHAT'S UP, KIDDO?
WHAT'S THE NAME OF THIS TOWN? WHERE AM I?
WHERE ARE YOU!? YOU'RE IN MOOSE FACTORY!
MOOSE FACTORY?! WHAT THE FUCK KIND OF NAME IS THAT FOR A TOWN?
I DON'T KNOW. WHAT KIND OF LANGUAGE IS THAT FOR A LITTLE GIRL TO BE USING?
I'M FROM NEW YORK. EVERYONE TALKS LIKE THAT THERE.
FAIR ENOUGH.

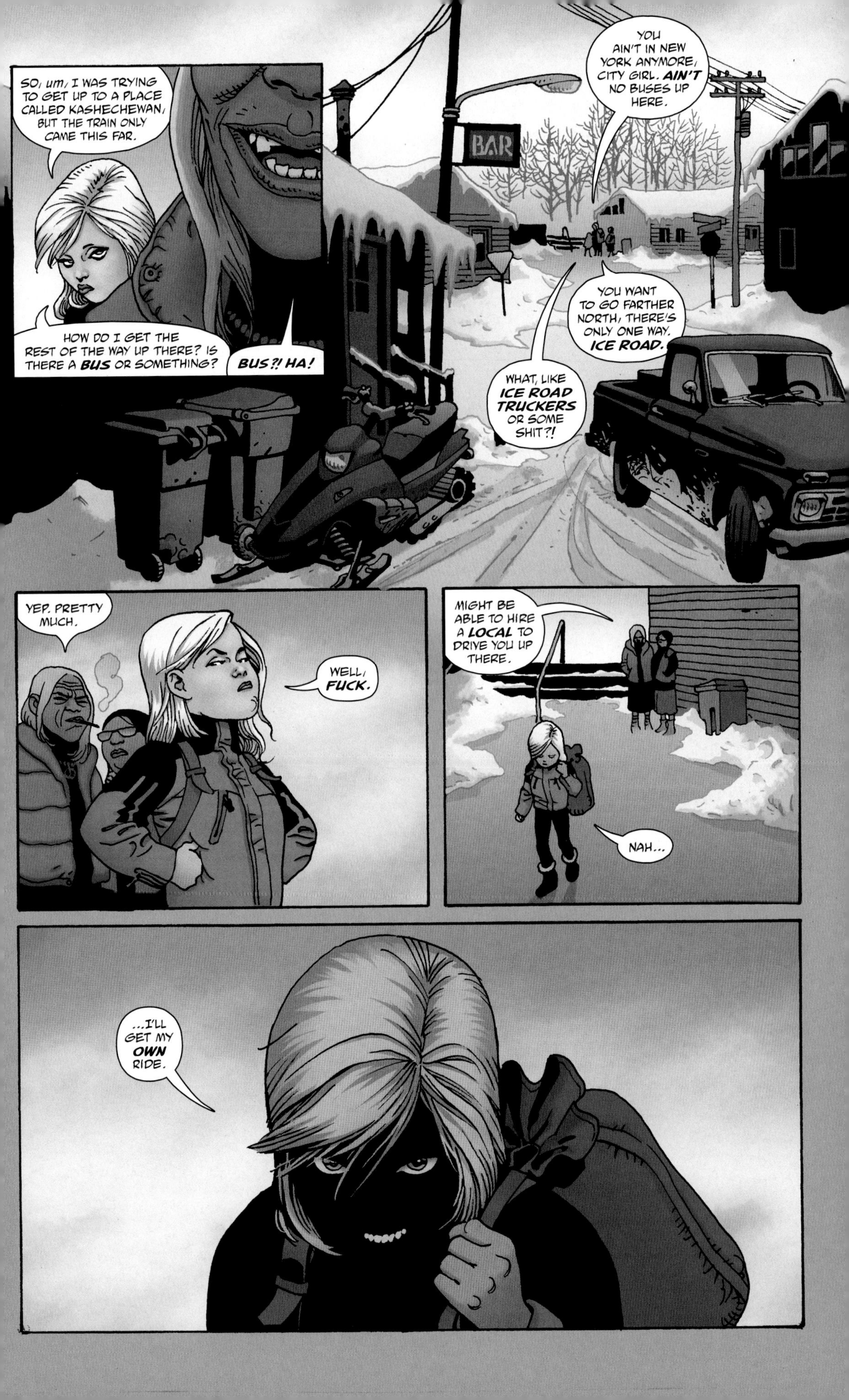

SO, um, I WAS TRYING TO GET UP TO A PLACE CALLED KASHECHEWAN, BUT THE TRAIN ONLY CAME THIS FAR.
HOW DO I GET THE REST OF THE WAY UP THERE? IS THERE A BUS OR SOMETHING?
BUS?! HA!
BAR
YOU AIN'T IN NEW YORK ANYMORE, CITY GIRL. AIN'T NO BUSES UP HERE.
YOU WANT TO GO FARTHER NORTH, THERE'S ONLY ONE WAY. ICE ROAD.
WHAT, LIKE ICE ROAD TRUCKERS OR SOME SHIT?!
YEP. PRETTY MUCH.
WELL, FUCK.
MIGHT BE ABLE TO HIRE A LOCAL TO DRIVE YOU UP THERE.
NAH...
...I'LL GET MY OWN RIDE.

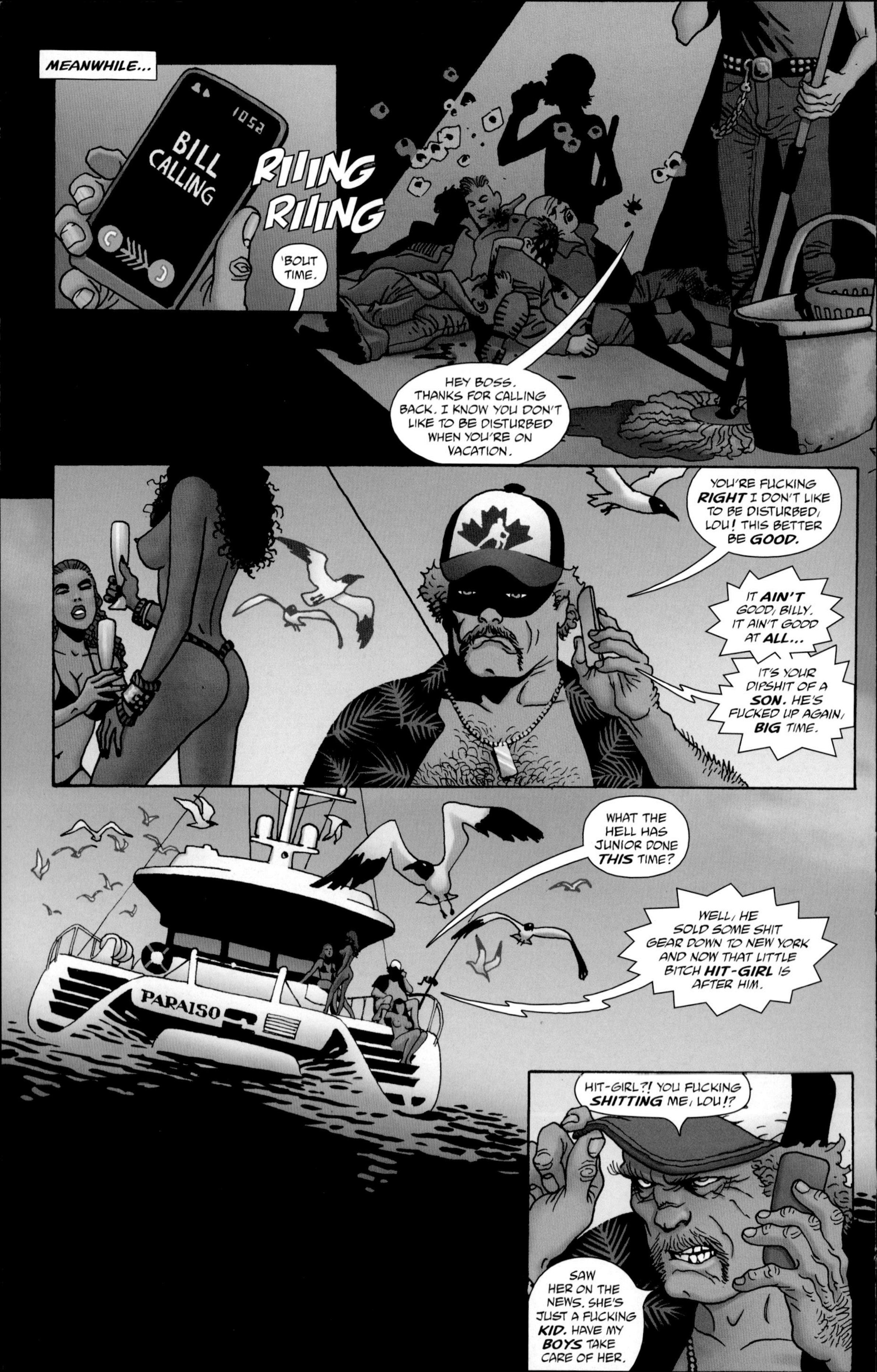
MEANWHILE...
1052
BILL CALLING
RIIING RIIING
'BOUT TIME.
HEY BOSS. THANKS FOR CALLING BACK. I KNOW YOU DON'T LIKE TO BE DISTURBED WHEN YOU'RE ON VACATION.
YOU'RE FUCKING RIGHT I DON'T LIKE TO BE DISTURBED, LOU! THIS BETTER BE GOOD.
IT AIN'T GOOD, BILLY. IT AIN'T GOOD AT ALL...
IT'S YOUR DIPSHIT OF A SON. HE'S FUCKED UP AGAIN, BIG TIME.
PARAISO
WHAT THE HELL HAS JUNIOR DONE THIS TIME?
WELL, HE SOLD SOME SHIT GEAR DOWN TO NEW YORK AND NOW THAT LITTLE BITCH HIT-GIRL IS AFTER HIM.
HIT-GIRL?! YOU FUCKING SHITTING ME, LOU!?
SAW HER ON THE NEWS. SHE'S JUST A FUCKING KID. HAVE MY BOYS TAKE CARE OF HER.

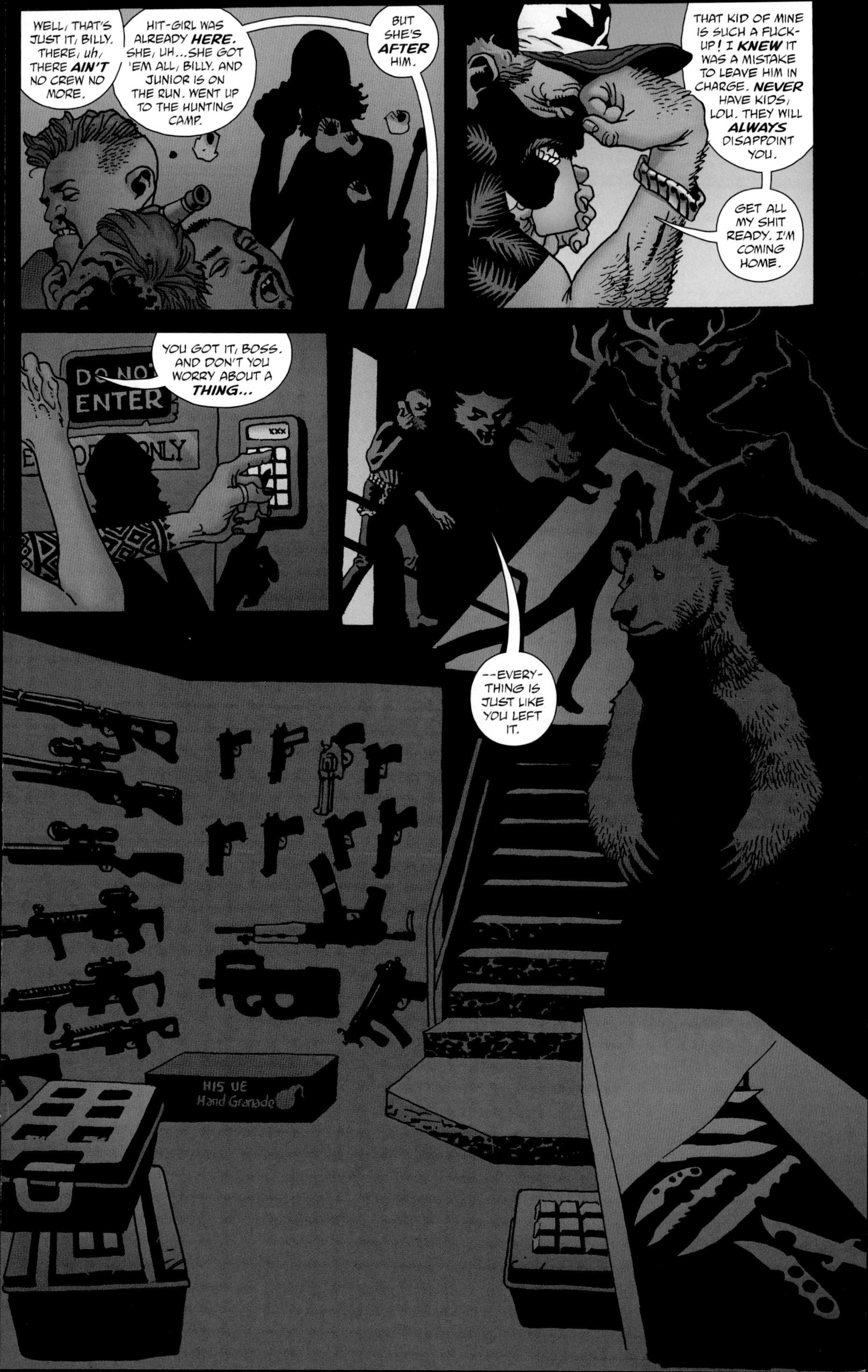
WELL, THAT'S JUST IT, BILLY. THERE, UH, THERE **AIN'T** NO CREW NO MORE.
HIT-GIRL WAS ALREADY **HERE.** SHE, UH...SHE GOT 'EM ALL, BILLY. AND JUNIOR IS ON THE RUN. WENT UP TO THE HUNTING CAMP.
BUT SHE'S **AFTER** HIM.
THAT KID OF MINE IS SUCH A FUCK-UP! I **KNEW** IT WAS A MISTAKE TO LEAVE HIM IN CHARGE. **NEVER** HAVE KIDS, LOU. THEY WILL **ALWAYS** DISAPPOINT YOU.
GET ALL MY SHIT READY. I'M COMING HOME.
YOU GOT IT, BOSS. AND DON'T YOU WORRY ABOUT A **THING...**
DO NOT ENTER
--EVERY-THING IS JUST LIKE YOU LEFT IT.
Hand Granade

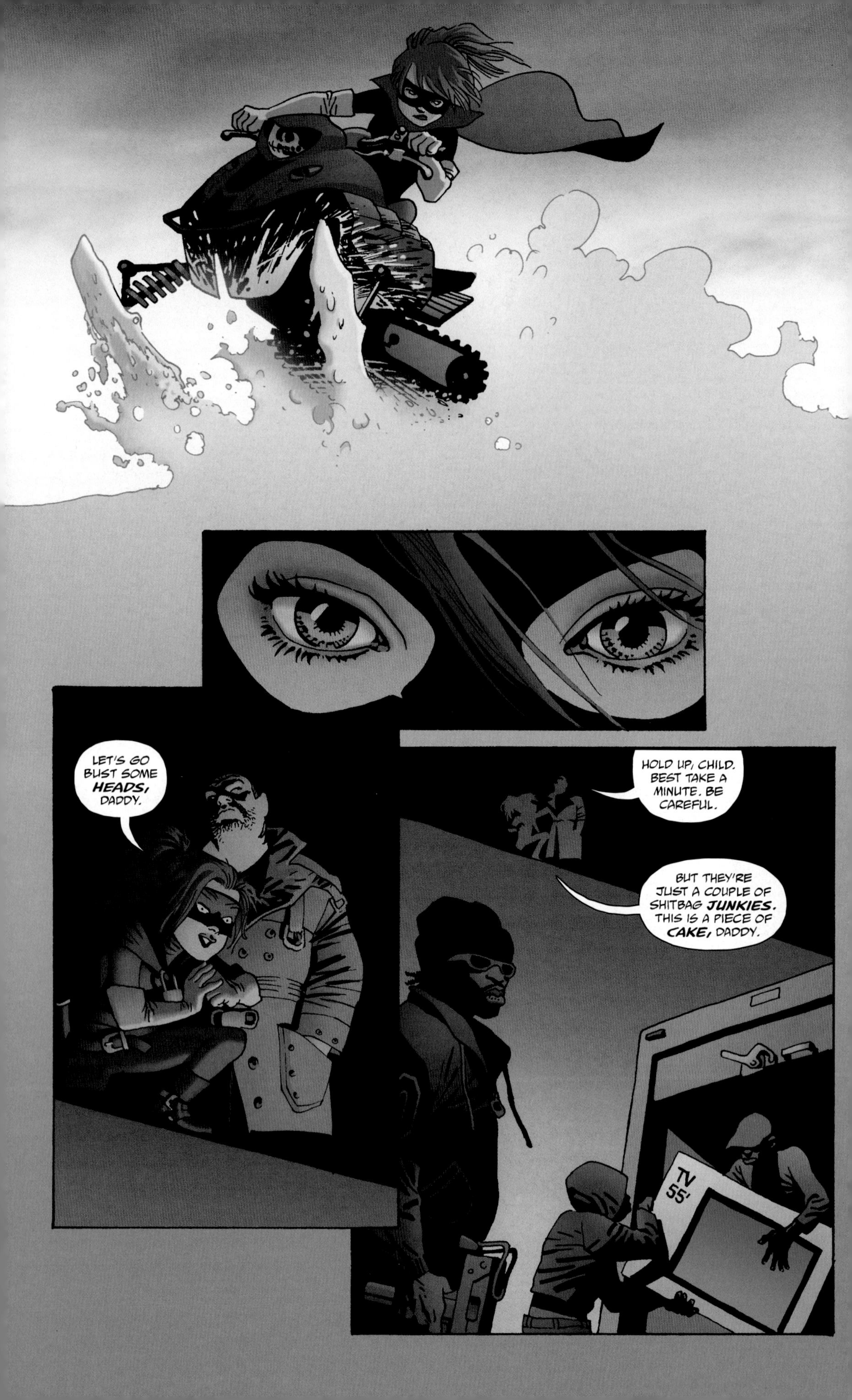

LET'S GO BUST SOME **HEADS,** DADDY.
HOLD UP, CHILD. BEST TAKE A MINUTE. BE CAREFUL.
BUT THEY'RE JUST A COUPLE OF SHITBAG **JUNKIES.** THIS IS A PIECE OF **CAKE,** DADDY.
TV 55'

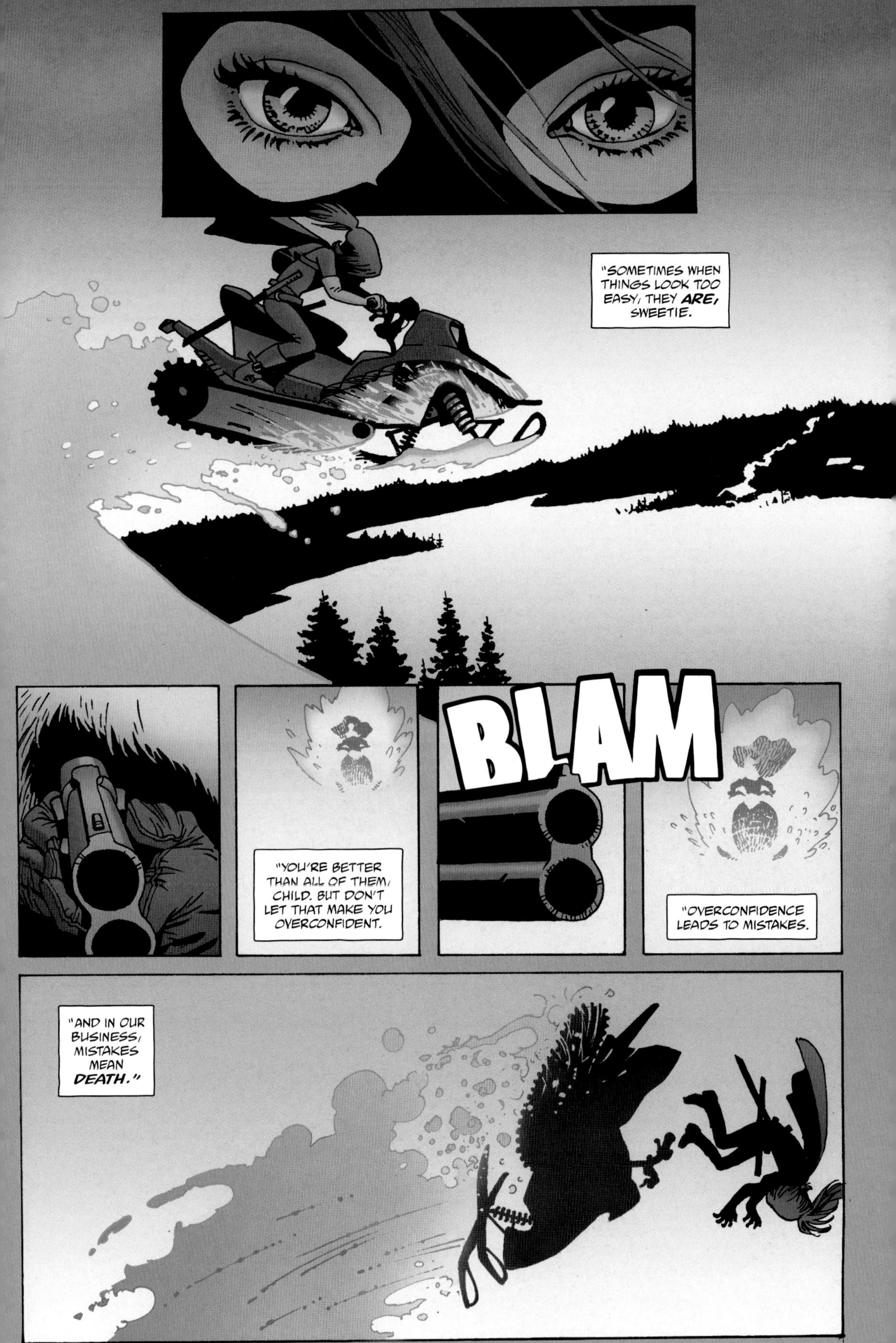

"SOMETIMES WHEN THINGS LOOK TOO EASY, THEY **ARE**, SWEETIE.
"YOU'RE BETTER THAN ALL OF THEM, CHILD. BUT DON'T LET THAT MAKE YOU OVERCONFIDENT.
BLAM
"OVERCONFIDENCE LEADS TO MISTAKES.
"AND IN OUR BUSINESS, MISTAKES MEAN **DEATH**."

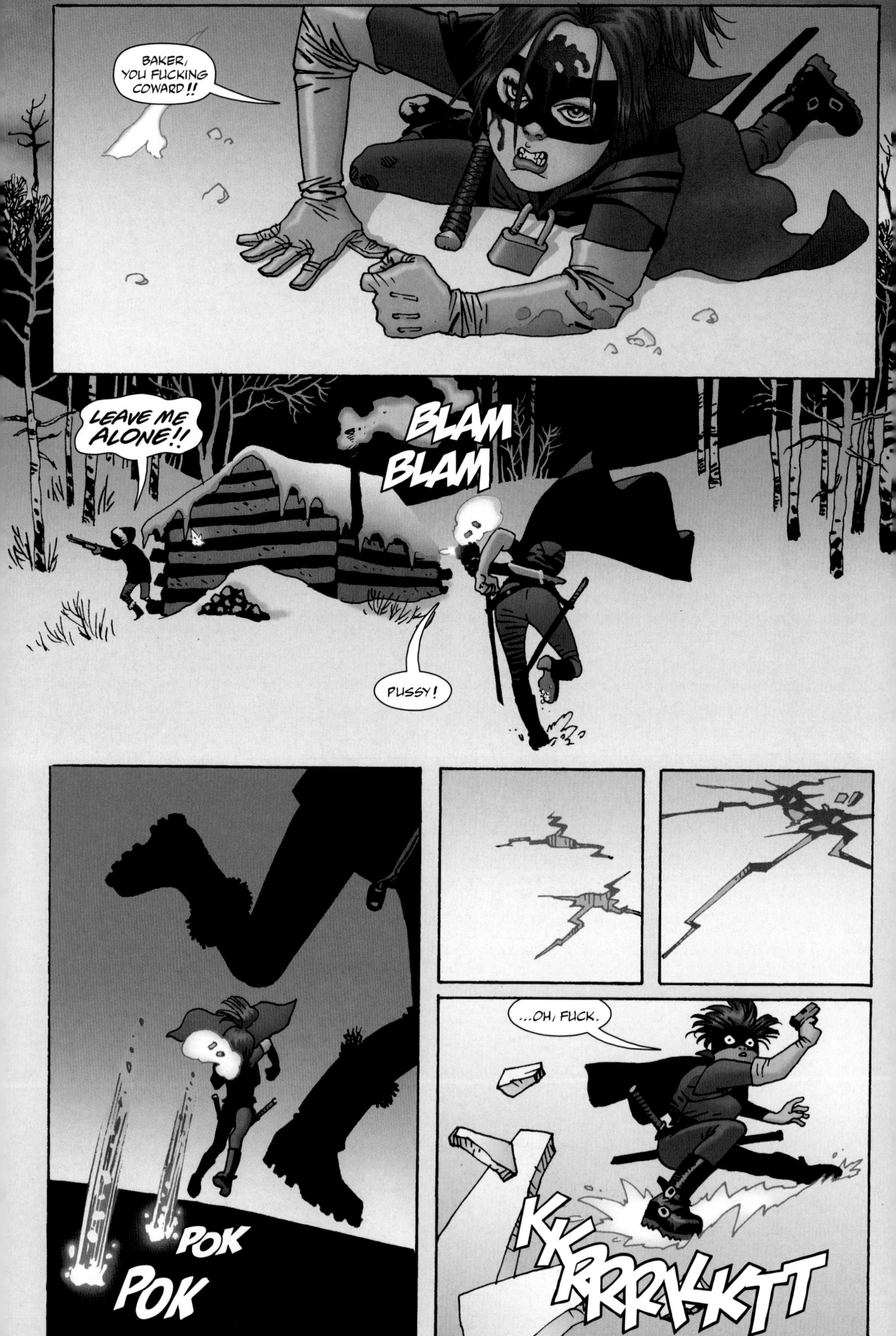
BAKER, YOU FUCKING COWARD!!
LEAVE ME ALONE!!
BLAM
BLAM
PUSSY!
POK
POK
...OH, FUCK.
KKRRRKKTT

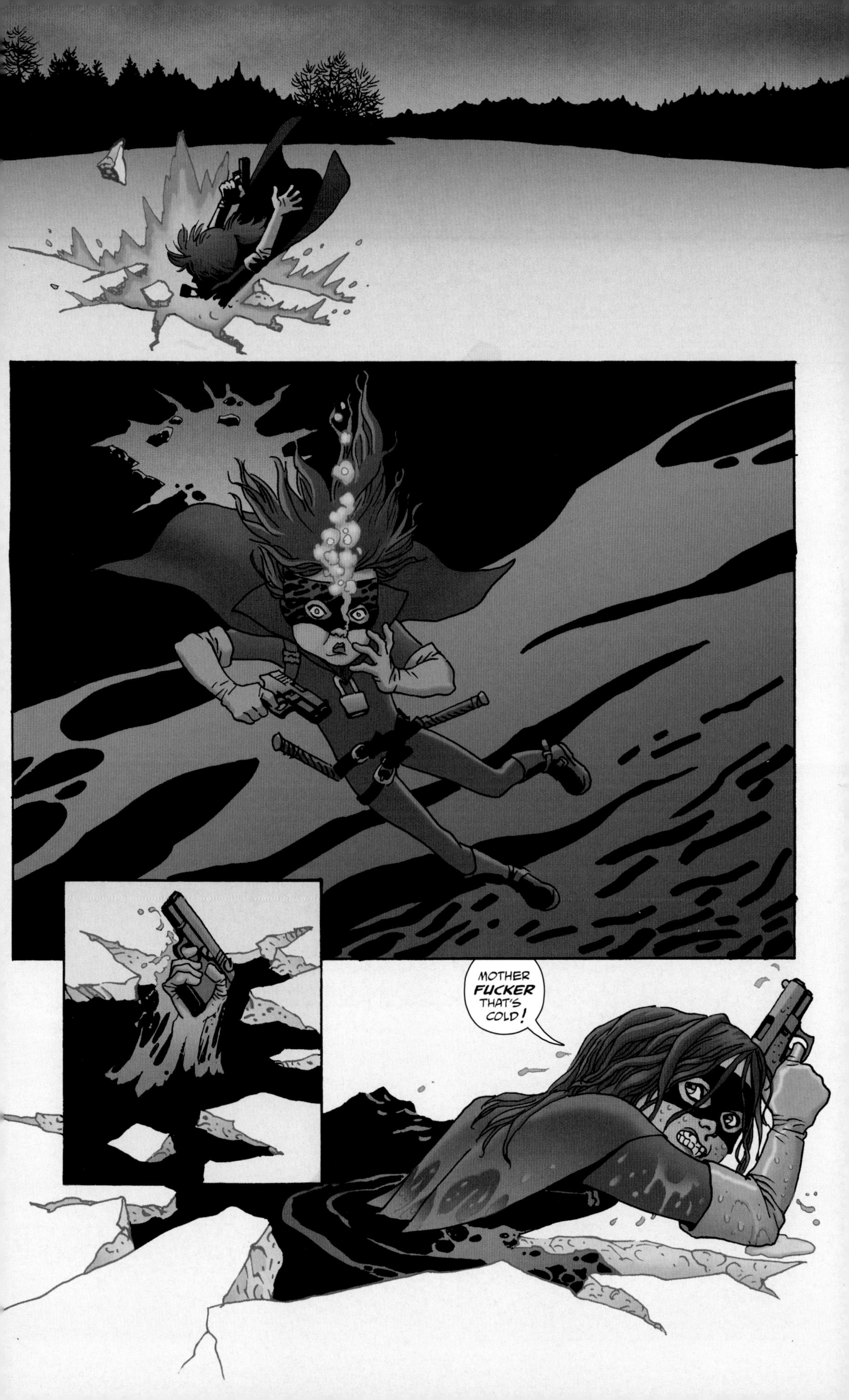
MOTHER FUCKER THAT'S COLD!

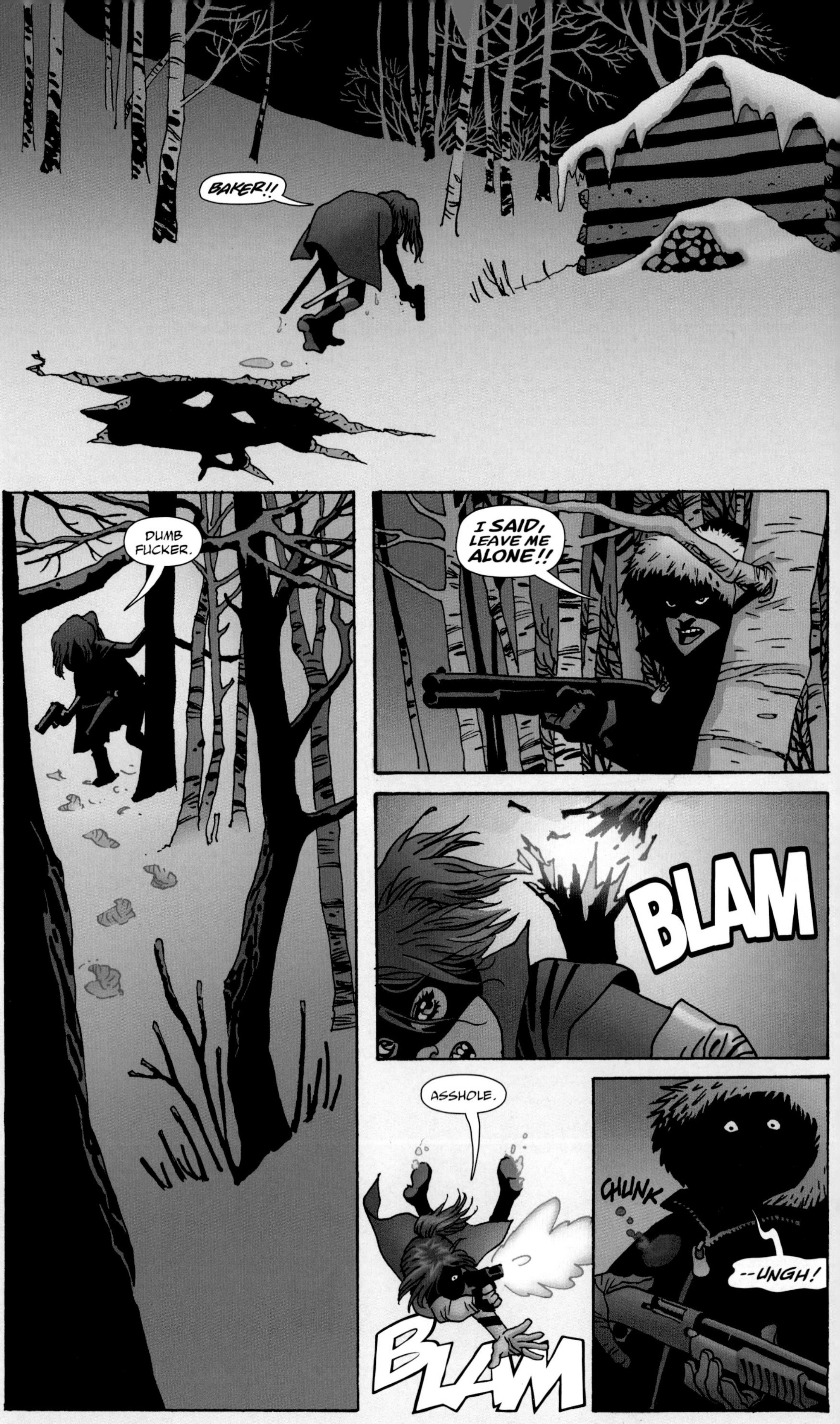
BAKER!!
DUMB FUCKER.
I SAID, LEAVE ME ALONE!!
BLAM
ASSHOLE.
BLAM
CHUNK
--UNGH!

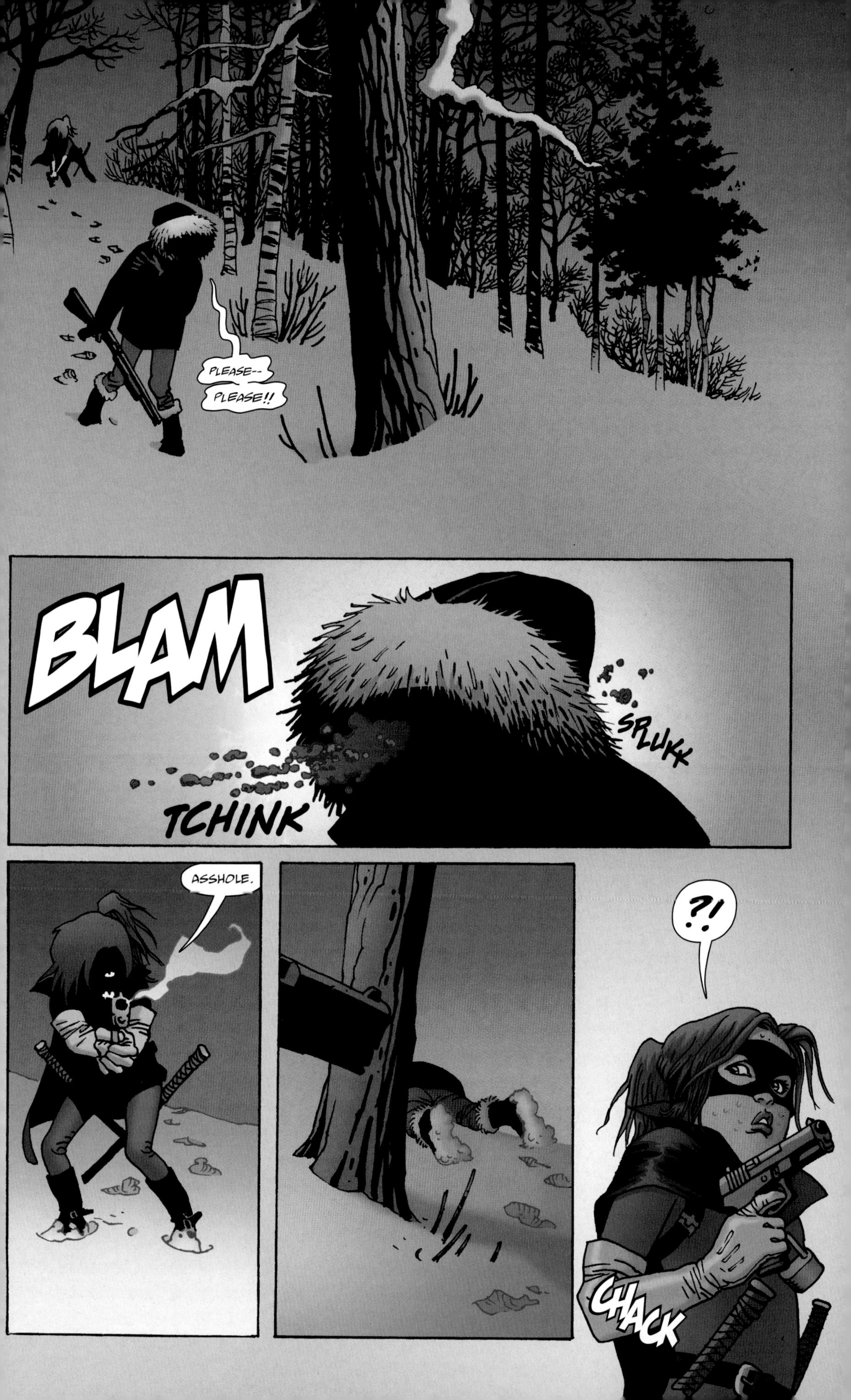

PLEASE--
PLEASE!!
BLAM
SPLUKK
TCHINK
ASSHOLE.
?!
CHACK

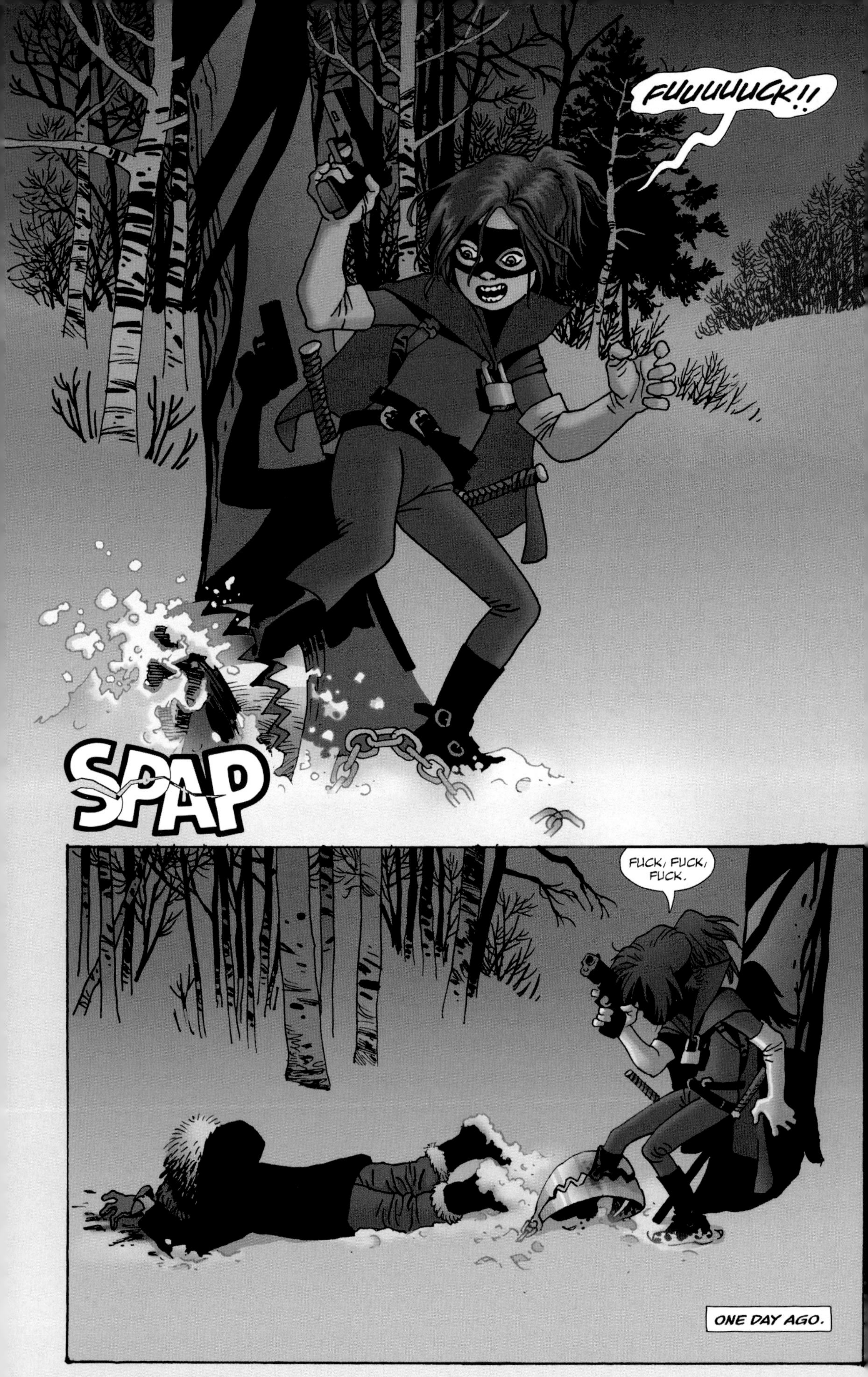
FUUUUUCK!!
SPAP
FUCK, FUCK, FUCK.
ONE DAY AGO.

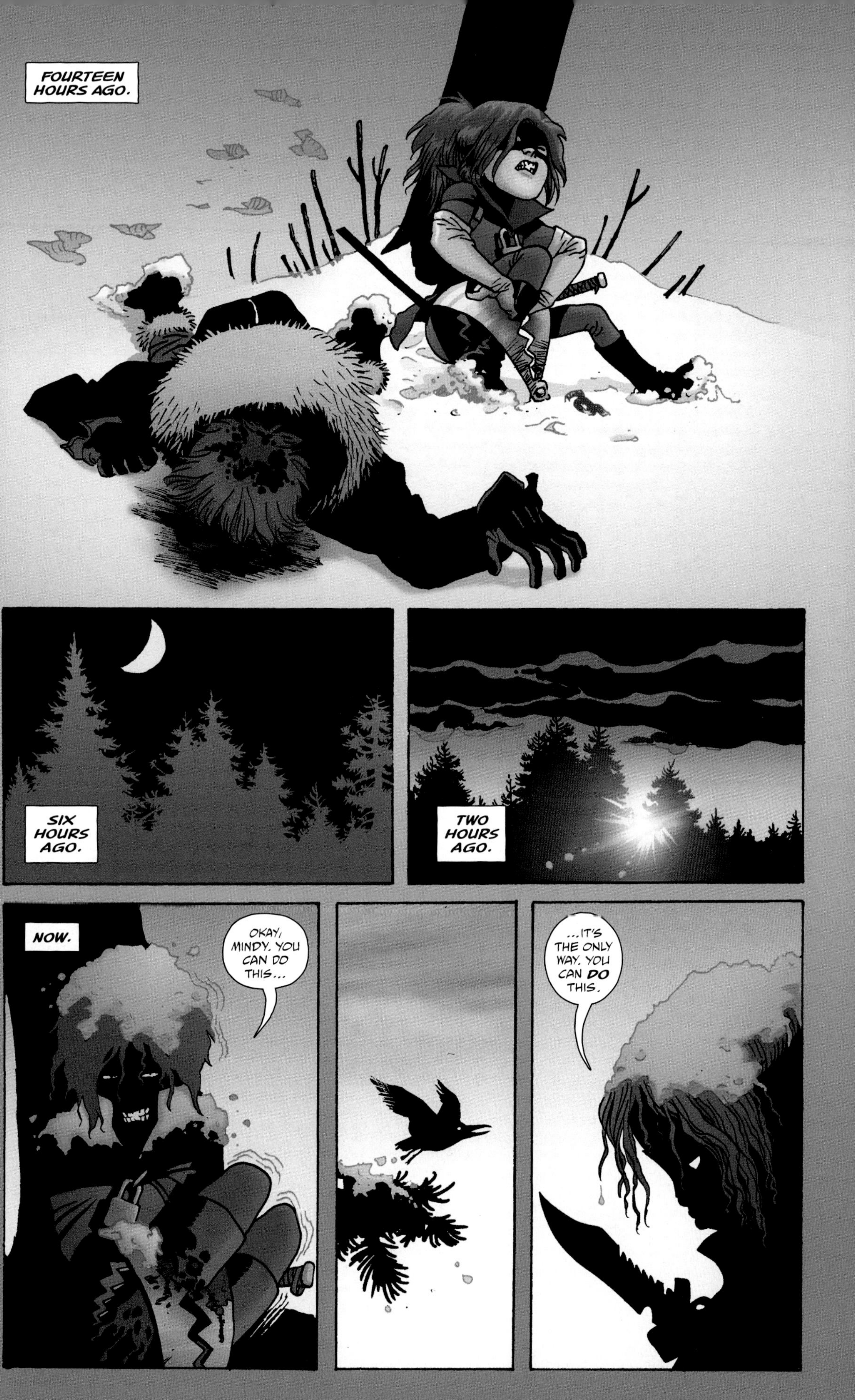
FOURTEEN HOURS AGO.
SIX HOURS AGO.
TWO HOURS AGO.
NOW.
OKAY, MINDY. YOU CAN DO THIS...
...IT'S THE ONLY WAY. YOU CAN DO THIS.

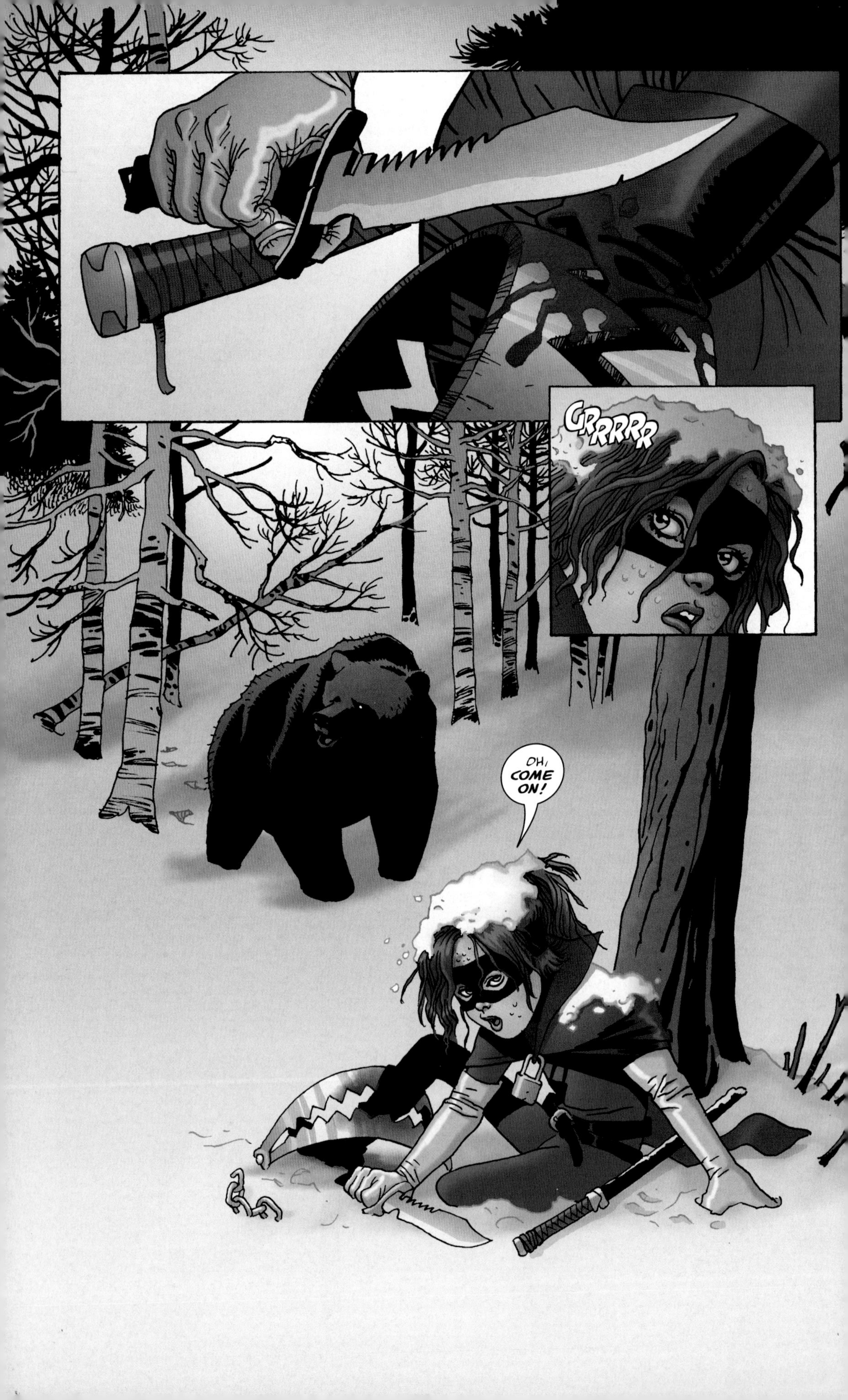
GRRRRR
OH, COME ON!

TWO

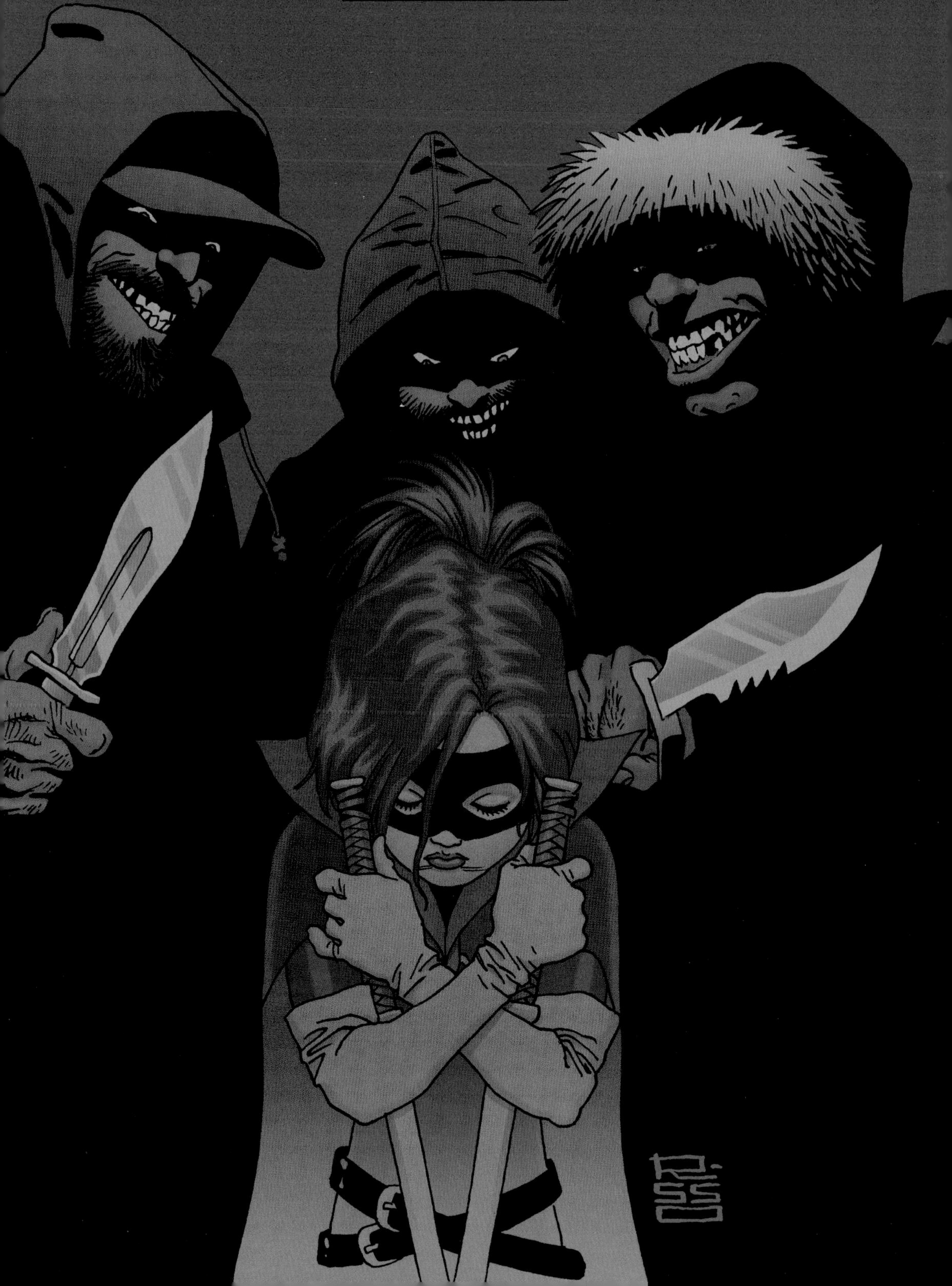

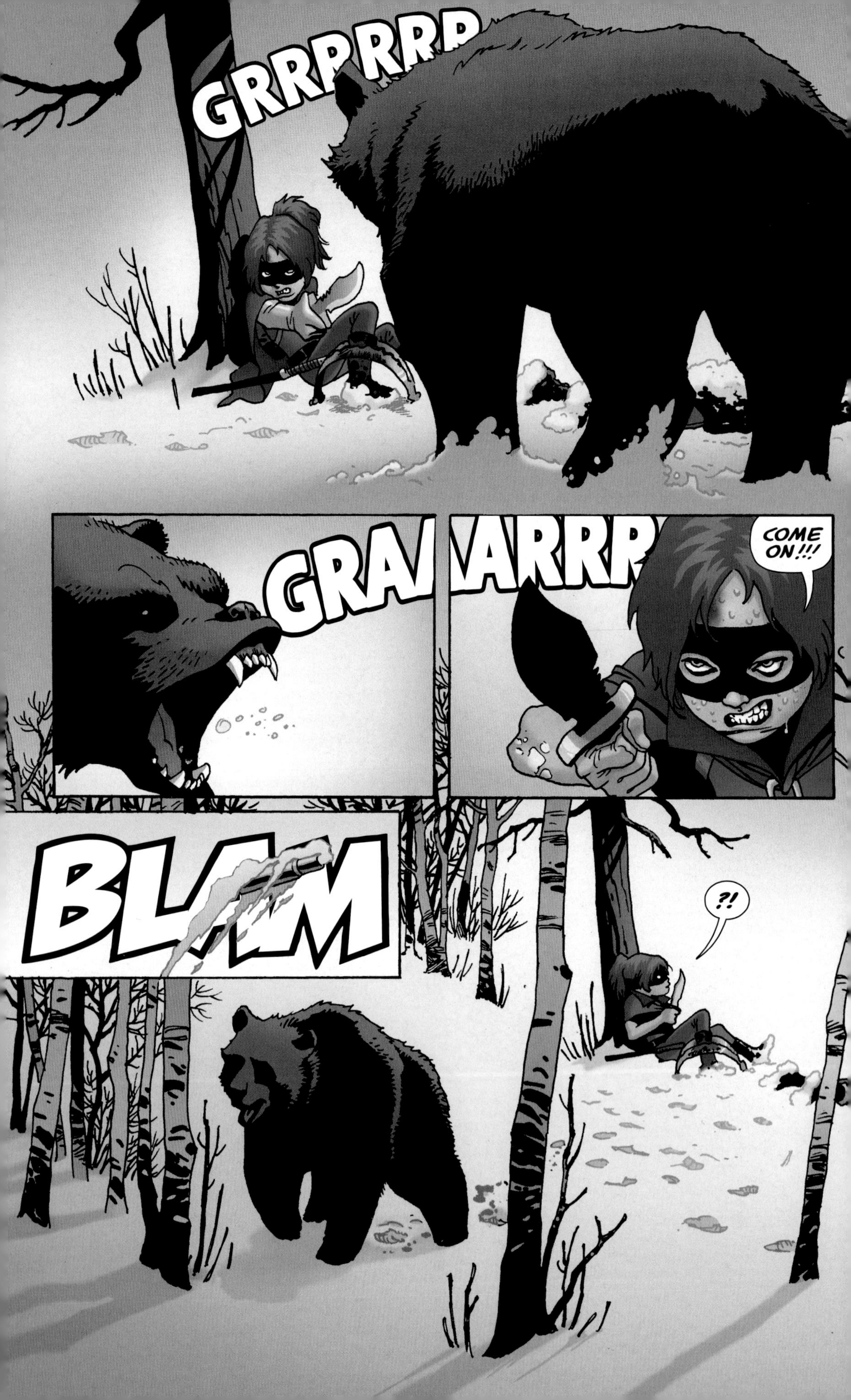
GRRRRRR
GRAAARRR
COME ON!!!
BLAM
?!

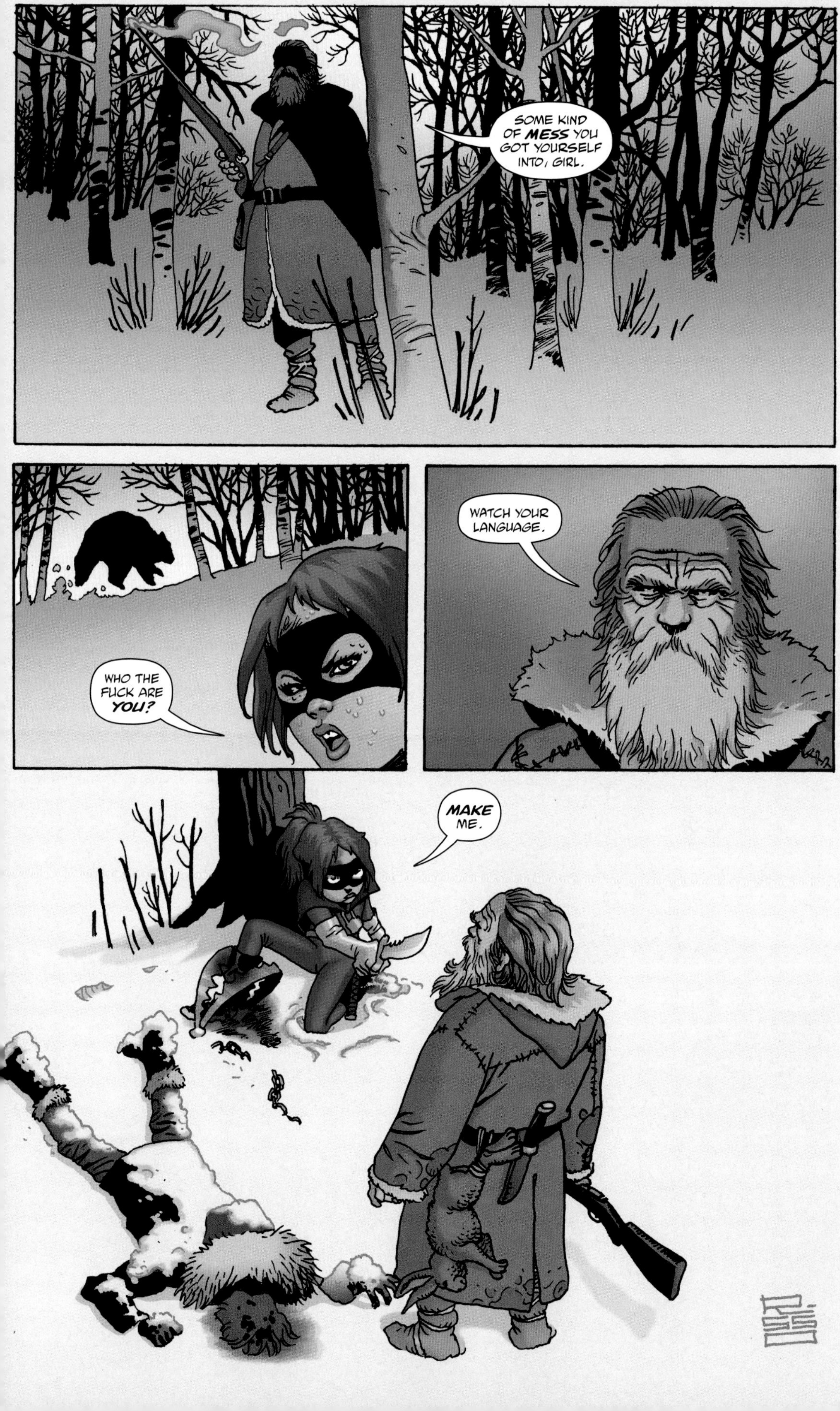
SOME KIND OF MESS YOU GOT YOURSELF INTO, GIRL.
WHO THE FUCK ARE YOU?
WATCH YOUR LANGUAGE.
MAKE ME.

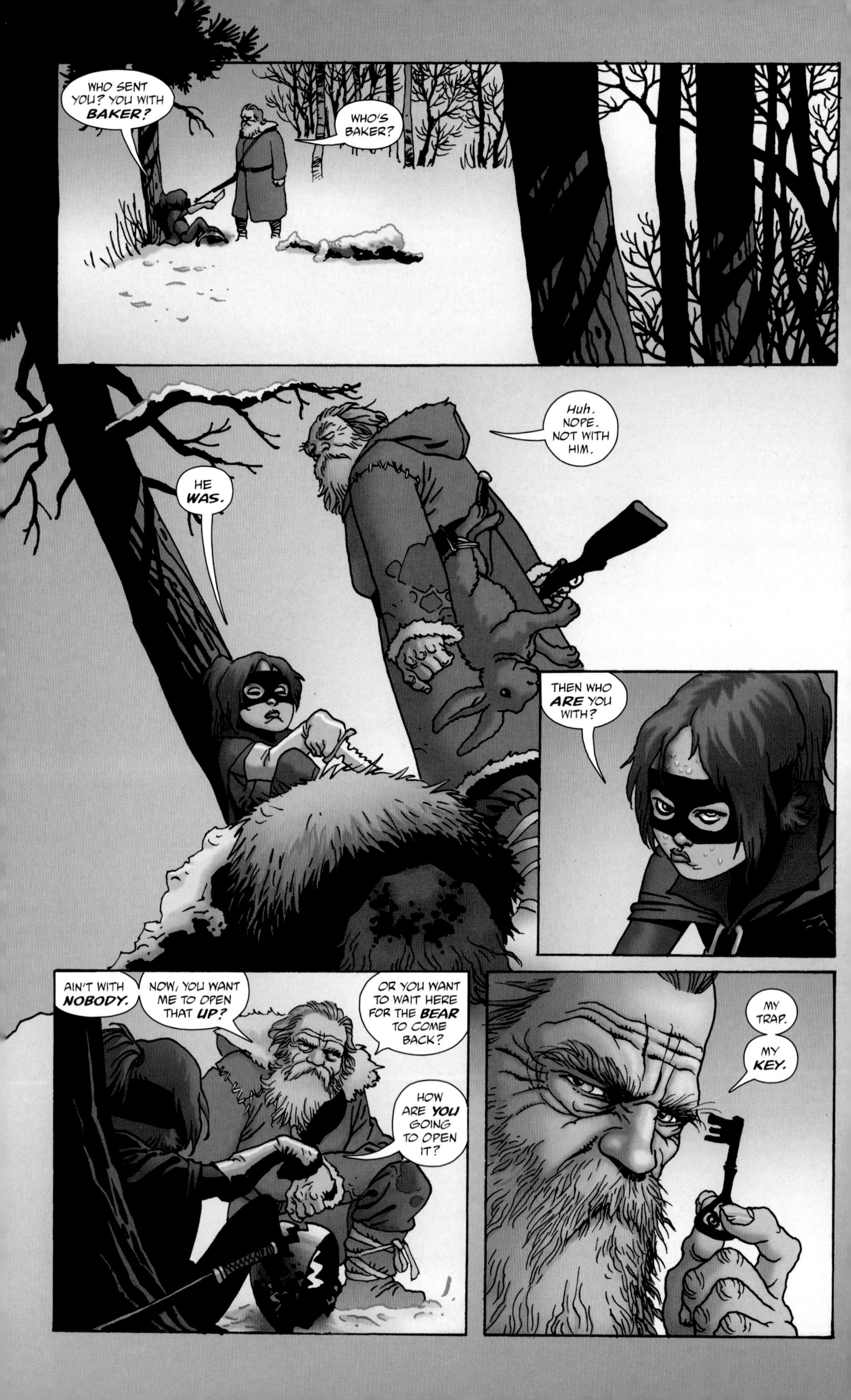
WHO SENT YOU? YOU WITH BAKER?
WHO'S BAKER?
Huh. NOPE. NOT WITH HIM.
HE WAS.
THEN WHO ARE YOU WITH?
AIN'T WITH NOBODY.
NOW, YOU WANT ME TO OPEN THAT UP?
OR YOU WANT TO WAIT HERE FOR THE BEAR TO COME BACK?
HOW ARE YOU GOING TO OPEN IT?
MY TRAP.
MY KEY.

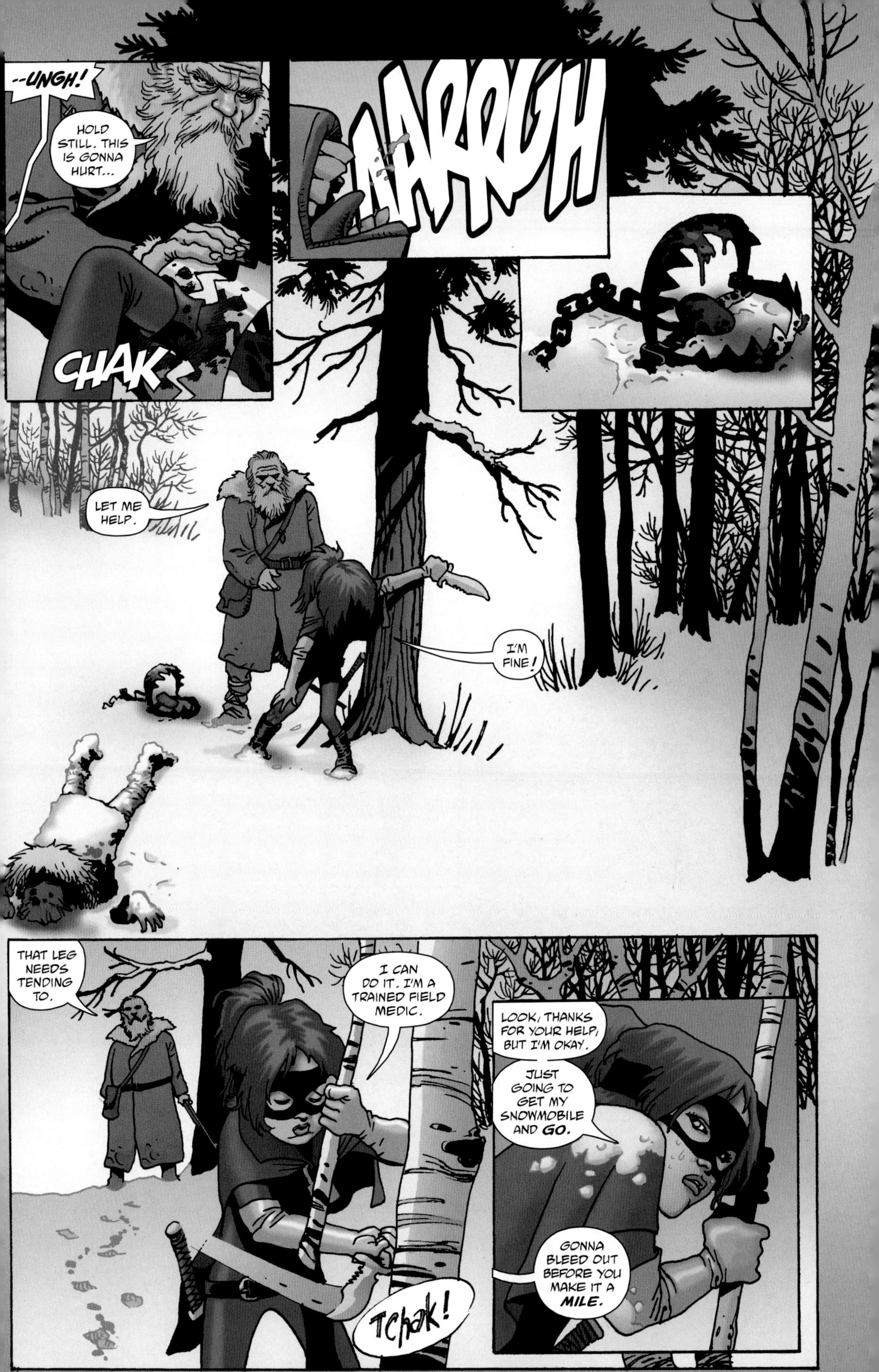
--UNGH!
HOLD STILL. THIS IS GONNA HURT...
CHAK
AARRGH
LET ME HELP.
I'M FINE!
THAT LEG NEEDS TENDING TO.
I CAN DO IT. I'M A TRAINED FIELD MEDIC.
TCHAK!
LOOK, THANKS FOR YOUR HELP, BUT I'M OKAY.
JUST GOING TO GET MY SNOWMOBILE AND GO.
GONNA BLEED OUT BEFORE YOU MAKE IT A MILE.

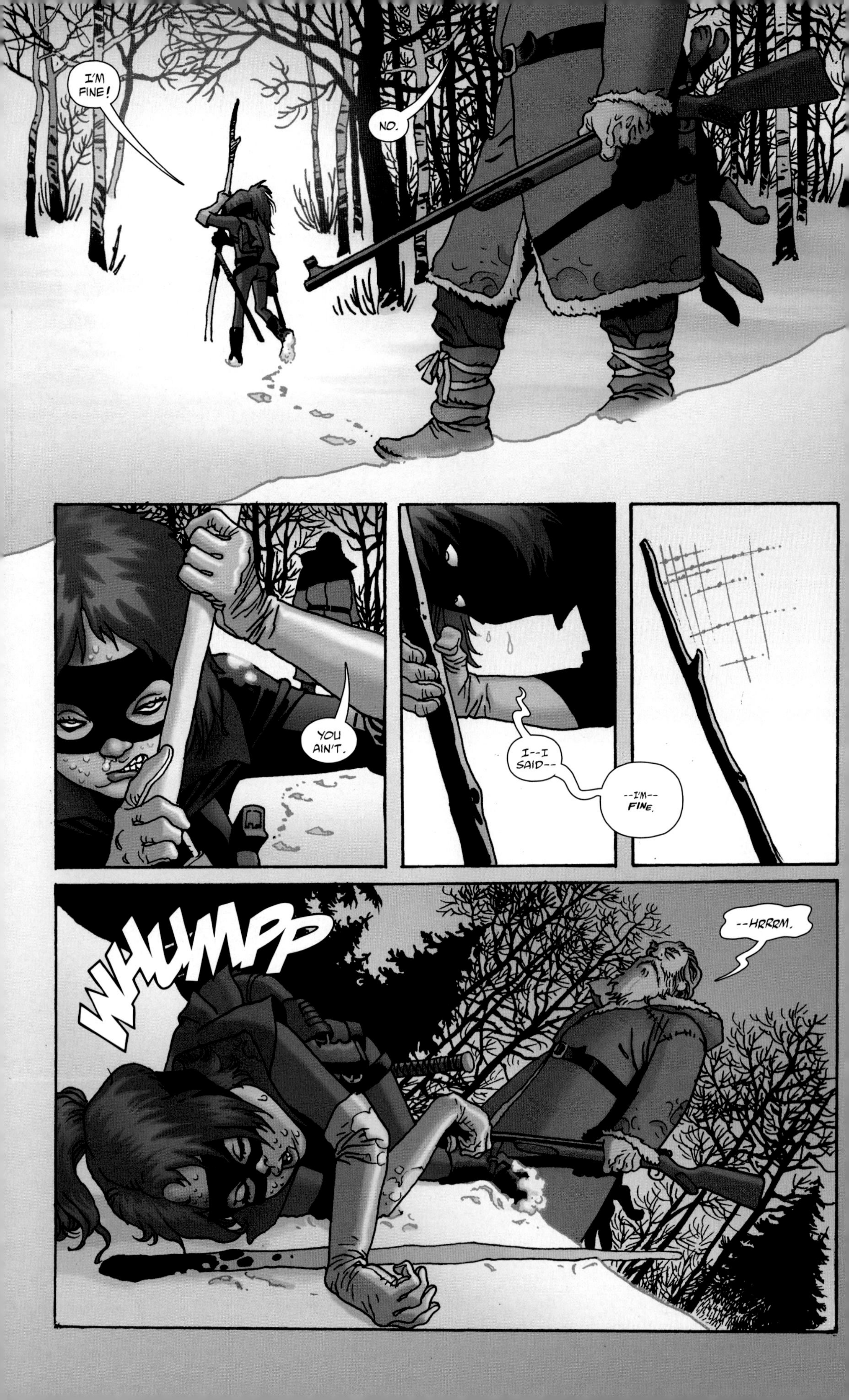
I'M FINE!
NO.
YOU AIN'T.
I--I SAID--
--I'M-- FINE.
WHUMPP
--HRRRM.

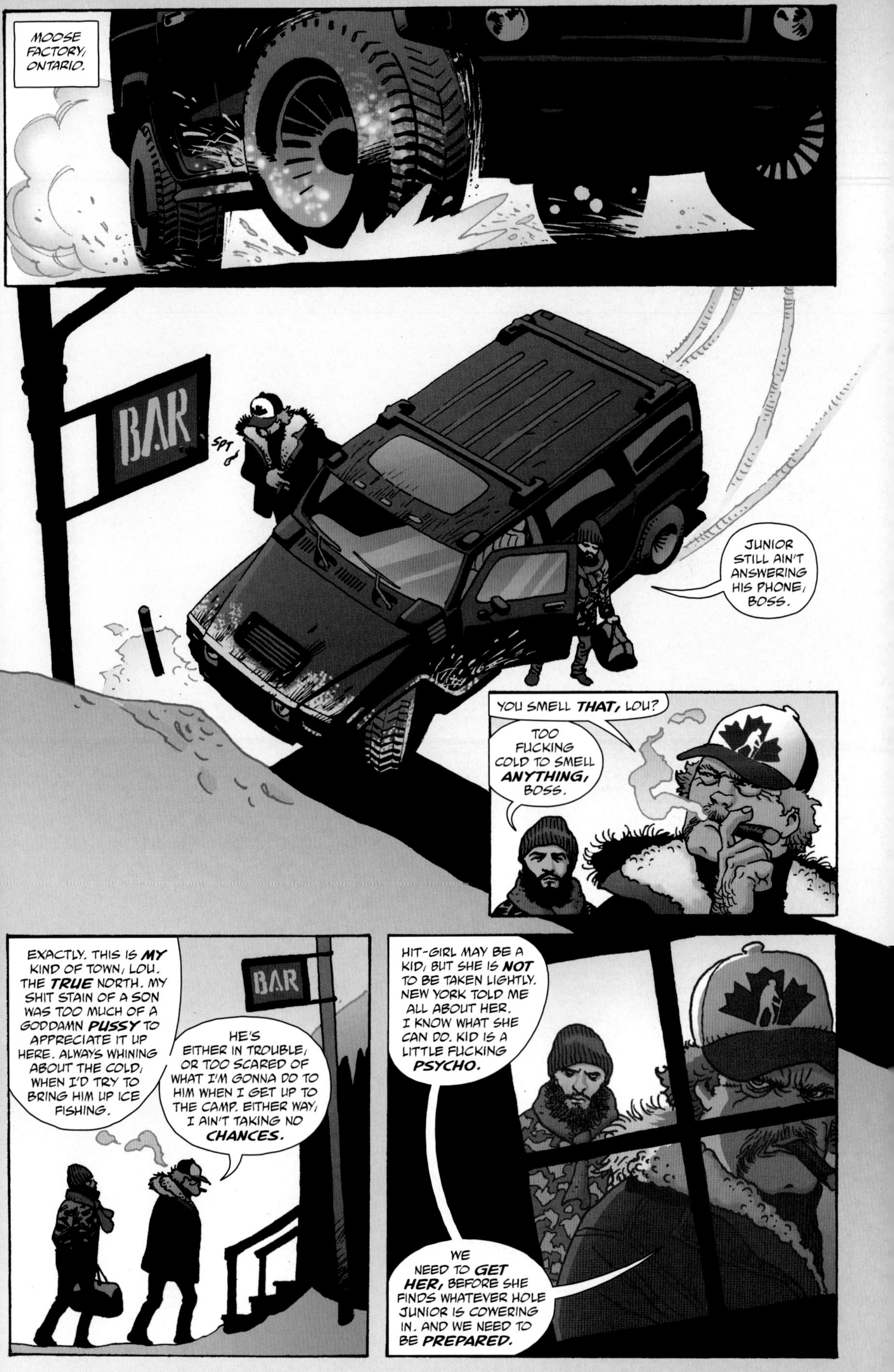
MOOSE FACTORY, ONTARIO.
BAR
SPT
JUNIOR STILL AIN'T ANSWERING HIS PHONE, BOSS.
YOU SMELL THAT, LOU?
TOO FUCKING COLD TO SMELL ANYTHING, BOSS.
EXACTLY. THIS IS MY KIND OF TOWN, LOU. THE TRUE NORTH. MY SHIT STAIN OF A SON WAS TOO MUCH OF A GODDAMN PUSSY TO APPRECIATE IT UP HERE. ALWAYS WHINING ABOUT THE COLD, WHEN I'D TRY TO BRING HIM UP ICE FISHING.
HE'S EITHER IN TROUBLE, OR TOO SCARED OF WHAT I'M GONNA DO TO HIM WHEN I GET UP TO THE CAMP. EITHER WAY, I AIN'T TAKING NO CHANCES.
BAR
HIT-GIRL MAY BE A KID, BUT SHE IS NOT TO BE TAKEN LIGHTLY. NEW YORK TOLD ME ALL ABOUT HER. I KNOW WHAT SHE CAN DO. KID IS A LITTLE FUCKING PSYCHO.
WE NEED TO GET HER, BEFORE SHE FINDS WHATEVER HOLE JUNIOR IS COWERING IN. AND WE NEED TO BE PREPARED.

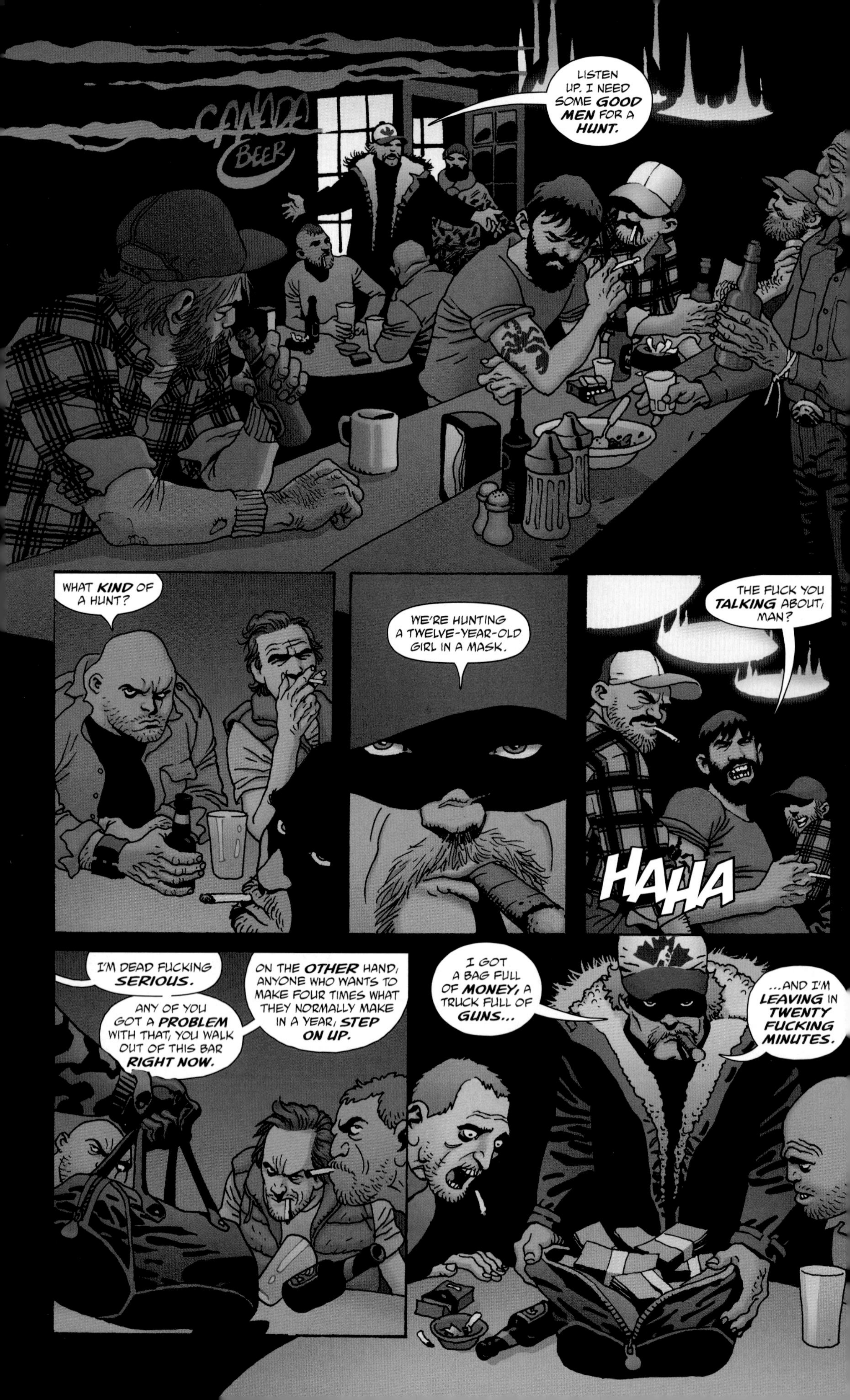
CANADA BEER
LISTEN UP. I NEED SOME GOOD MEN FOR A HUNT.
WHAT KIND OF A HUNT?
WE'RE HUNTING A TWELVE-YEAR-OLD GIRL IN A MASK.
THE FUCK YOU TALKING ABOUT, MAN?
HAHA
I'M DEAD FUCKING SERIOUS.
ANY OF YOU GOT A PROBLEM WITH THAT, YOU WALK OUT OF THIS BAR RIGHT NOW.
ON THE OTHER HAND, ANYONE WHO WANTS TO MAKE FOUR TIMES WHAT THEY NORMALLY MAKE IN A YEAR, STEP ON UP.
I GOT A BAG FULL OF MONEY, A TRUCK FULL OF GUNS...
...AND I'M LEAVING IN TWENTY FUCKING MINUTES.

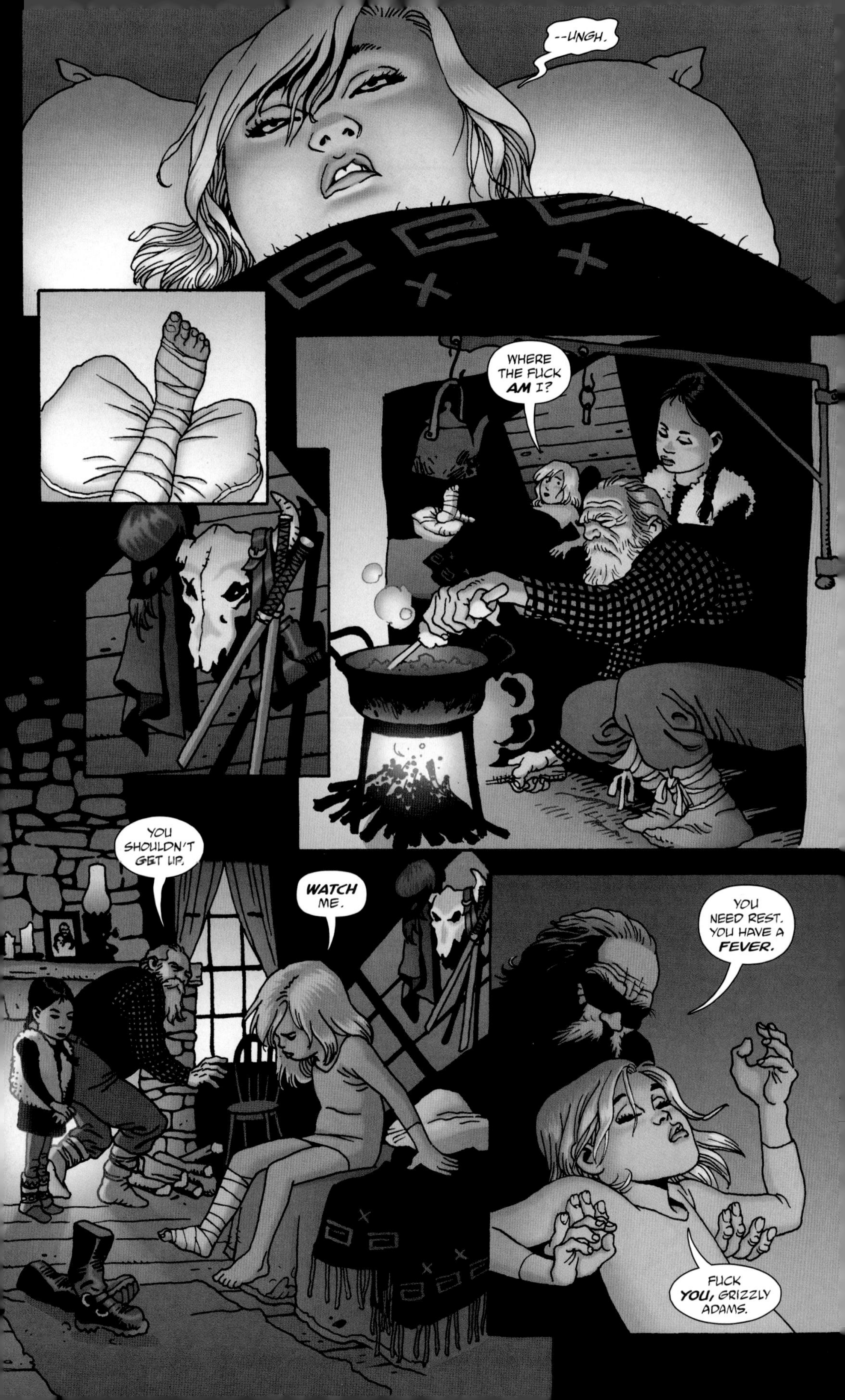
--UNGH.
WHERE THE FUCK AM I?
YOU SHOULDN'T GET UP.
WATCH ME.
YOU NEED REST. YOU HAVE A FEVER.
FUCK YOU, GRIZZLY ADAMS.

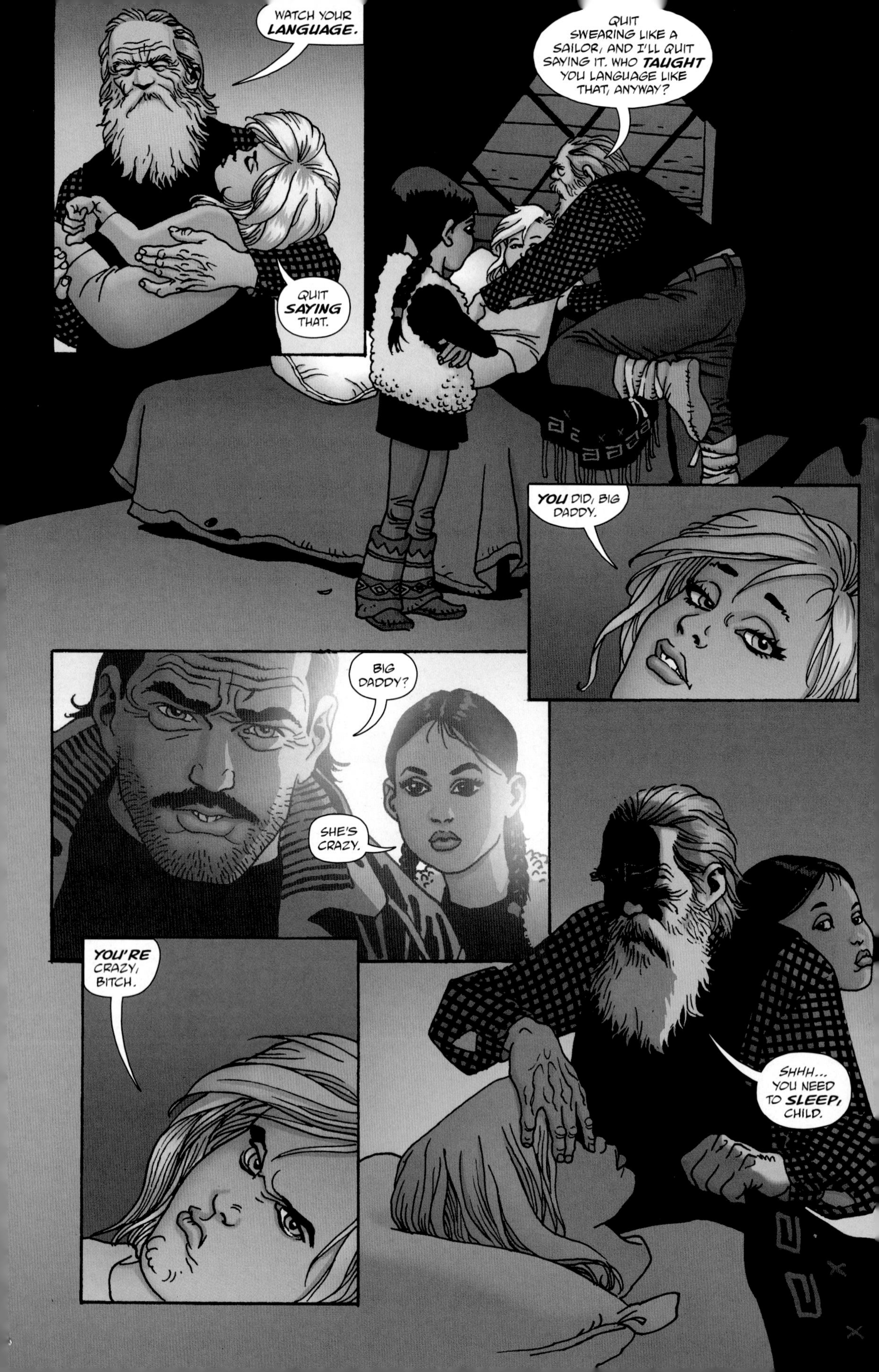
WATCH YOUR LANGUAGE.
QUIT SAYING THAT.
QUIT SWEARING LIKE A SAILOR, AND I'LL QUIT SAYING IT. WHO TAUGHT YOU LANGUAGE LIKE THAT, ANYWAY?
YOU DID, BIG DADDY.
BIG DADDY?
SHE'S CRAZY.
YOU'RE CRAZY, BITCH.
SHHH... YOU NEED TO SLEEP, CHILD.

...SLEEP.

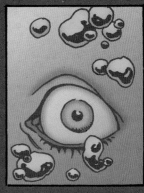

--MRRRFF!!

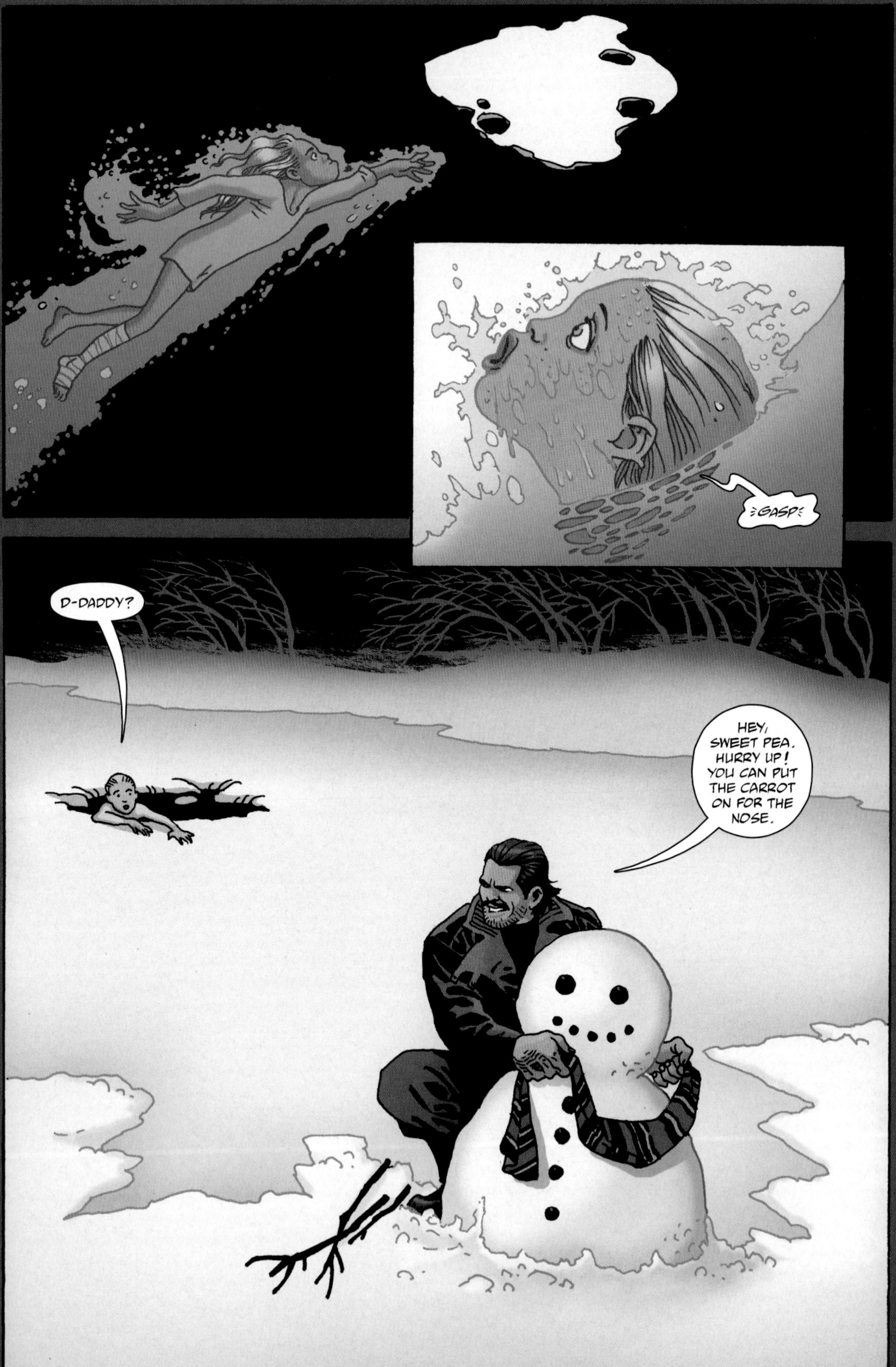
GASP
D-DADDY?
HEY, SWEET PEA. HURRY UP! YOU CAN PUT THE CARROT ON FOR THE NOSE.

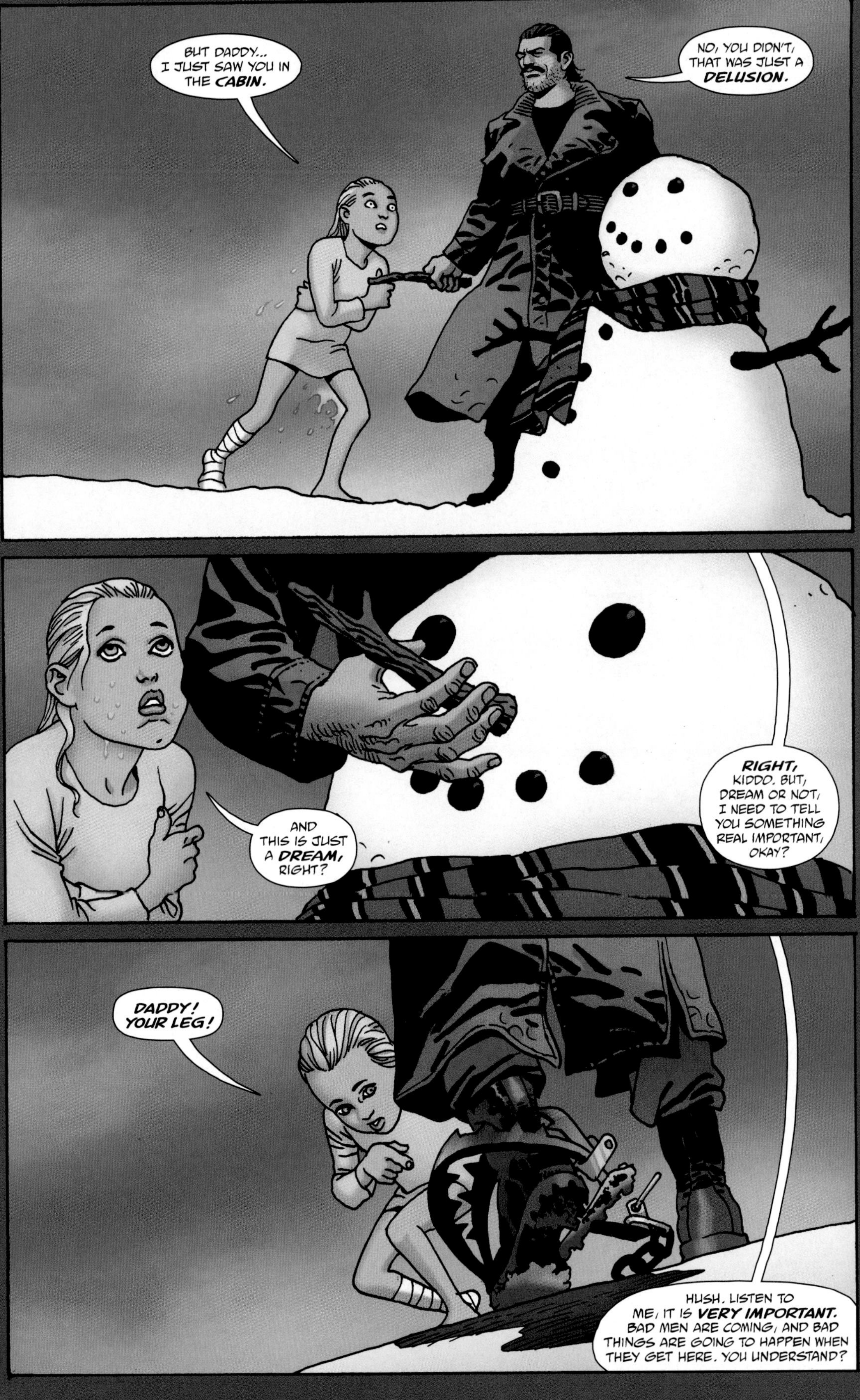
BUT DADDY... I JUST SAW YOU IN THE CABIN.
NO, YOU DIDN'T, THAT WAS JUST A DELUSION.
AND THIS IS JUST A DREAM, RIGHT?
RIGHT, KIDDO. BUT, DREAM OR NOT, I NEED TO TELL YOU SOMETHING REAL IMPORTANT, OKAY?
DADDY! YOUR LEG!
HUSH. LISTEN TO ME, IT IS VERY IMPORTANT. BAD MEN ARE COMING, AND BAD THINGS ARE GOING TO HAPPEN WHEN THEY GET HERE. YOU UNDERSTAND?

I'LL GET YOU OUT, DADDY!

THAT DOESN'T MATTER, CHILD. IT'S NOT REAL.

YOU NEED TO PROMISE ME YOU WON'T FORGET WHAT I TOLD YOU!

I--I PROMISE.

GOOD GIRL. NOW *REPEAT* IT.

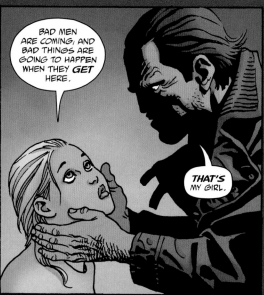

BAD MEN ARE COMING, AND BAD THINGS ARE GOING TO HAPPEN WHEN THEY *GET* HERE.

THAT'S MY GIRL.

NOW WAKE UP. YOU'RE HUNGRY, AND SOMETHING SMELLS GOOD.

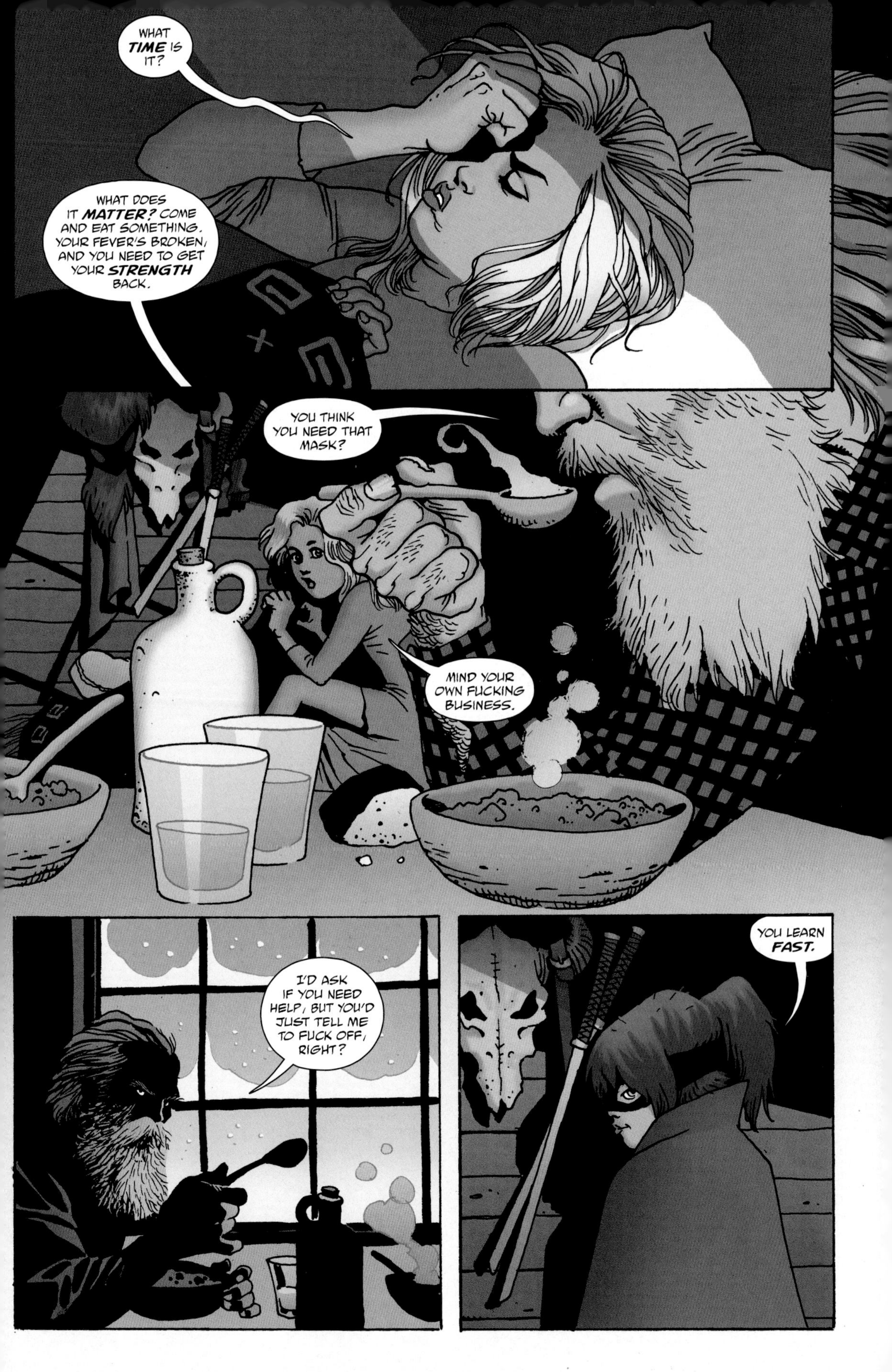
WHAT TIME IS IT?
WHAT DOES IT MATTER? COME AND EAT SOMETHING. YOUR FEVER'S BROKEN, AND YOU NEED TO GET YOUR STRENGTH BACK.
YOU THINK YOU NEED THAT MASK?
MIND YOUR OWN FUCKING BUSINESS.
I'D ASK IF YOU NEED HELP, BUT YOU'D JUST TELL ME TO FUCK OFF, RIGHT?
YOU LEARN FAST.

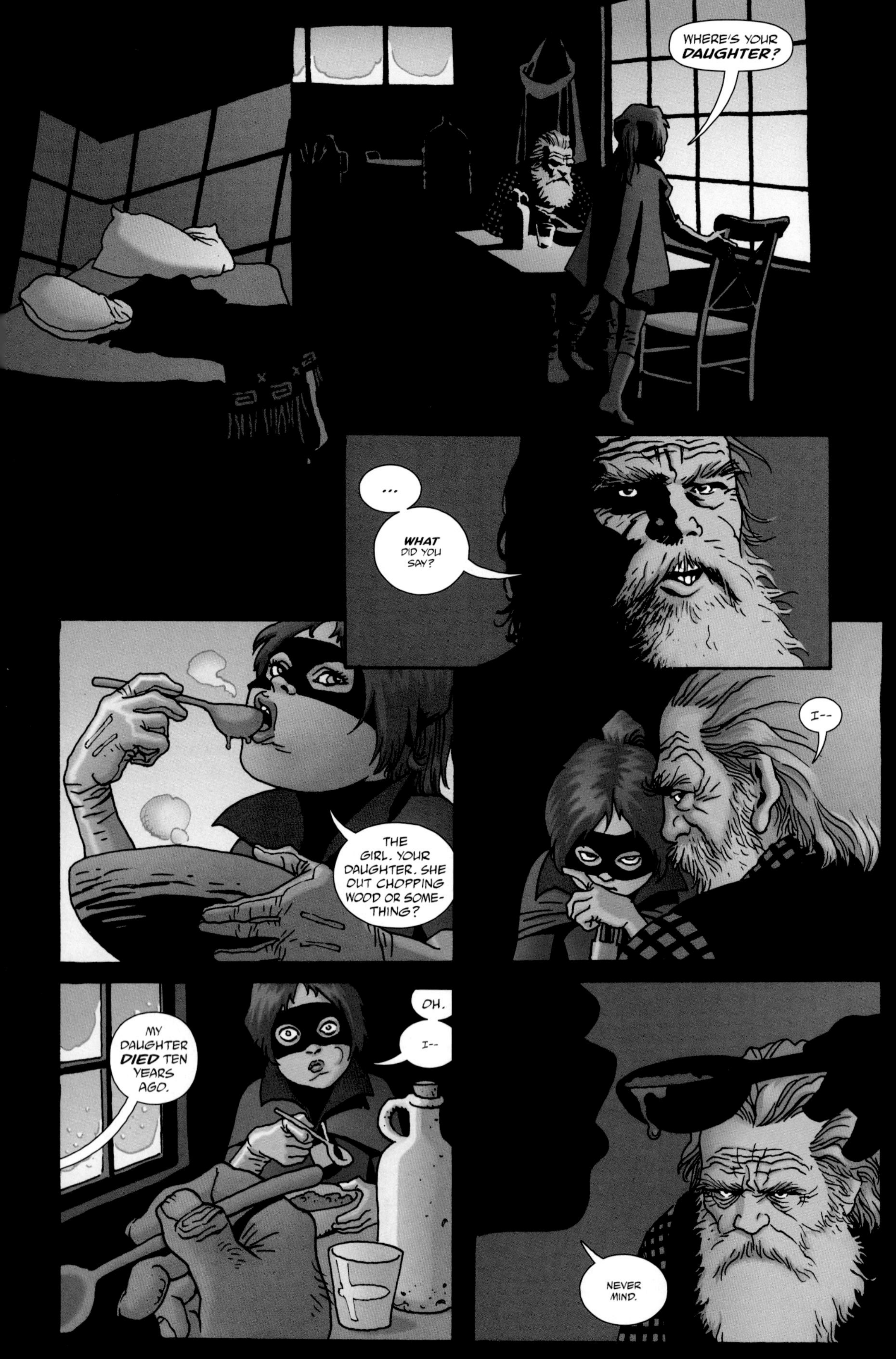
WHERE'S YOUR DAUGHTER?
...
WHAT DID YOU SAY?
THE GIRL. YOUR DAUGHTER. SHE OUT CHOPPING WOOD OR SOME-THING?
I--
MY DAUGHTER DIED TEN YEARS AGO.
OH.
I--
NEVER MIND.

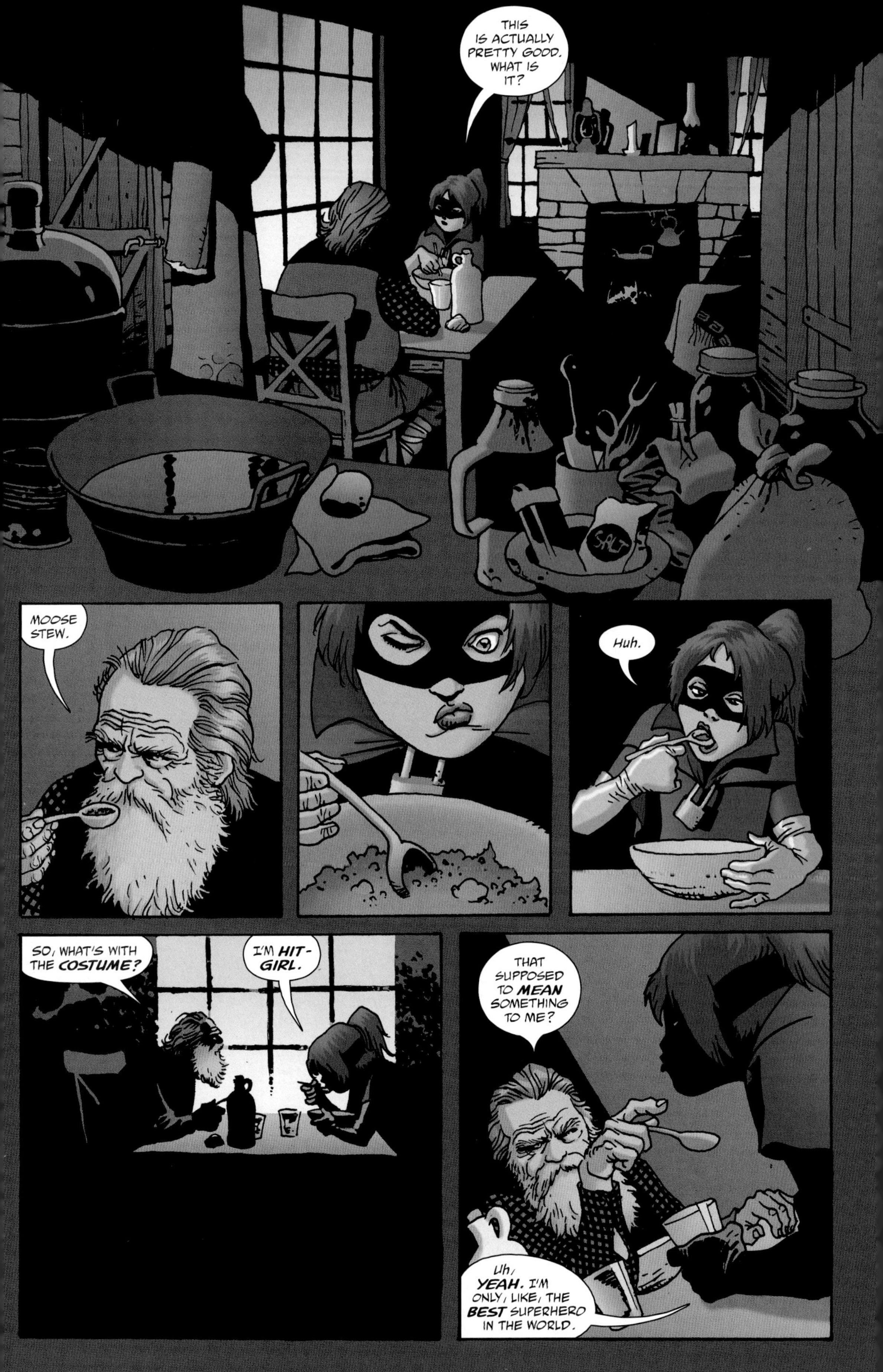
THIS IS ACTUALLY PRETTY GOOD. WHAT IS IT?
SALT
MOOSE STEW.
Huh.
SO, WHAT'S WITH THE COSTUME?
I'M HIT-GIRL.
THAT SUPPOSED TO MEAN SOMETHING TO ME?
Uh, YEAH. I'M ONLY, LIKE, THE BEST SUPERHERO IN THE WORLD.

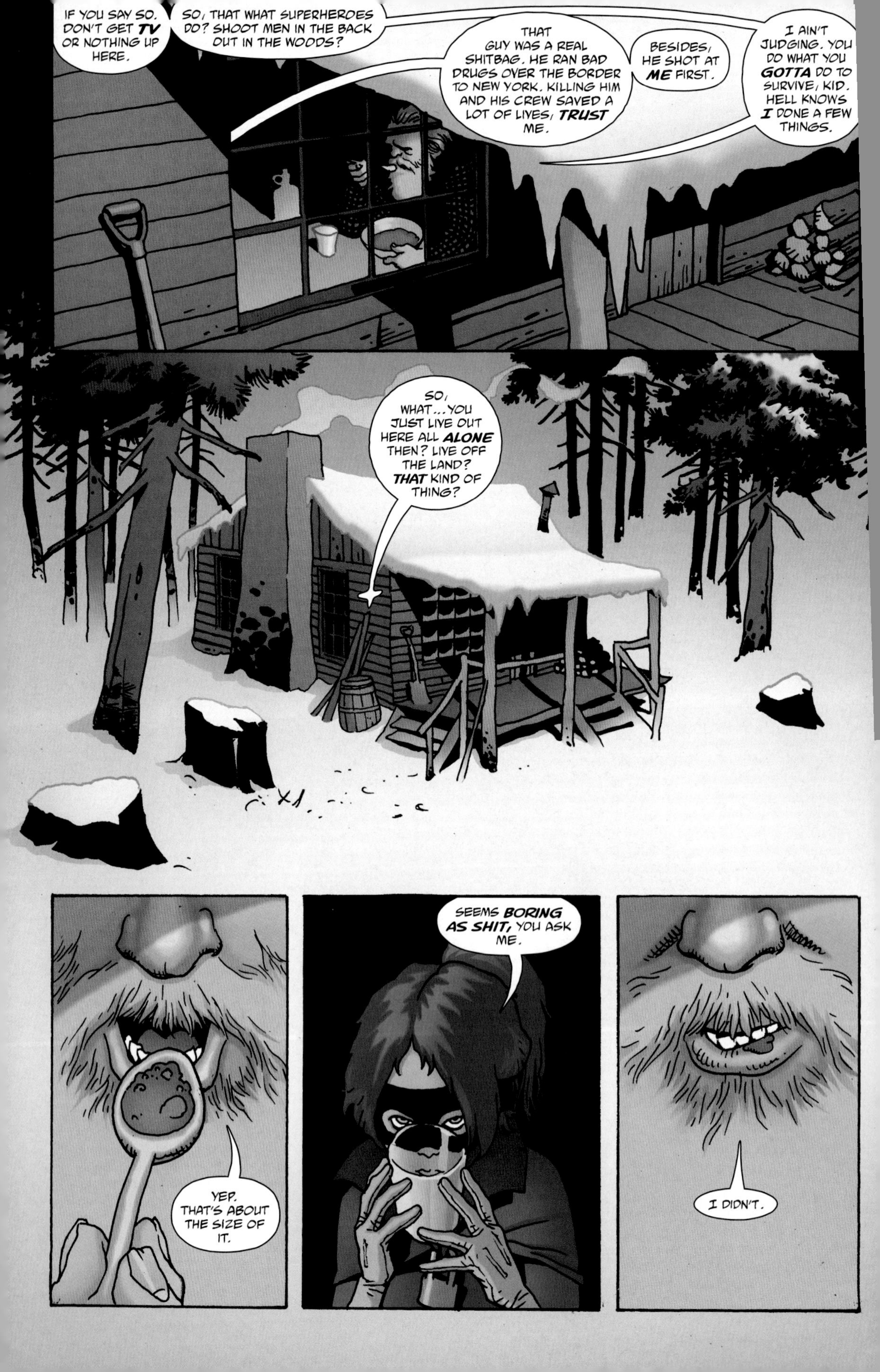
IF YOU SAY SO. DON'T GET TV OR NOTHING UP HERE.
SO, THAT WHAT SUPERHEROES DO? SHOOT MEN IN THE BACK OUT IN THE WOODS?
THAT GUY WAS A REAL SHITBAG. HE RAN BAD DRUGS OVER THE BORDER TO NEW YORK. KILLING HIM AND HIS CREW SAVED A LOT OF LIVES, TRUST ME.
BESIDES, HE SHOT AT ME FIRST.
I AIN'T JUDGING. YOU DO WHAT YOU GOTTA DO TO SURVIVE, KID. HELL KNOWS I DONE A FEW THINGS.
SO, WHAT... YOU JUST LIVE OUT HERE ALL ALONE THEN? LIVE OFF THE LAND? THAT KIND OF THING?
YEP. THAT'S ABOUT THE SIZE OF IT.
SEEMS BORING AS SHIT, YOU ASK ME.
I DIDN'T.

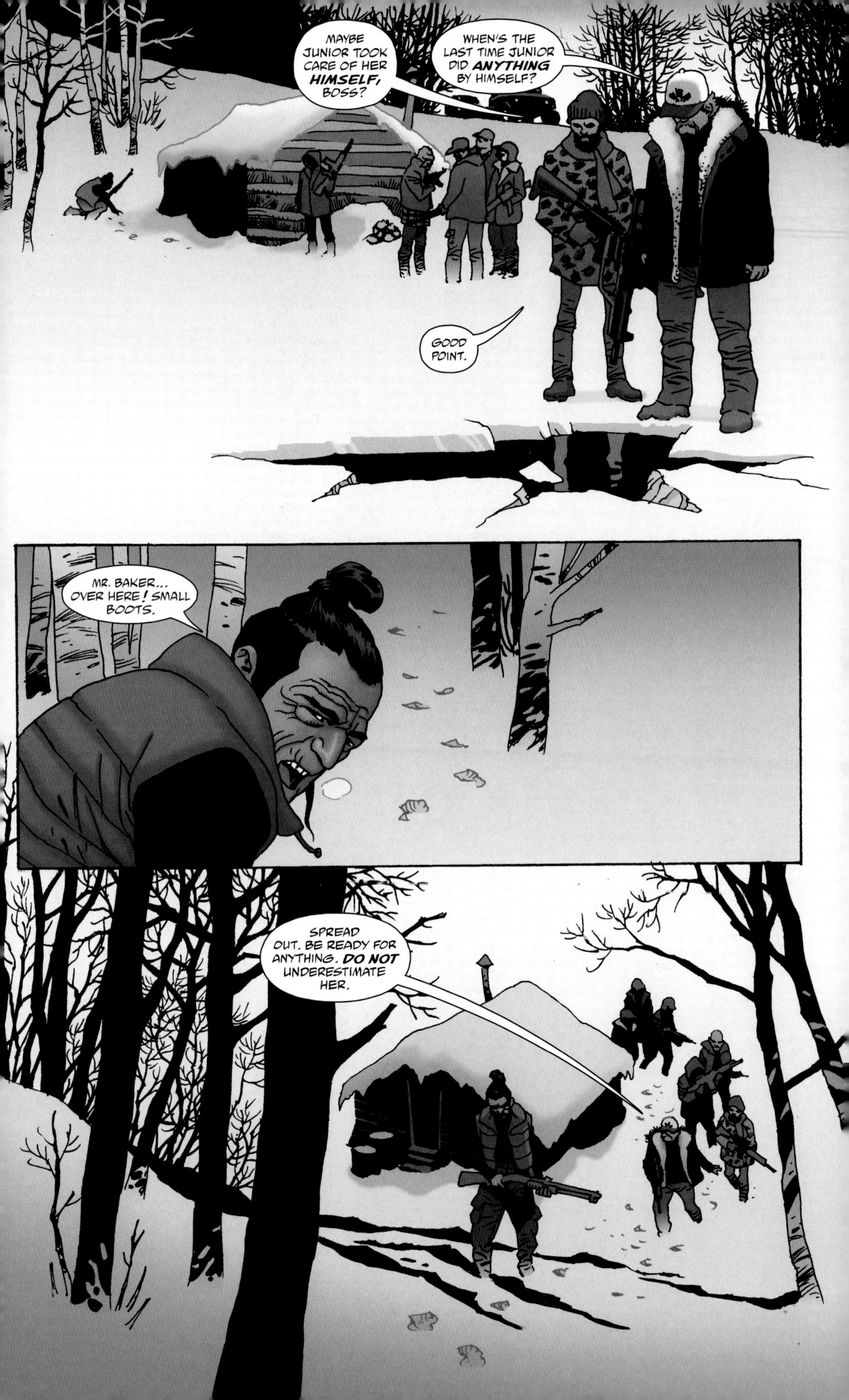

MAYBE JUNIOR TOOK CARE OF HER **HIMSELF,** BOSS?
WHEN'S THE LAST TIME JUNIOR DID **ANYTHING** BY HIMSELF?
GOOD POINT.
MR. BAKER... OVER HERE! SMALL BOOTS.
SPREAD OUT. BE READY FOR ANYTHING. **DO NOT** UNDERESTIMATE HER.

YO! OVER HERE.

AH, SHIT.

I'M SORRY, BOSS.

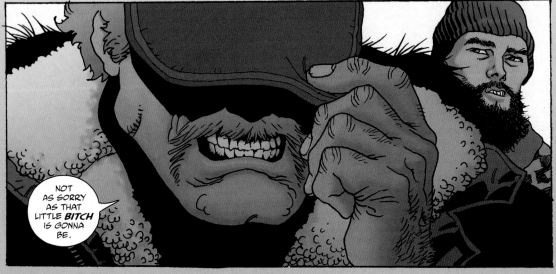

NOT AS SORRY AS THAT LITTLE *BITCH* IS GONNA BE.

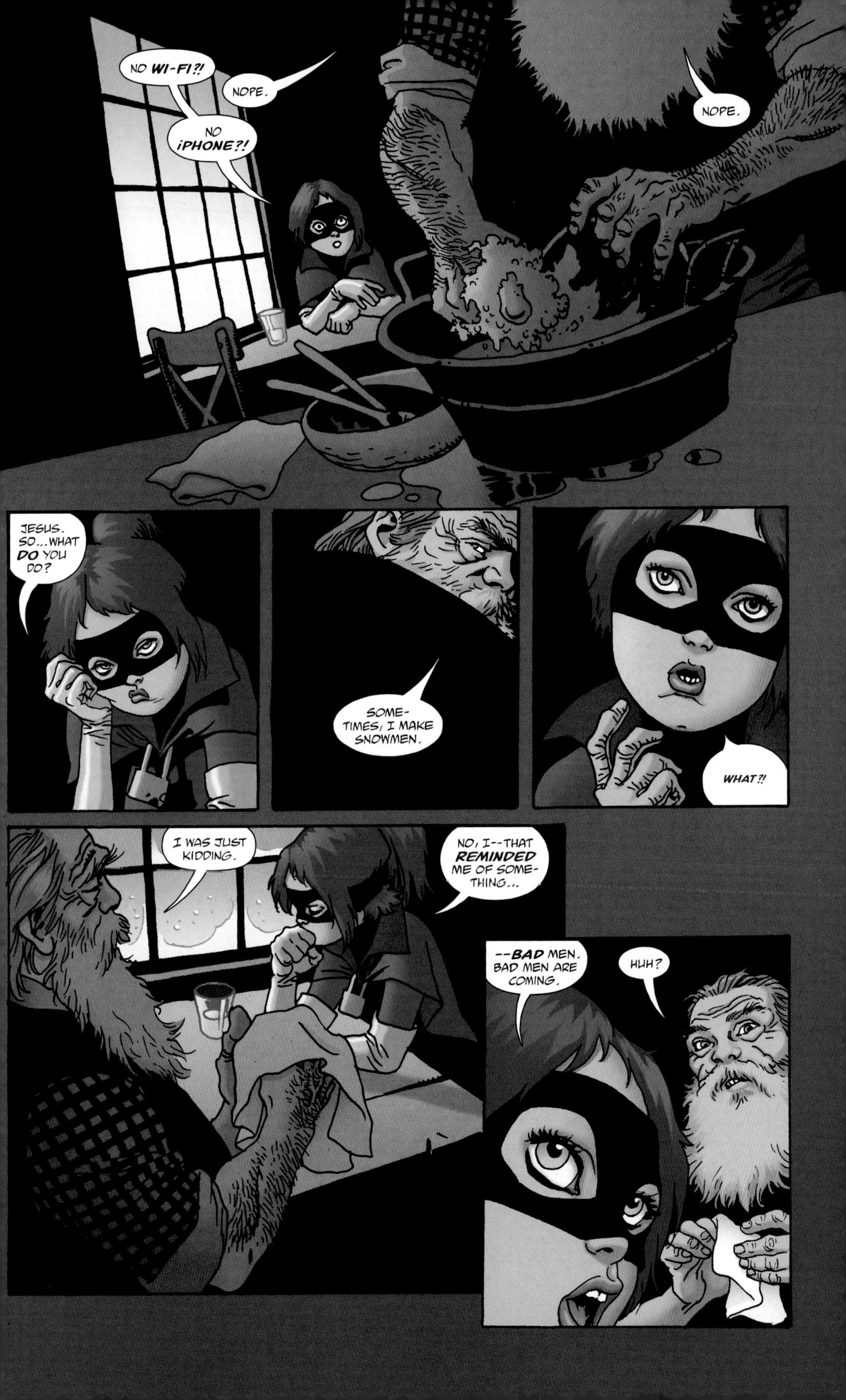
NO **WI-FI**?!
NOPE.
NO **iPHONE**?!
NOPE.
JESUS. SO...WHAT **DO** YOU DO?
SOME-TIMES, I MAKE SNOWMEN.
WHAT?!
I WAS JUST KIDDING.
NO, I--THAT **REMINDED** ME OF SOME-THING...
--**BAD** MEN. BAD MEN ARE COMING.
HUH?

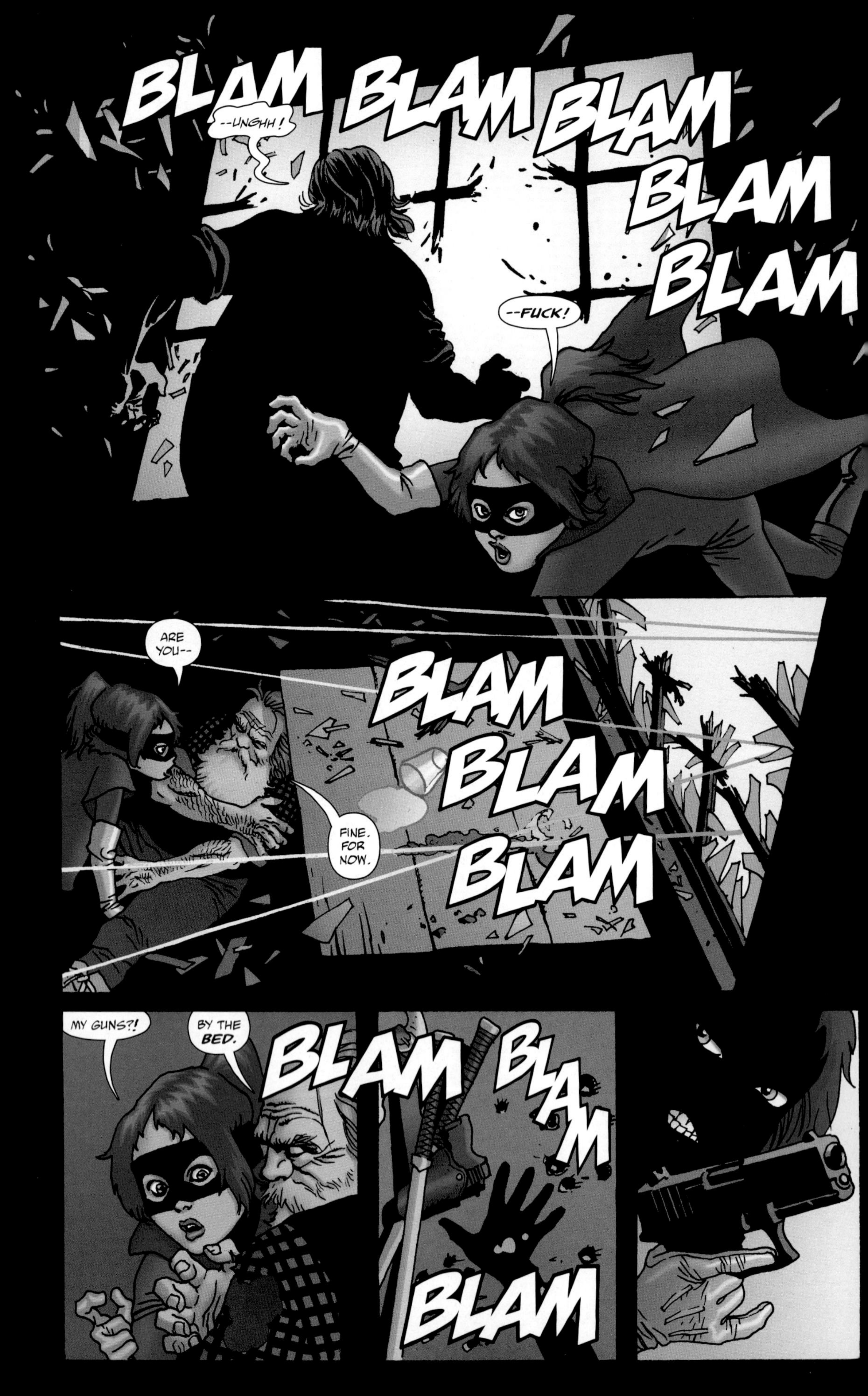
BLAM BLAM BLAM
--UNGHH!
BLAM
BLAM
--FUCK!
ARE YOU--
BLAM
BLAM
FINE. FOR NOW.
BLAM
MY GUNS?!
BY THE BED.
BLAM
BLAM
BLAM

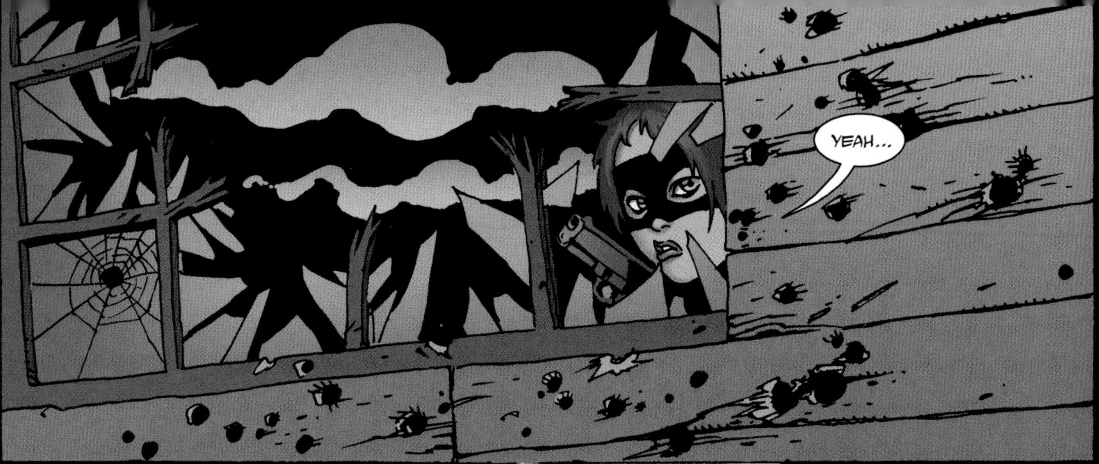
YEAH...

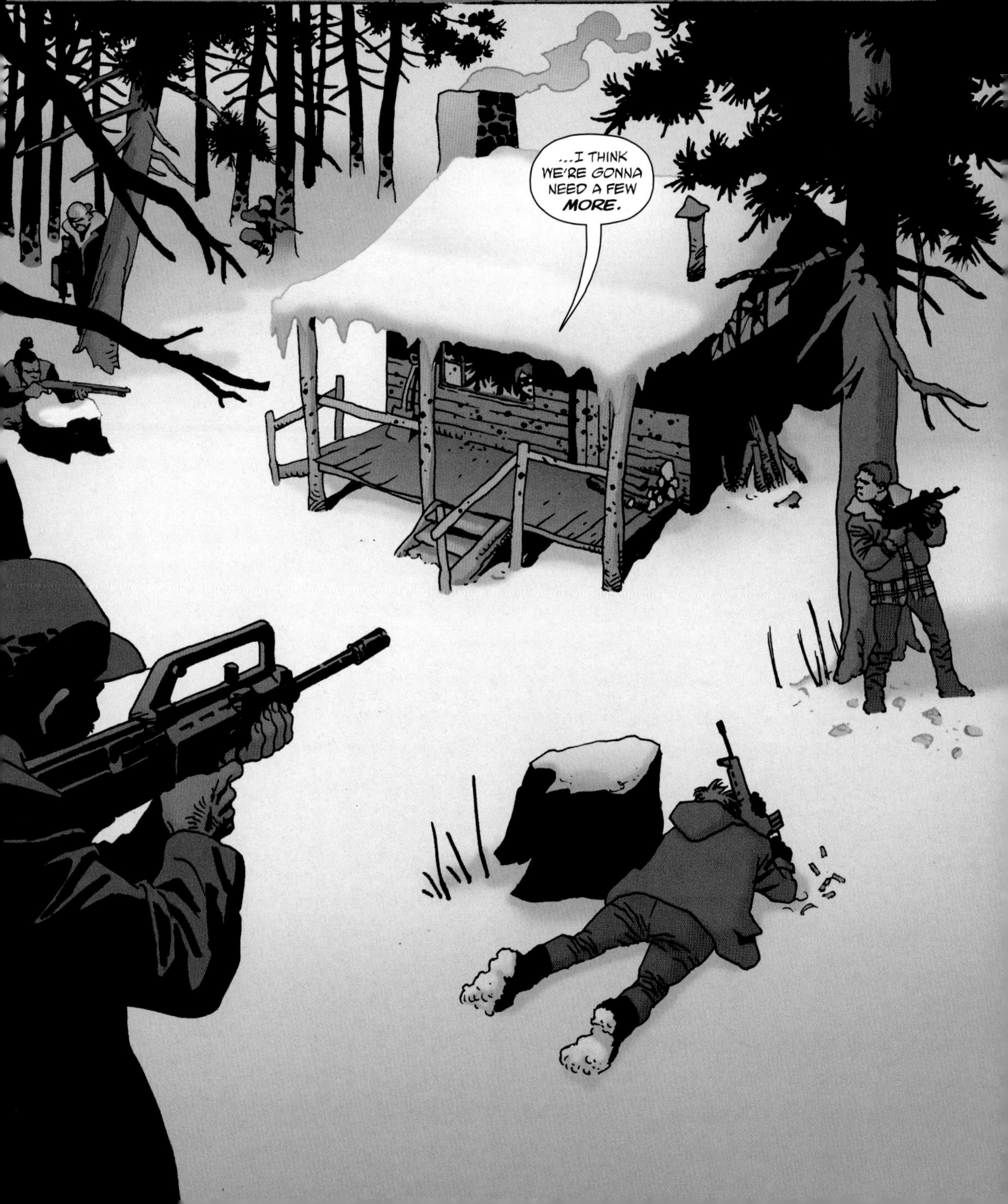
...I THINK WE'RE GONNA NEED A FEW MORE.

THREE

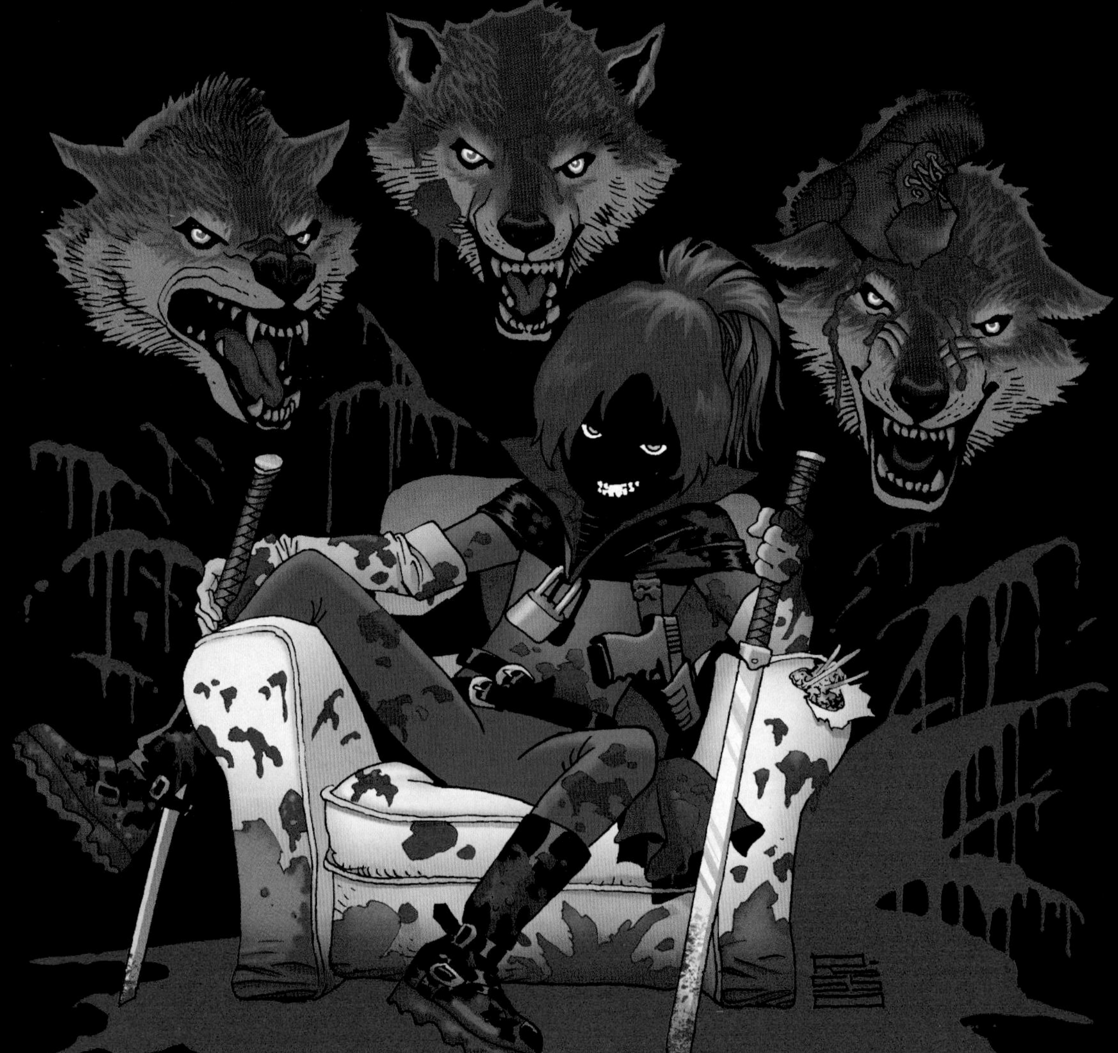

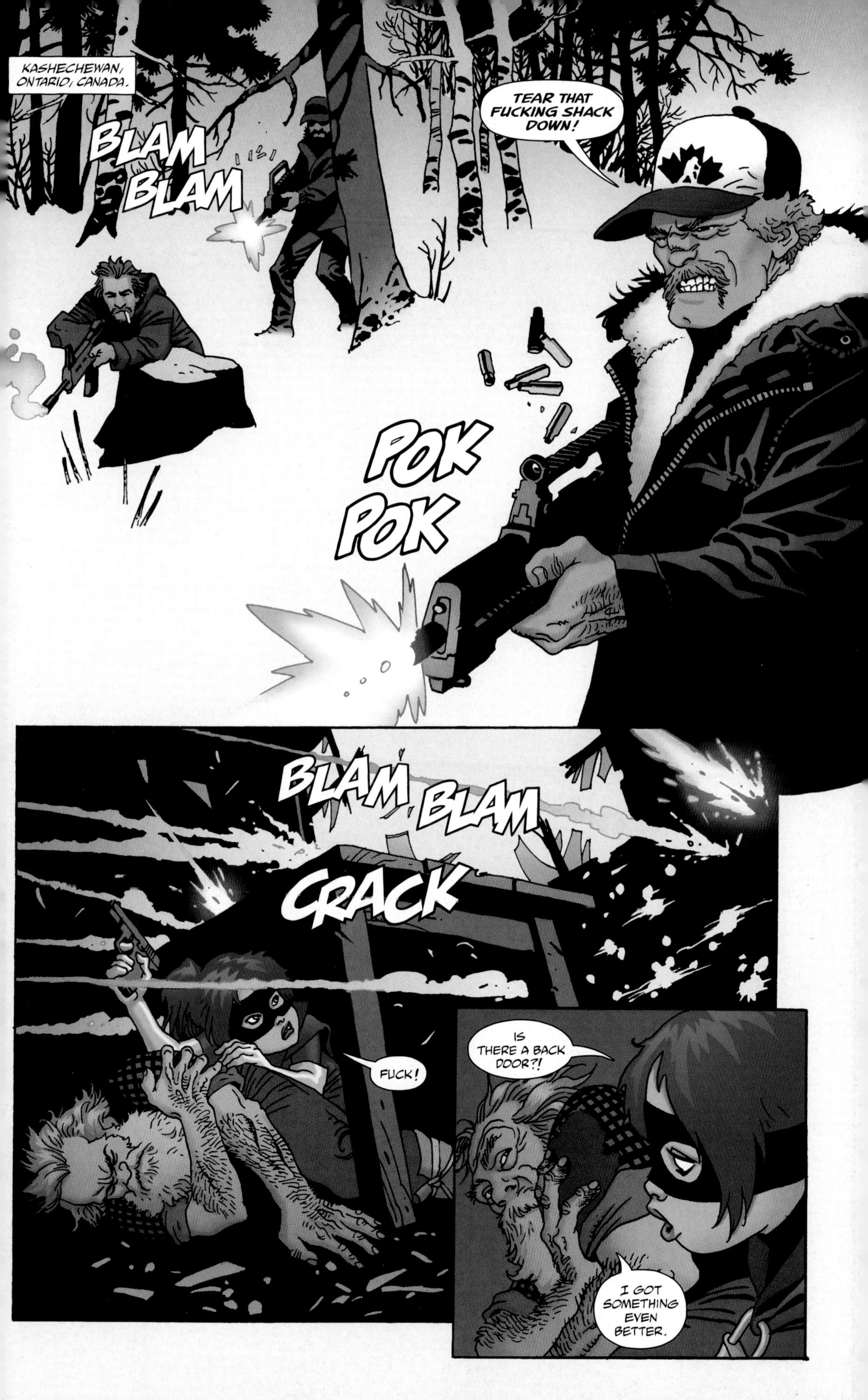
KASHECHEWAN, ONTARIO, CANADA.
BLAM BLAM
TEAR THAT FUCKING SHACK DOWN!
POK POK
BLAM BLAM
CRACK
FUCK!
IS THERE A BACK DOOR?!
I GOT SOMETHING EVEN BETTER.

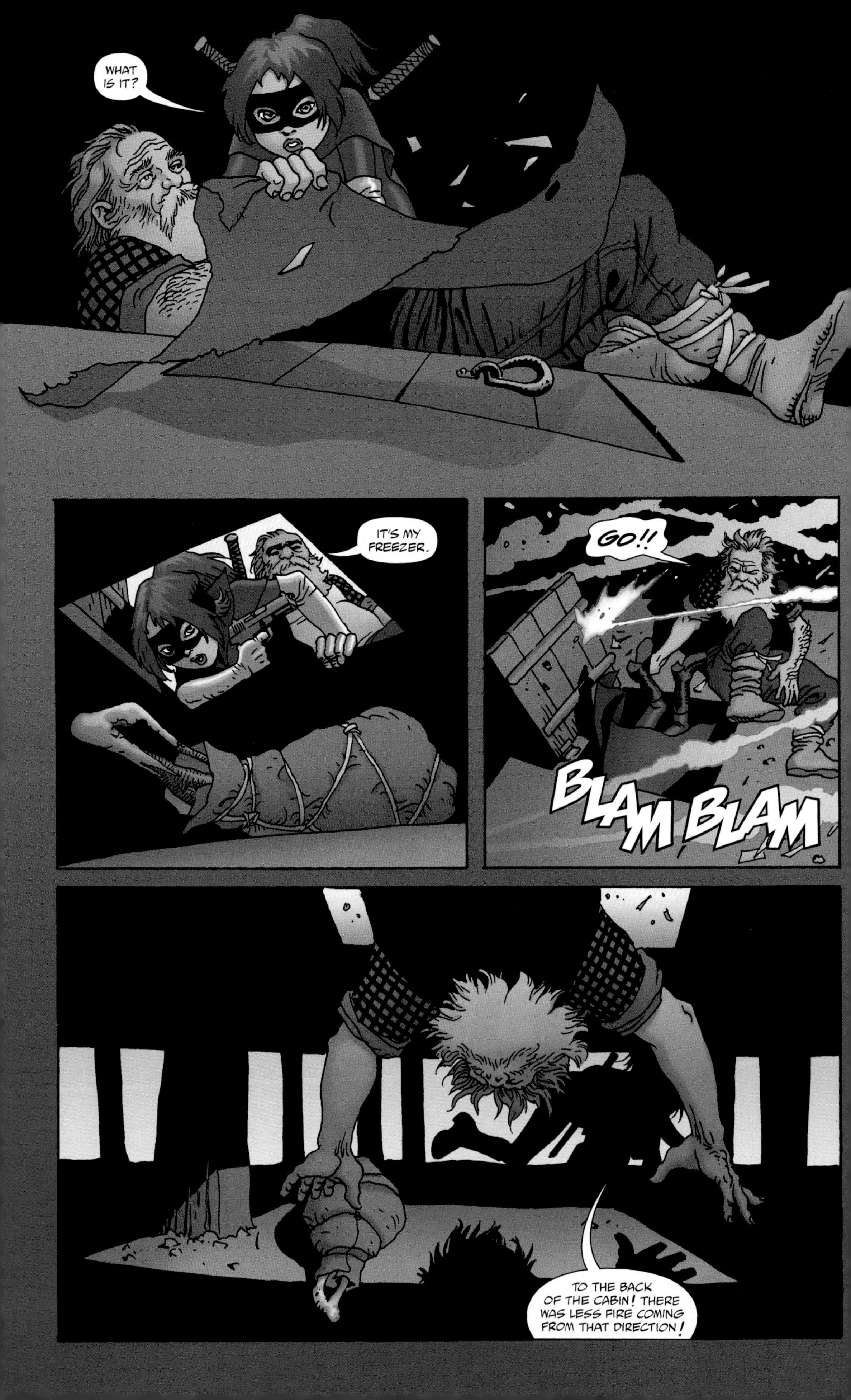
WHAT IS IT?
IT'S MY FREEZER.
GO!!
BLAM BLAM
TO THE BACK OF THE CABIN! THERE WAS LESS FIRE COMING FROM THAT DIRECTION!

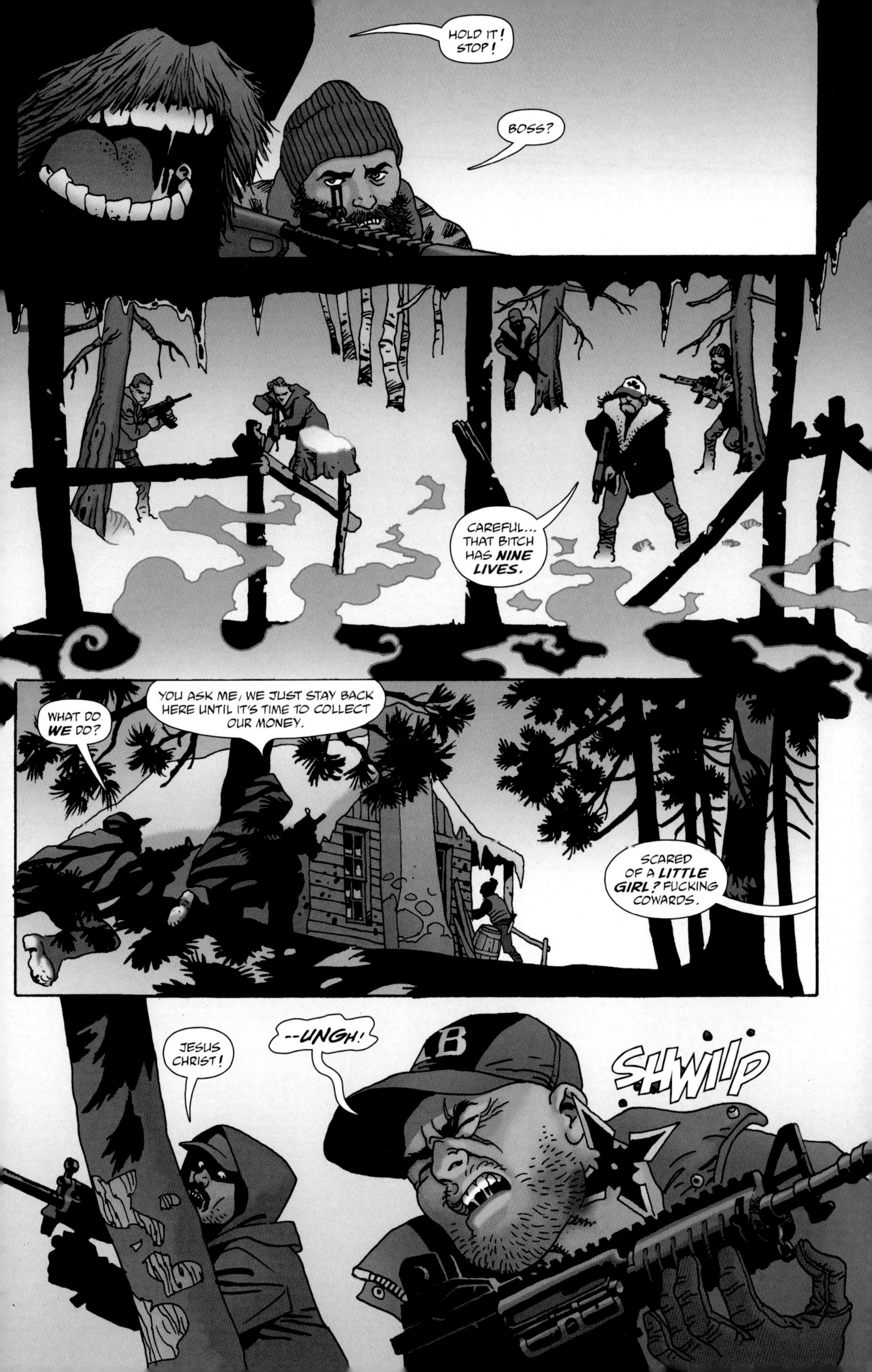
HOLD IT! STOP!
BOSS?
CAREFUL... THAT BITCH HAS NINE LIVES.
WHAT DO WE DO?
YOU ASK ME, WE JUST STAY BACK HERE UNTIL IT'S TIME TO COLLECT OUR MONEY.
SCARED OF A LITTLE GIRL? FUCKING COWARDS.
JESUS CHRIST!
--UNGH!
SHWIIP

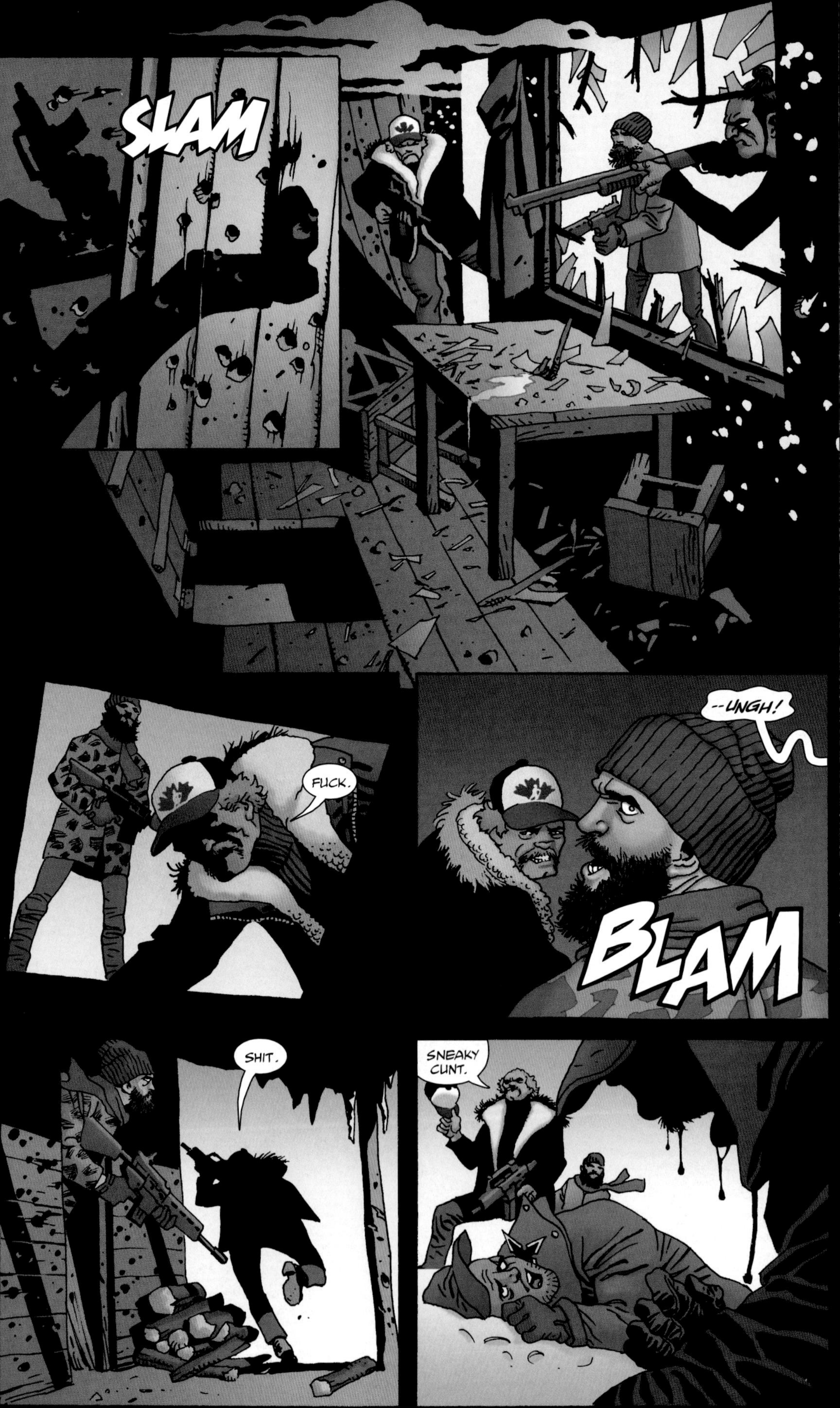
SLAM
FUCK.
--UNGH!
BLAM
SHIT.
SNEAKY CUNT.

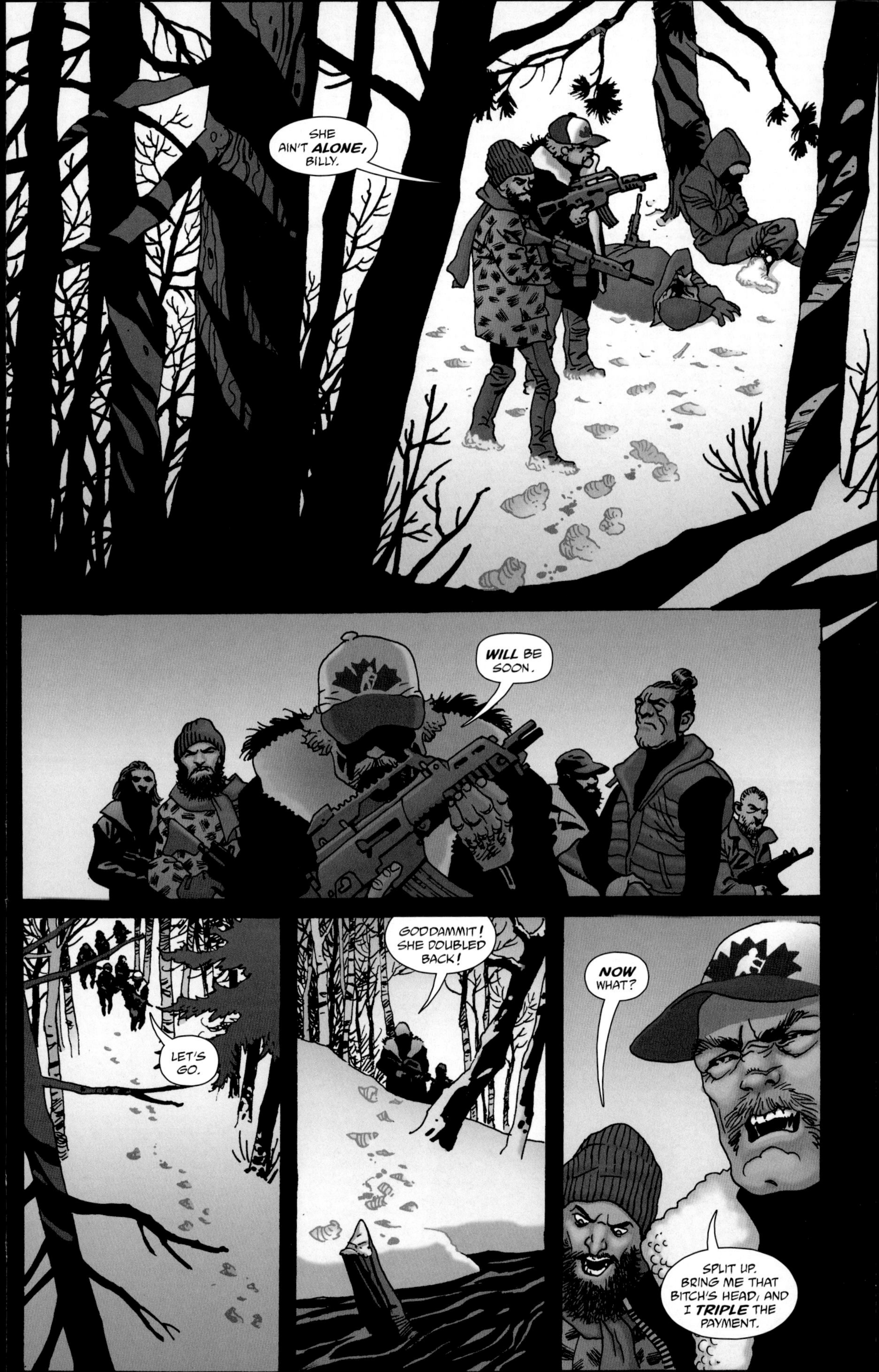
SHE AIN'T ALONE, BILLY.
WILL BE SOON.
LET'S GO.
GODDAMMIT! SHE DOUBLED BACK!
NOW WHAT?
SPLIT UP. BRING ME THAT BITCH'S HEAD, AND I TRIPLE THE PAYMENT.

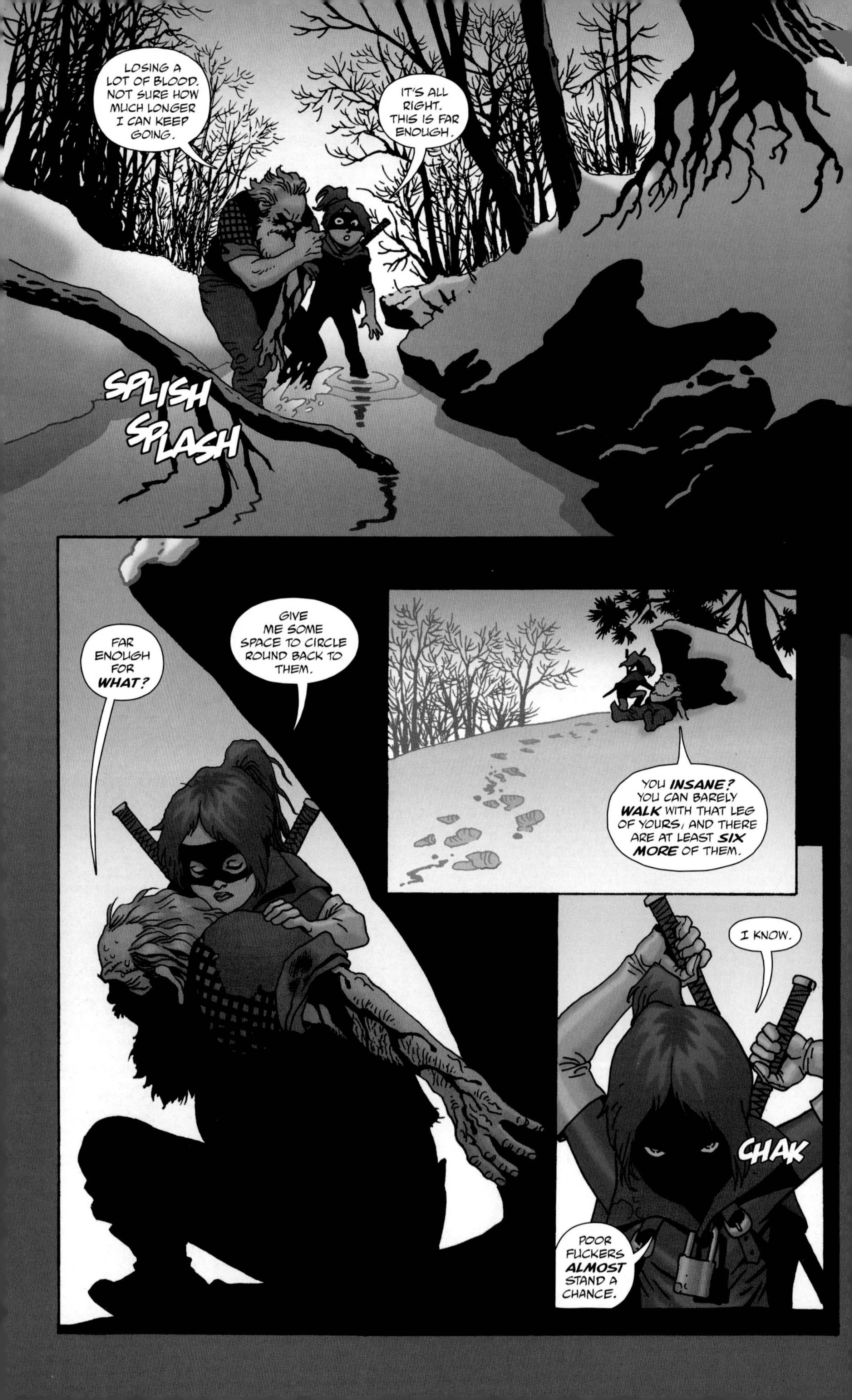
LOSING A LOT OF BLOOD. NOT SURE HOW MUCH LONGER I CAN KEEP GOING.
IT'S ALL RIGHT. THIS IS FAR ENOUGH.
SPLISH
SPLASH
FAR ENOUGH FOR WHAT?
GIVE ME SOME SPACE TO CIRCLE ROUND BACK TO THEM.
YOU INSANE? YOU CAN BARELY WALK WITH THAT LEG OF YOURS, AND THERE ARE AT LEAST SIX MORE OF THEM.
I KNOW.
CHAK
POOR FUCKERS ALMOST STAND A CHANCE.

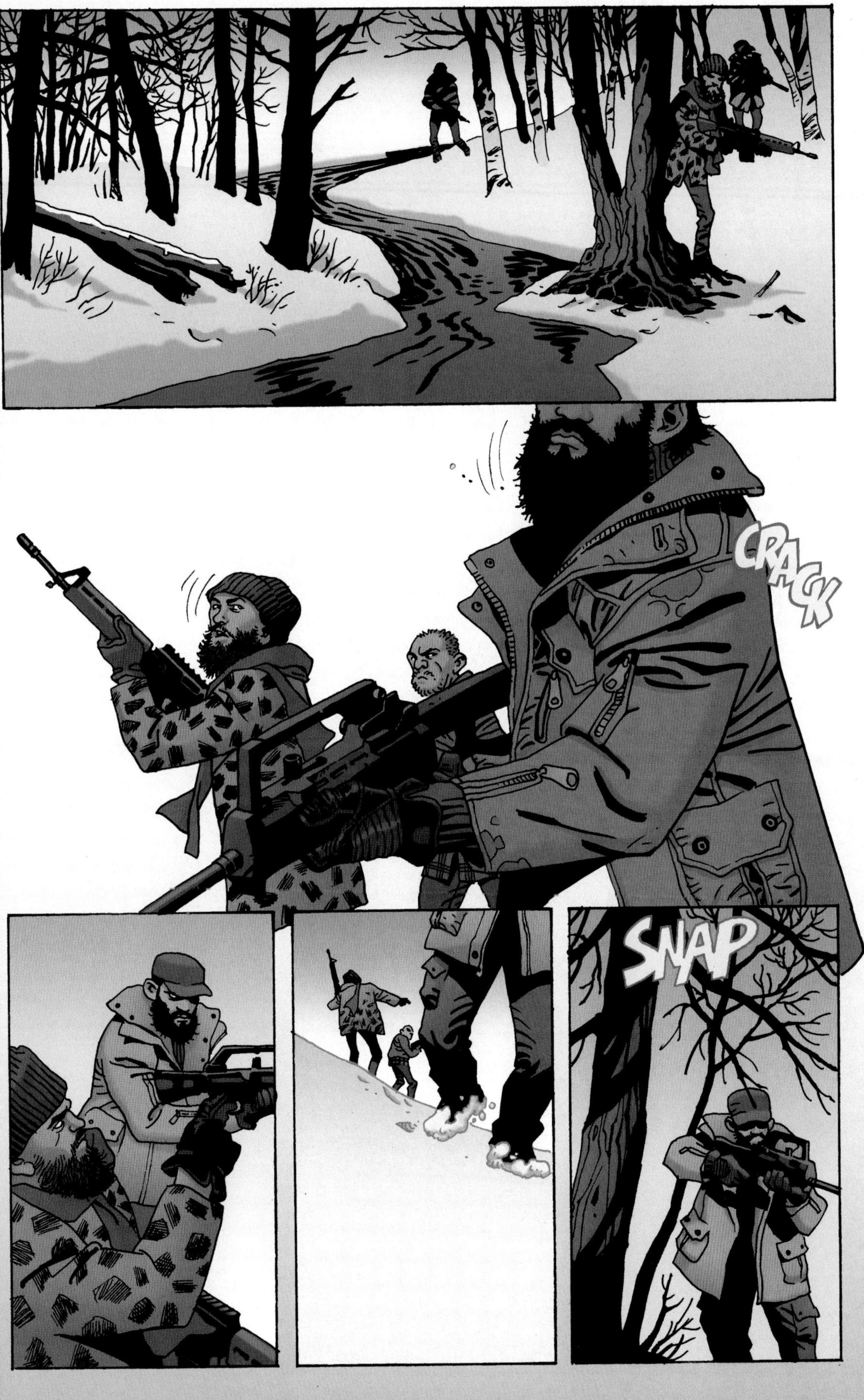
CRACK
SNAP

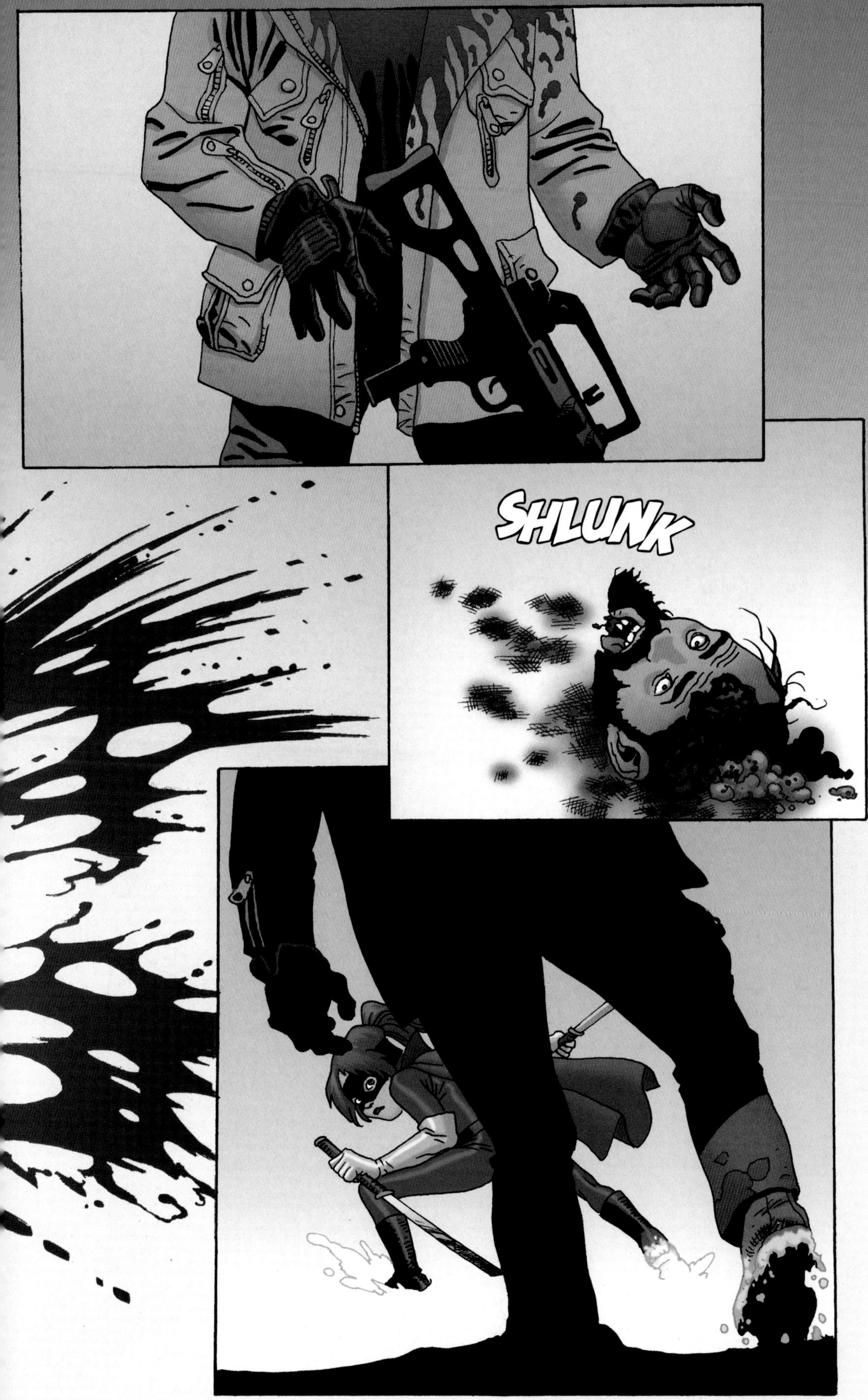
SHLUNK

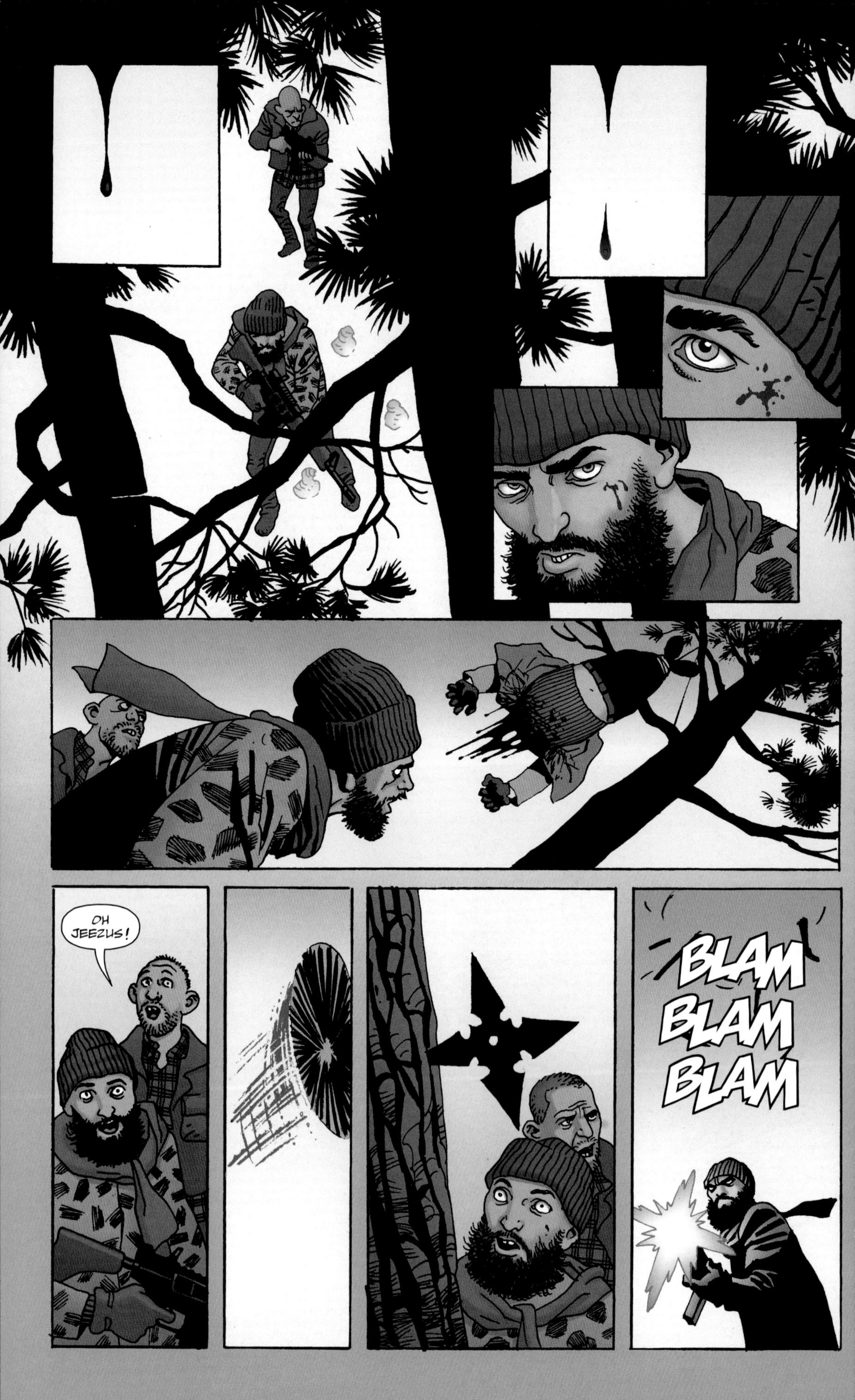
OH JEEZUS!
BLAM
BLAM
BLAM

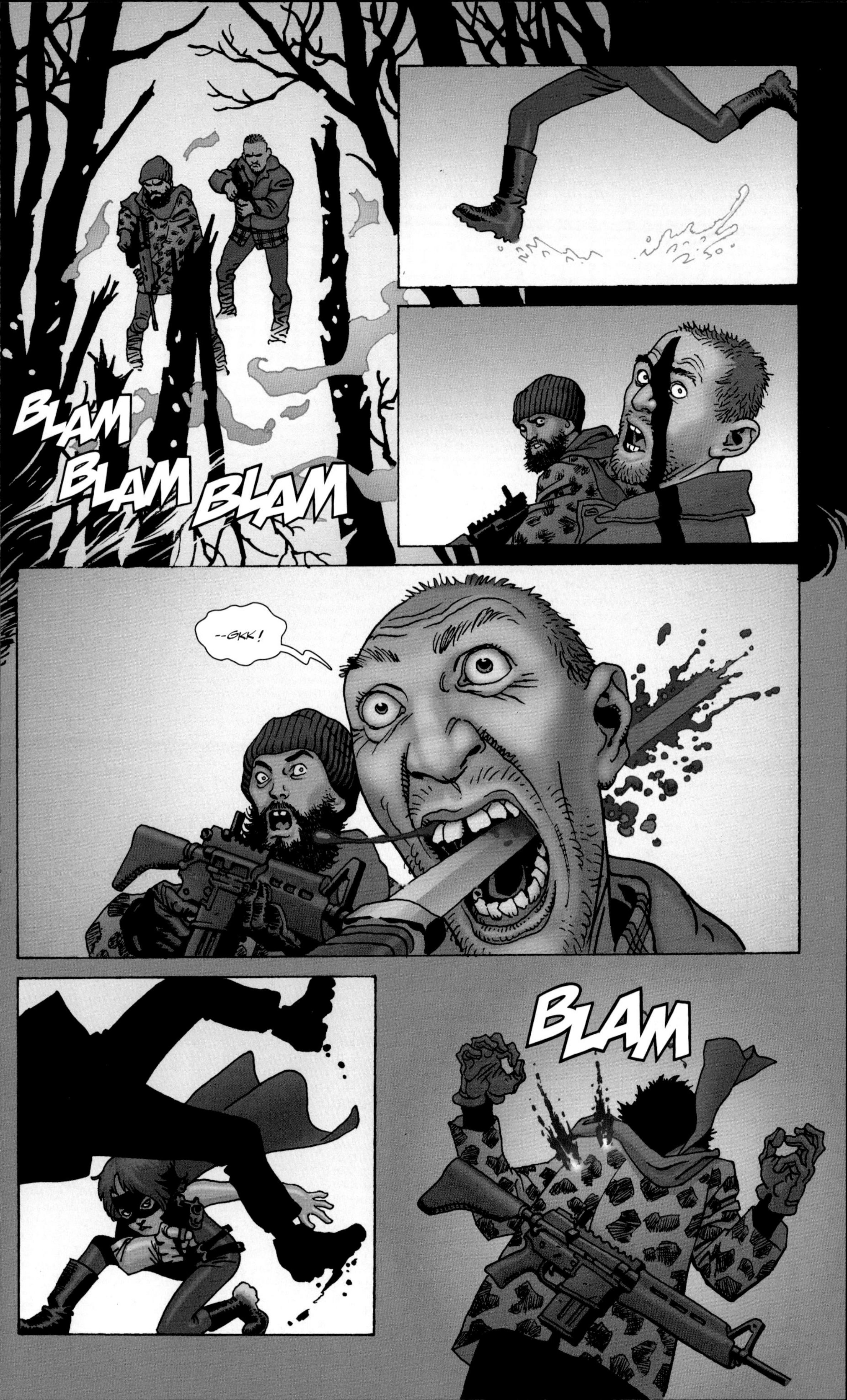
BLAM
BLAM
BLAM
--GKK!
BLAM

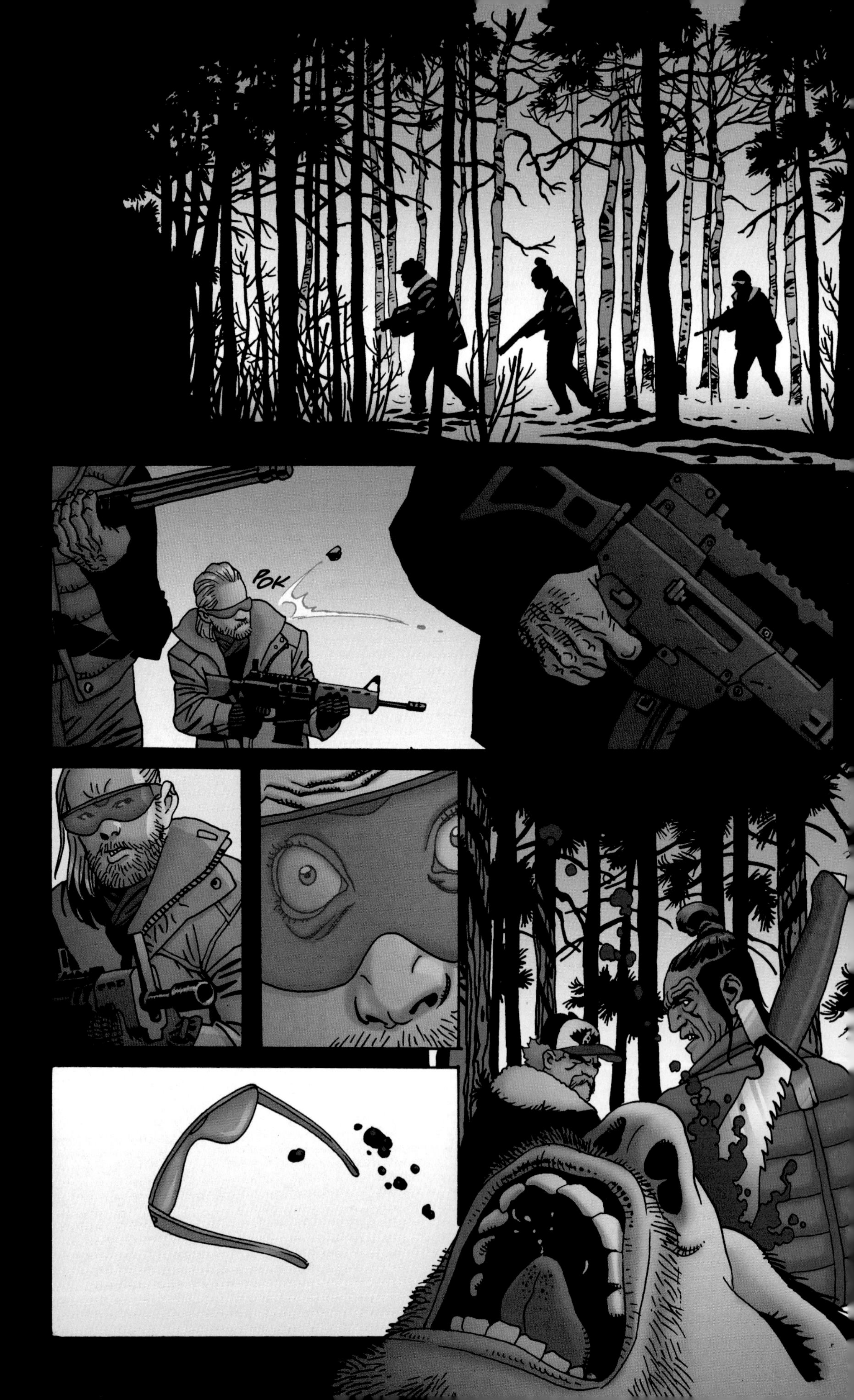
POK

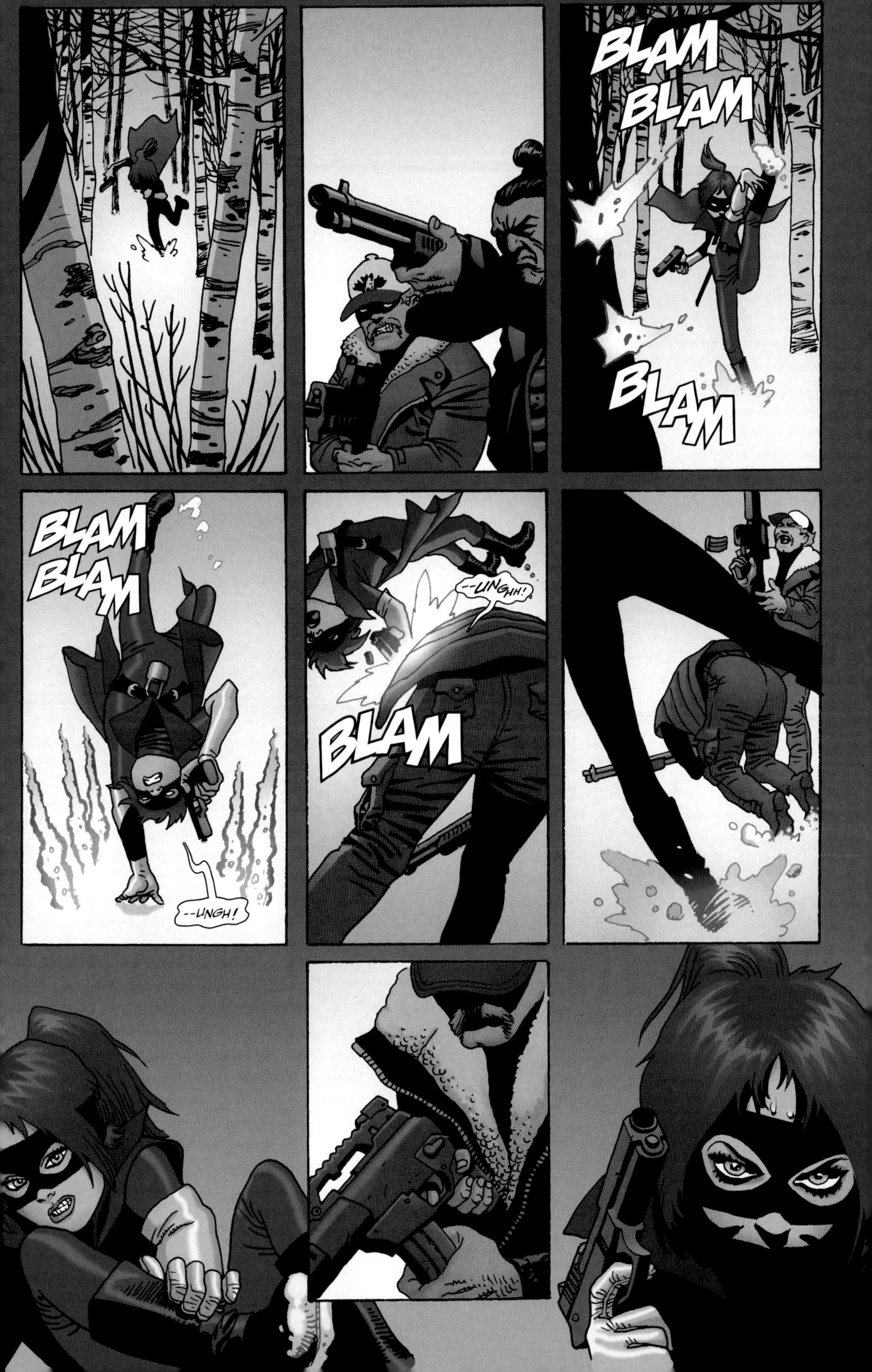
BLAM
BLAM
BLAM
BLAM
BLAM
--UNGH!
--UNGHH!
BLAM

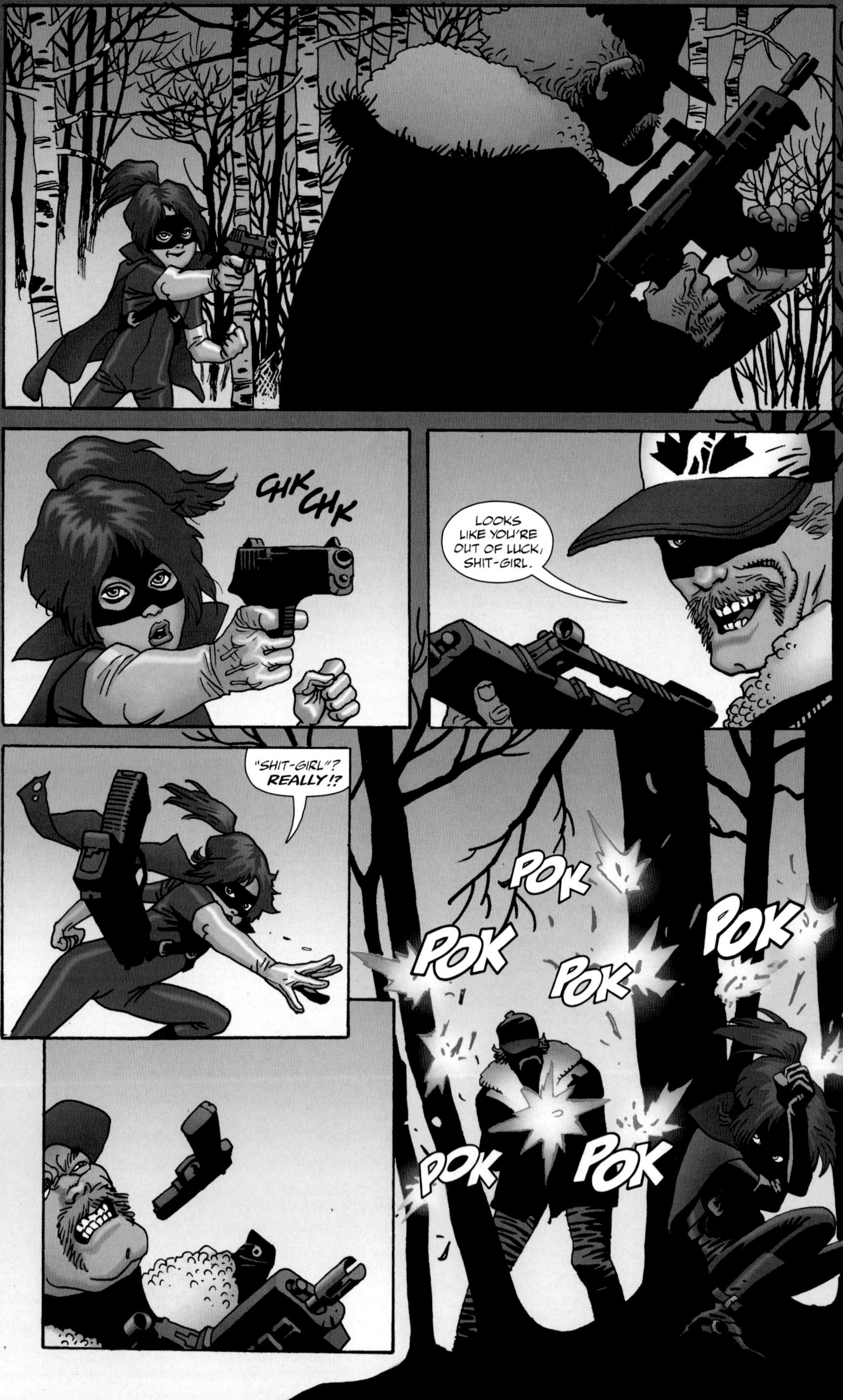
CHK CHK
LOOKS LIKE YOU'RE OUT OF LUCK, SHIT-GIRL.
"SHIT-GIRL"? REALLY!?
POK
POK
POK
POK
POK
POK

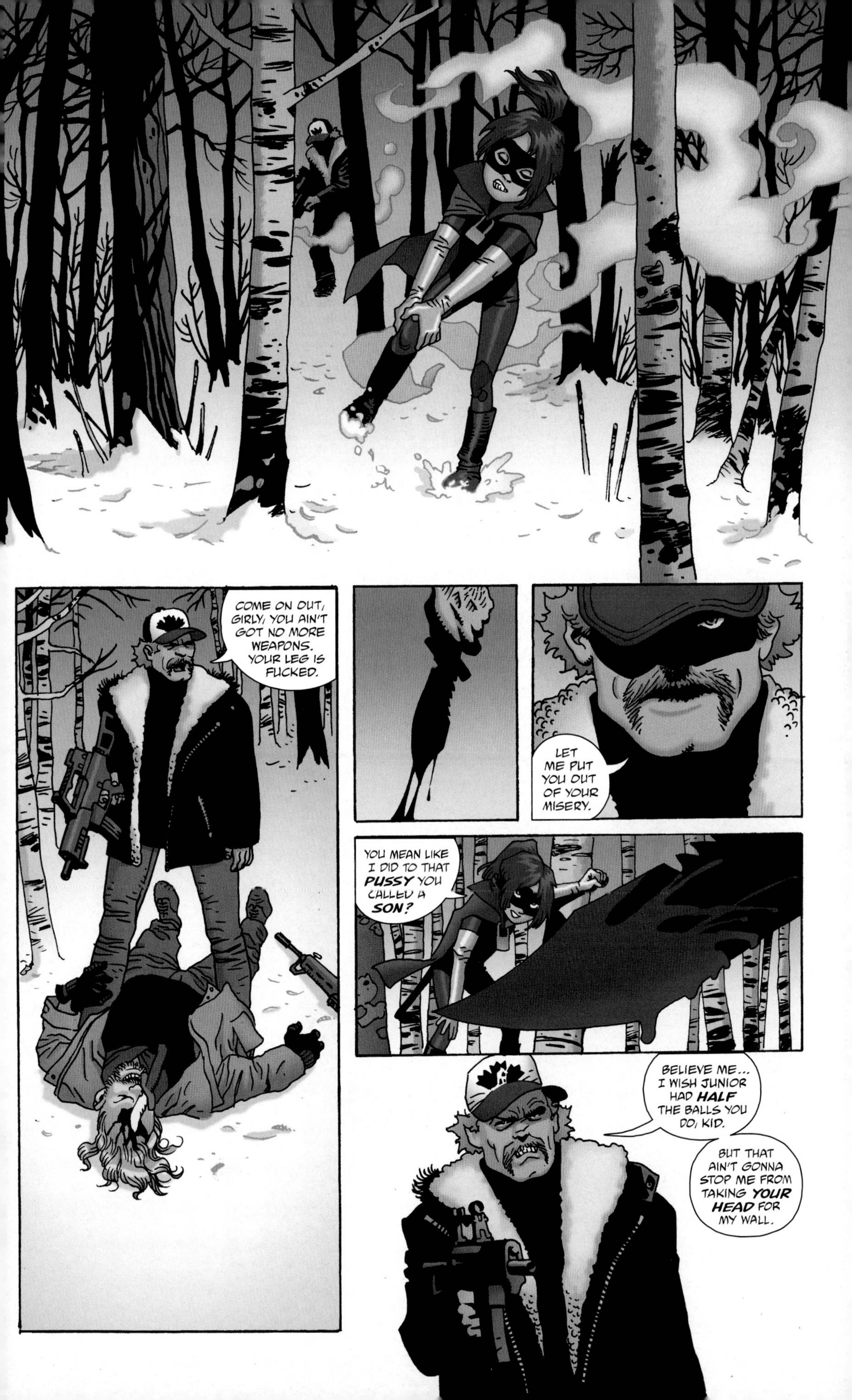
COME ON OUT, GIRLY, YOU AIN'T GOT NO MORE WEAPONS. YOUR LEG IS FUCKED.
LET ME PUT YOU OUT OF YOUR MISERY.
YOU MEAN LIKE I DID TO THAT **PUSSY** YOU CALLED A **SON?**
BELIEVE ME... I WISH JUNIOR HAD **HALF** THE BALLS YOU DO, KID.
BUT THAT AIN'T GONNA STOP ME FROM TAKING **YOUR HEAD** FOR MY WALL.

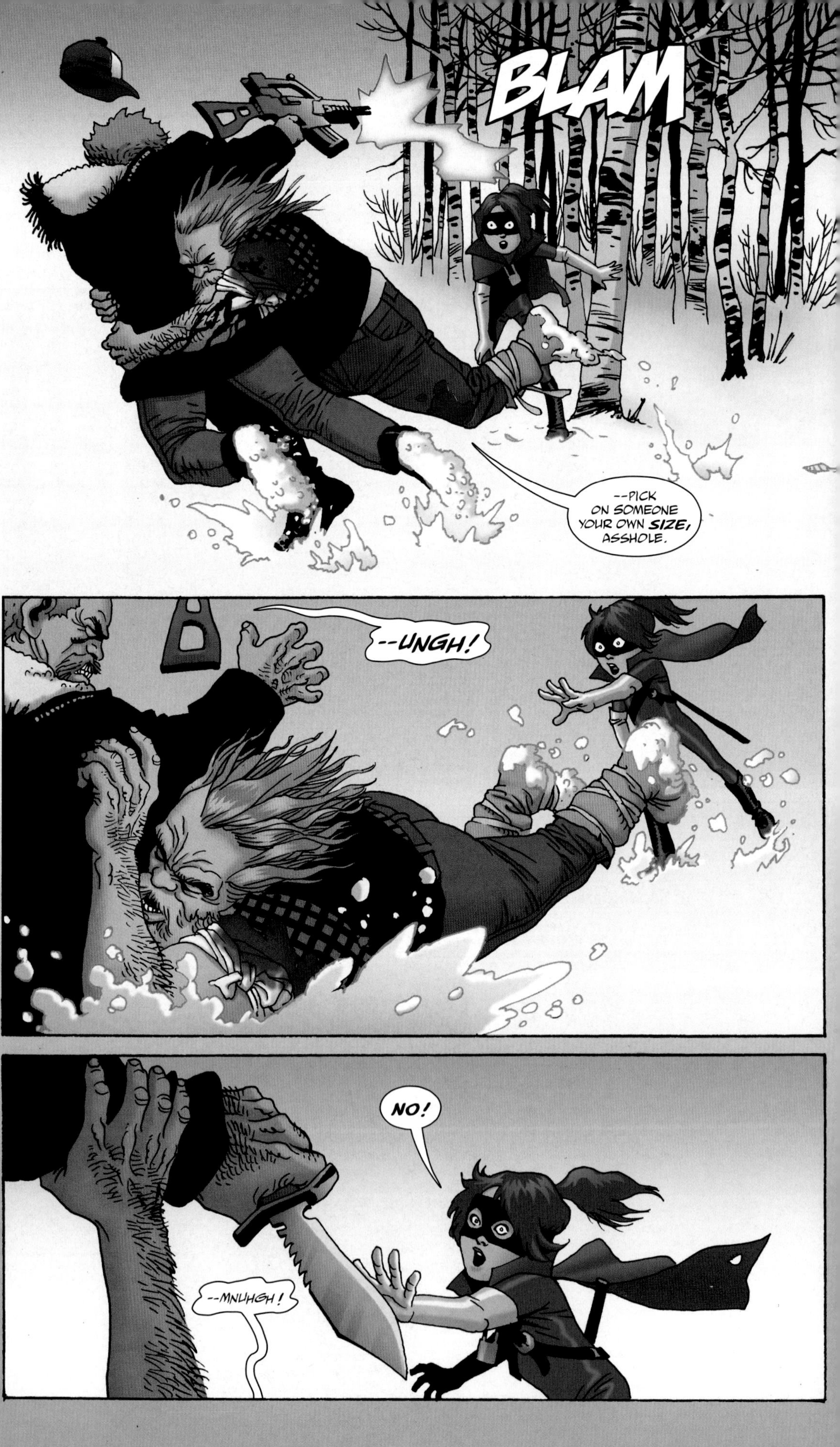
BLAM
--PICK ON SOMEONE YOUR OWN SIZE, ASSHOLE.
--UNGH!
NO!
--MNUHGH!

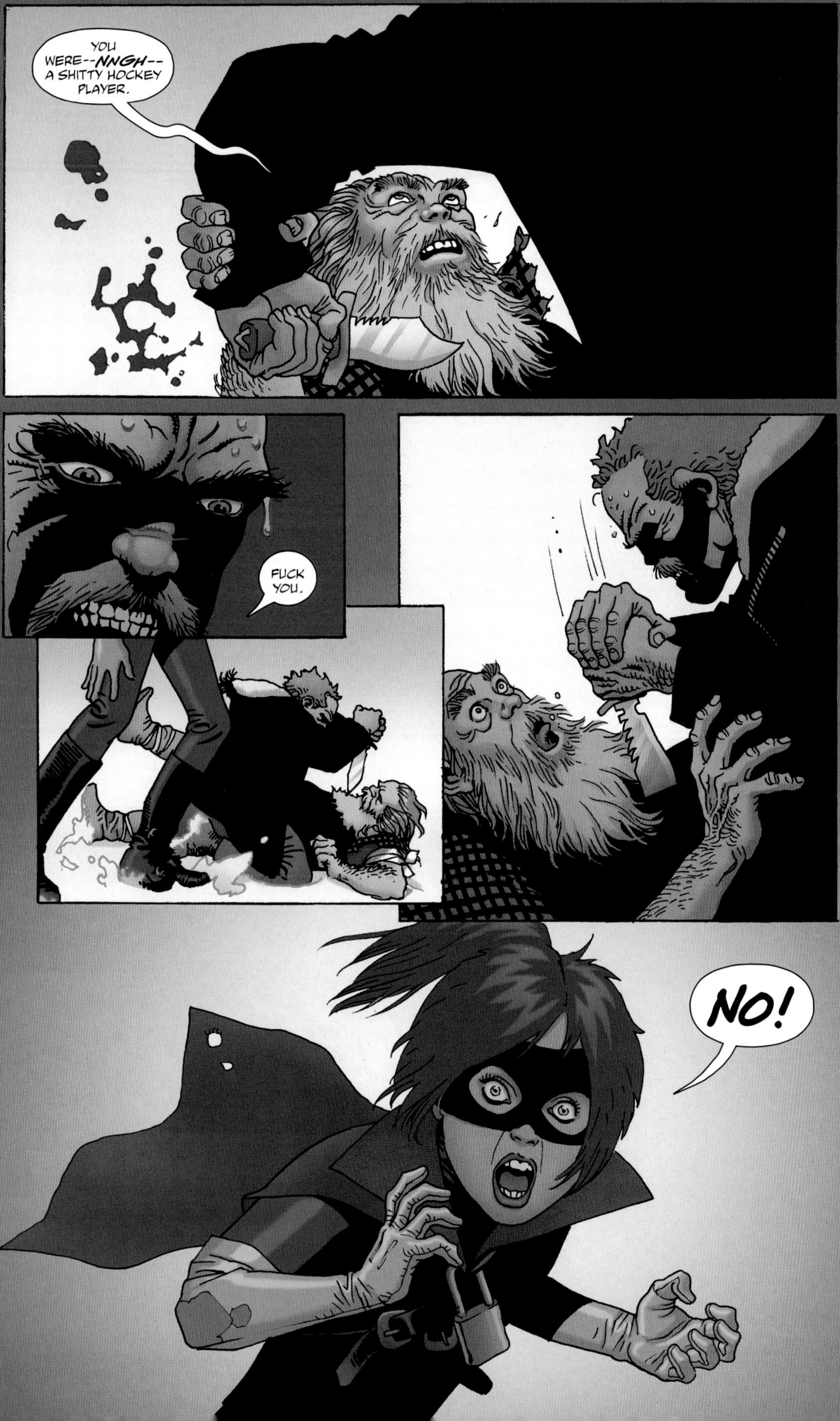

YOU WERE--NNGH--A SHITTY HOCKEY PLAYER.
FUCK YOU.
NO!

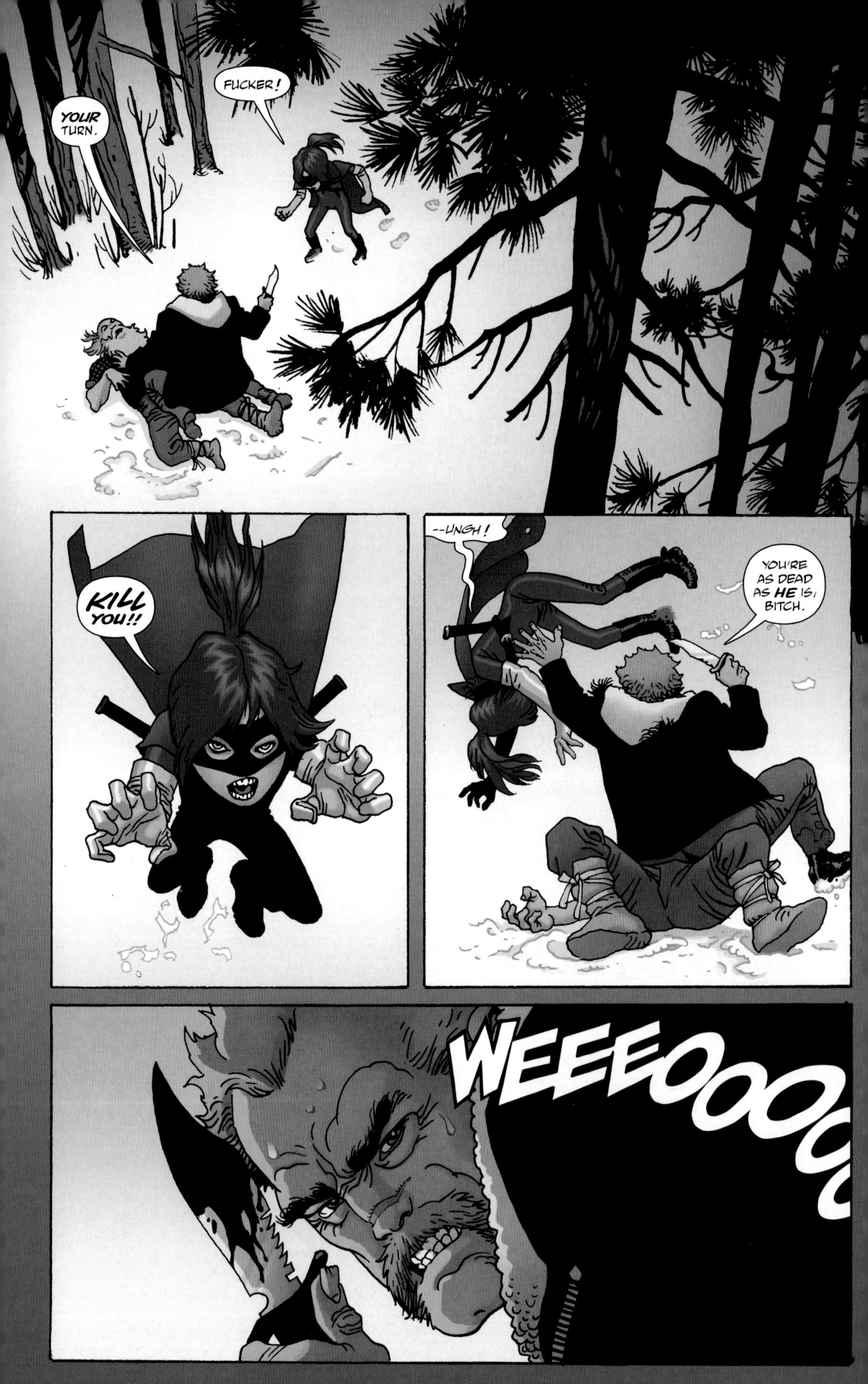
YOUR TURN.
FUCKER!
KILL YOU!!
--UNGH!
YOU'RE AS DEAD AS HE IS, BITCH.
WEEEOOOO

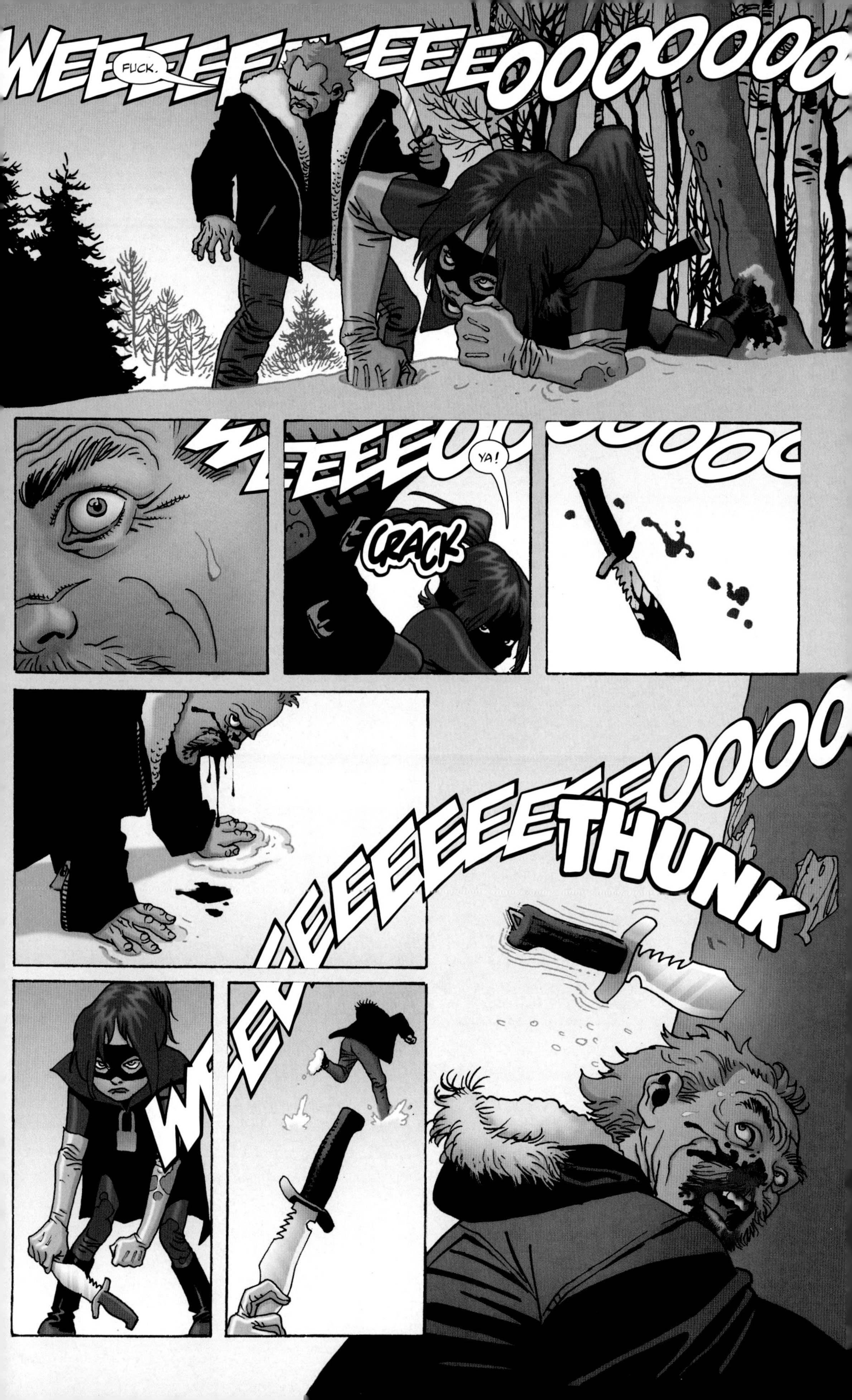
WEEEEEEEEEOOOOOOO
FUCK.
WEEEEEO
YA!
CRACK
OOOOOO
WEEEEEEEEEEOOOOO
THUNK

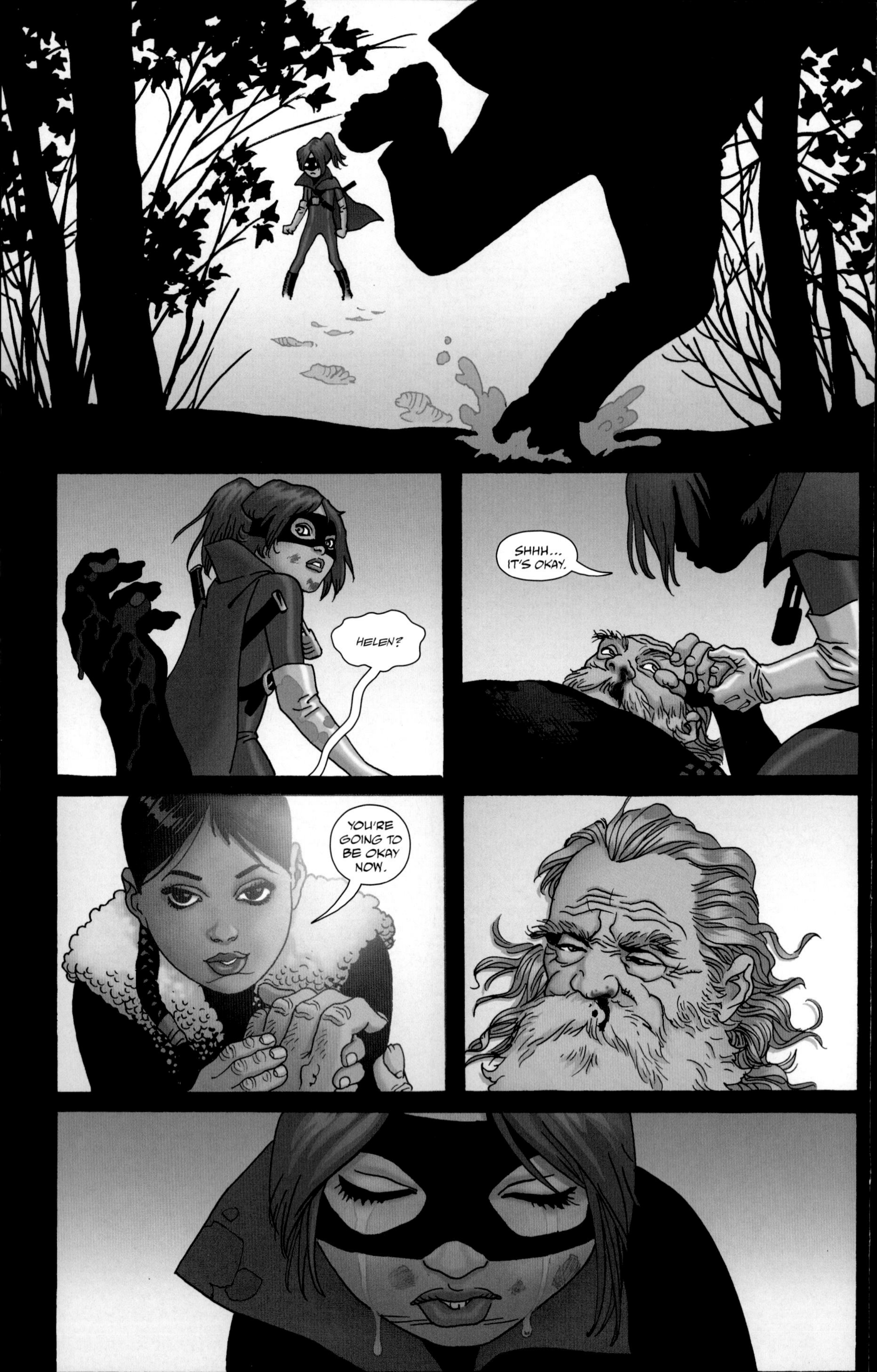
HELEN?
SHHH... IT'S OKAY.
YOU'RE GOING TO BE OKAY NOW.

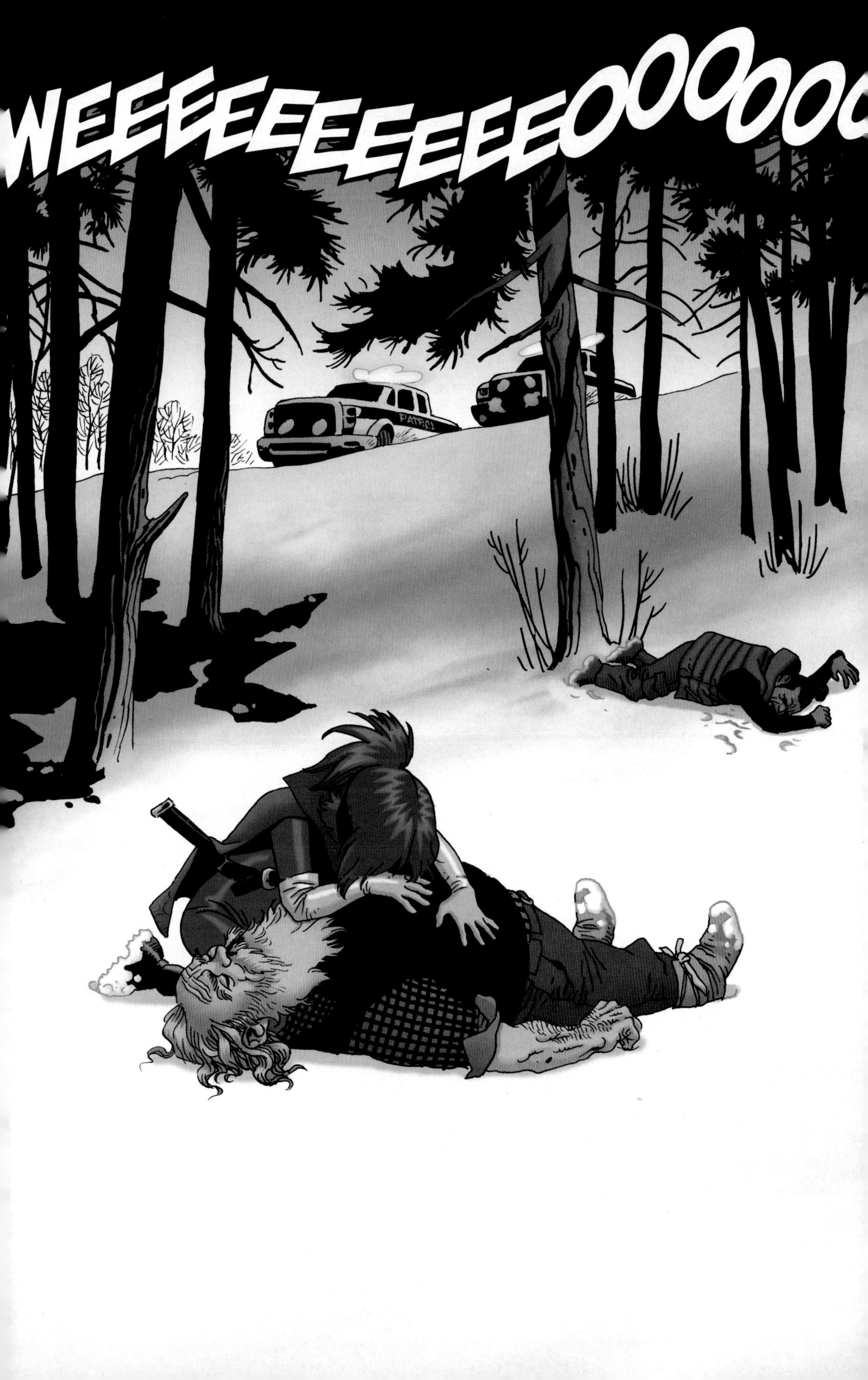
WEEEEEEEEEEOOOOO

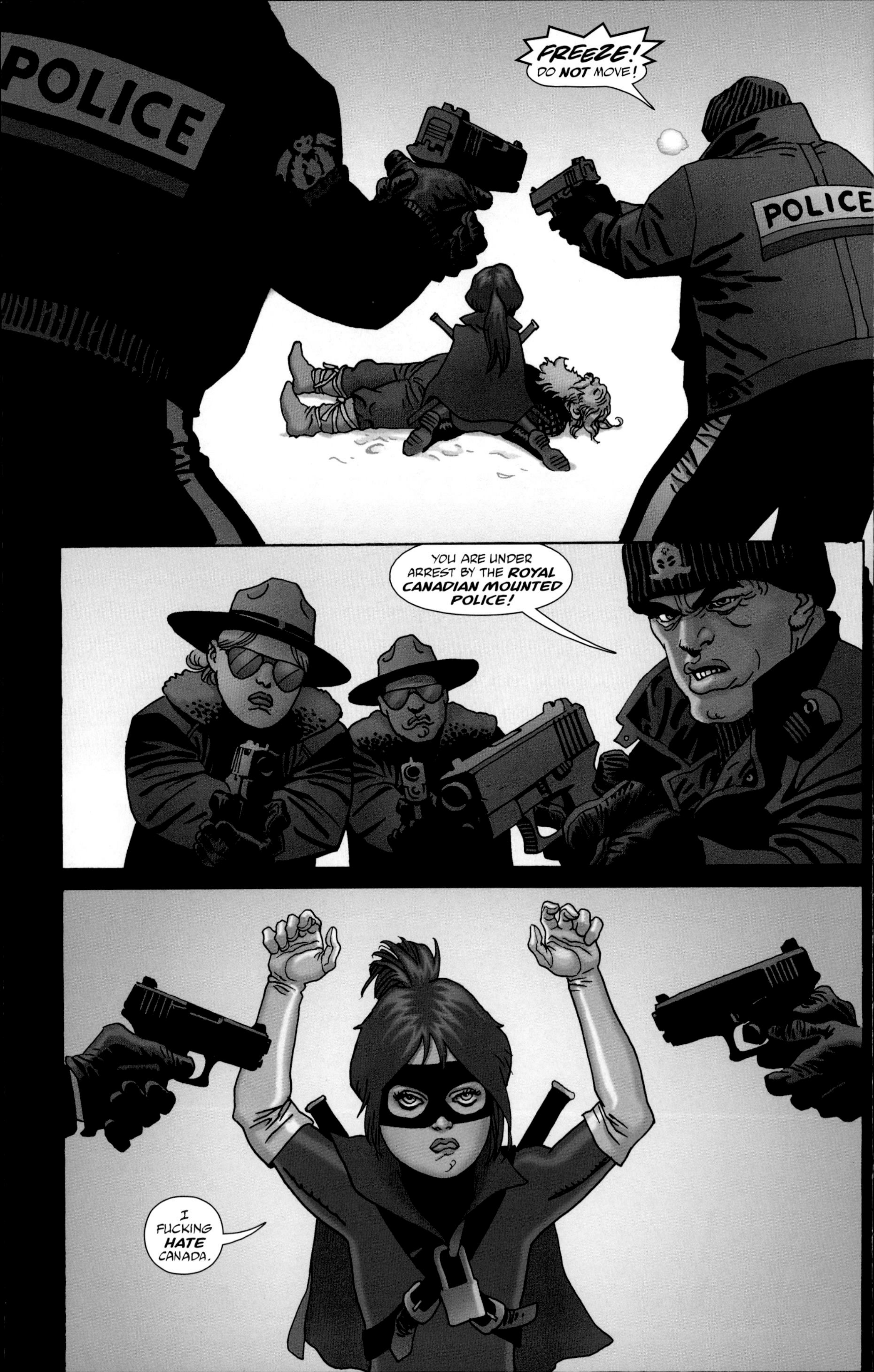
FREEZE! DO NOT MOVE!
POLICE
POLICE
YOU ARE UNDER ARREST BY THE ROYAL CANADIAN MOUNTED POLICE!
I FUCKING HATE CANADA.

FOUR

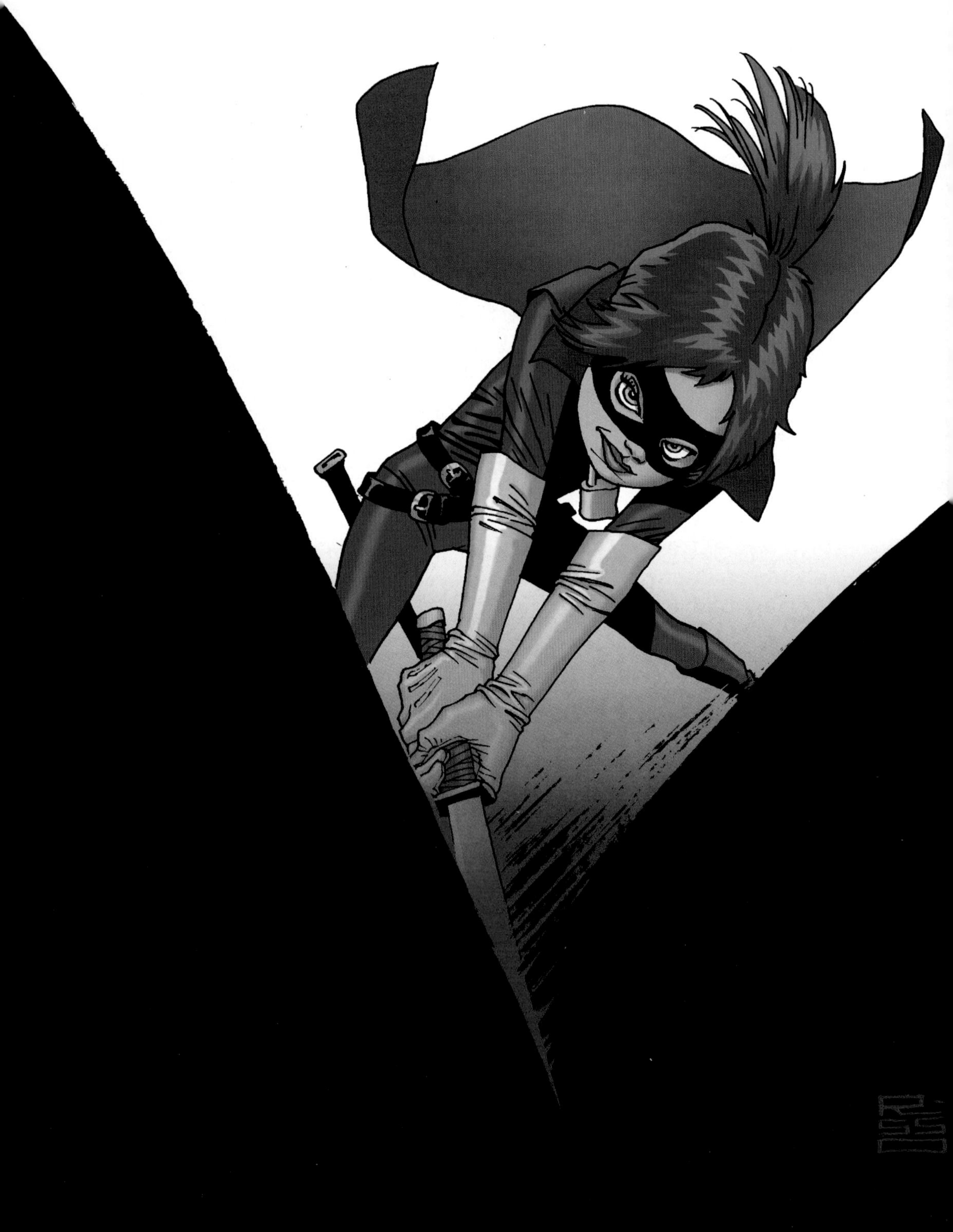

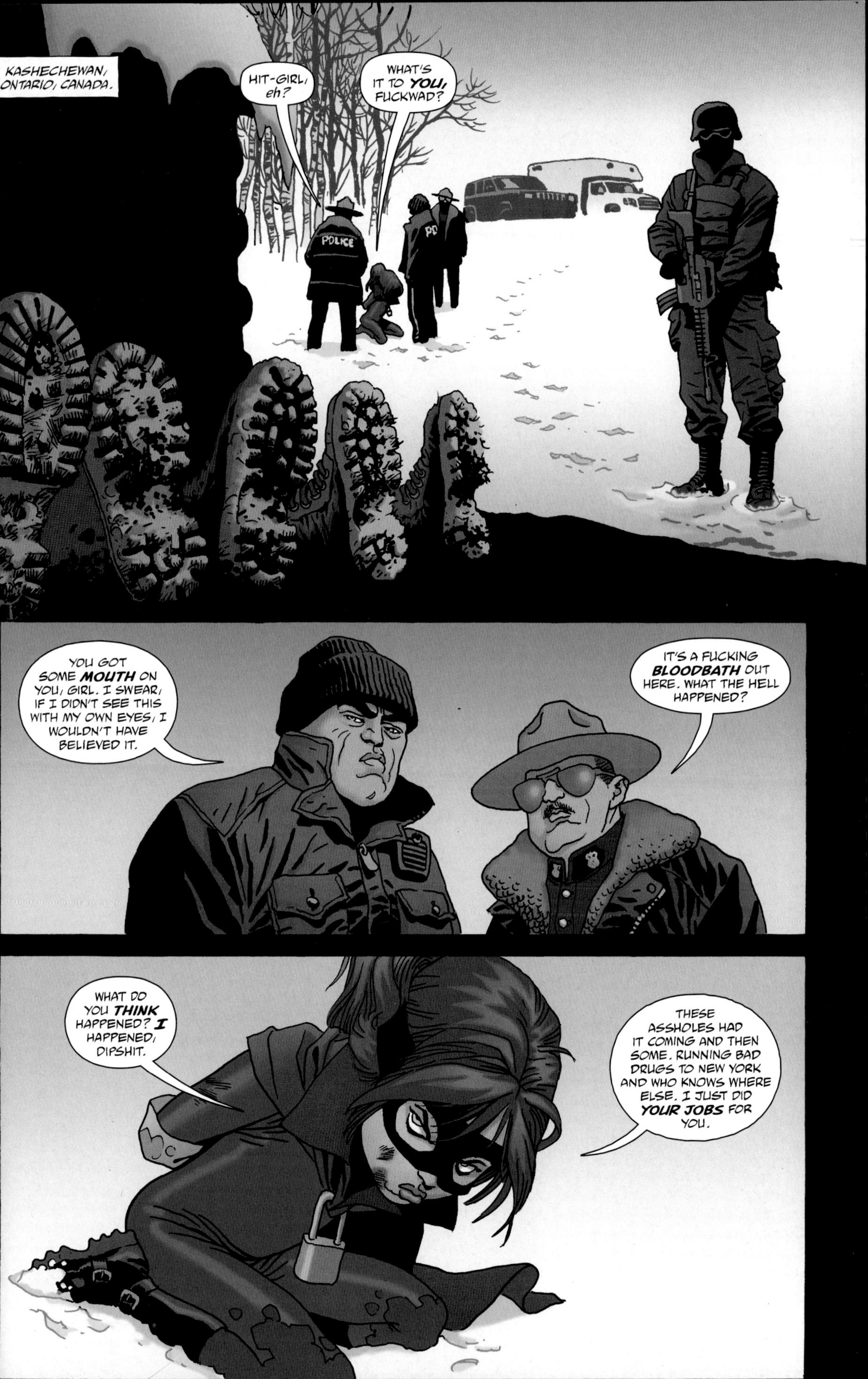
KASHECHEWAN, ONTARIO, CANADA.
HIT-GIRL, eh?
WHAT'S IT TO YOU, FUCKWAD?
YOU GOT SOME MOUTH ON YOU, GIRL. I SWEAR, IF I DIDN'T SEE THIS WITH MY OWN EYES, I WOULDN'T HAVE BELIEVED IT.
IT'S A FUCKING BLOODBATH OUT HERE. WHAT THE HELL HAPPENED?
WHAT DO YOU THINK HAPPENED? I HAPPENED, DIPSHIT.
THESE ASSHOLES HAD IT COMING AND THEN SOME. RUNNING BAD DRUGS TO NEW YORK AND WHO KNOWS WHERE ELSE. I JUST DID YOUR JOBS FOR YOU.

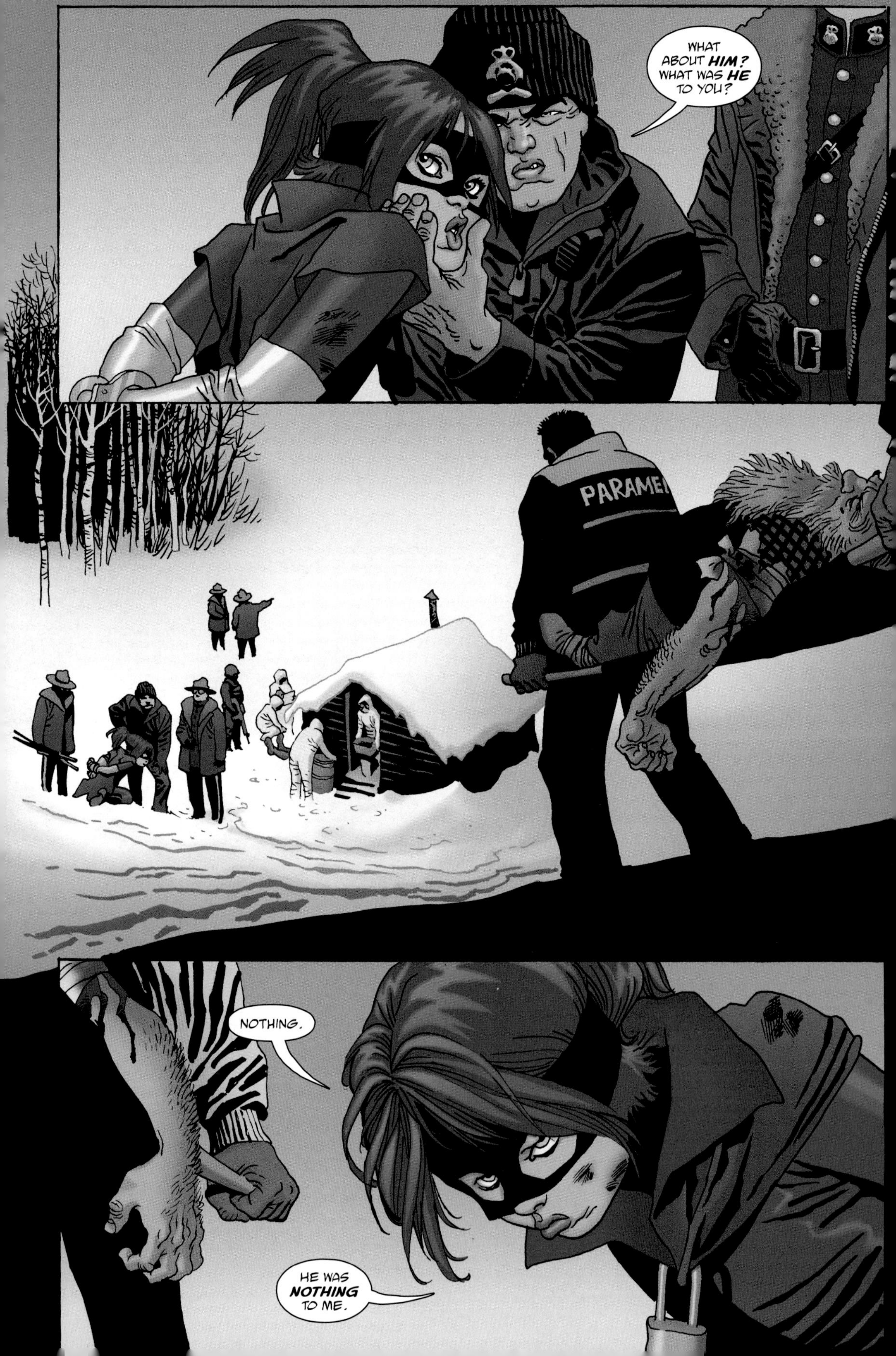
WHAT ABOUT HIM? WHAT WAS HE TO YOU?
PARAMEI
NOTHING.
HE WAS NOTHING TO ME.

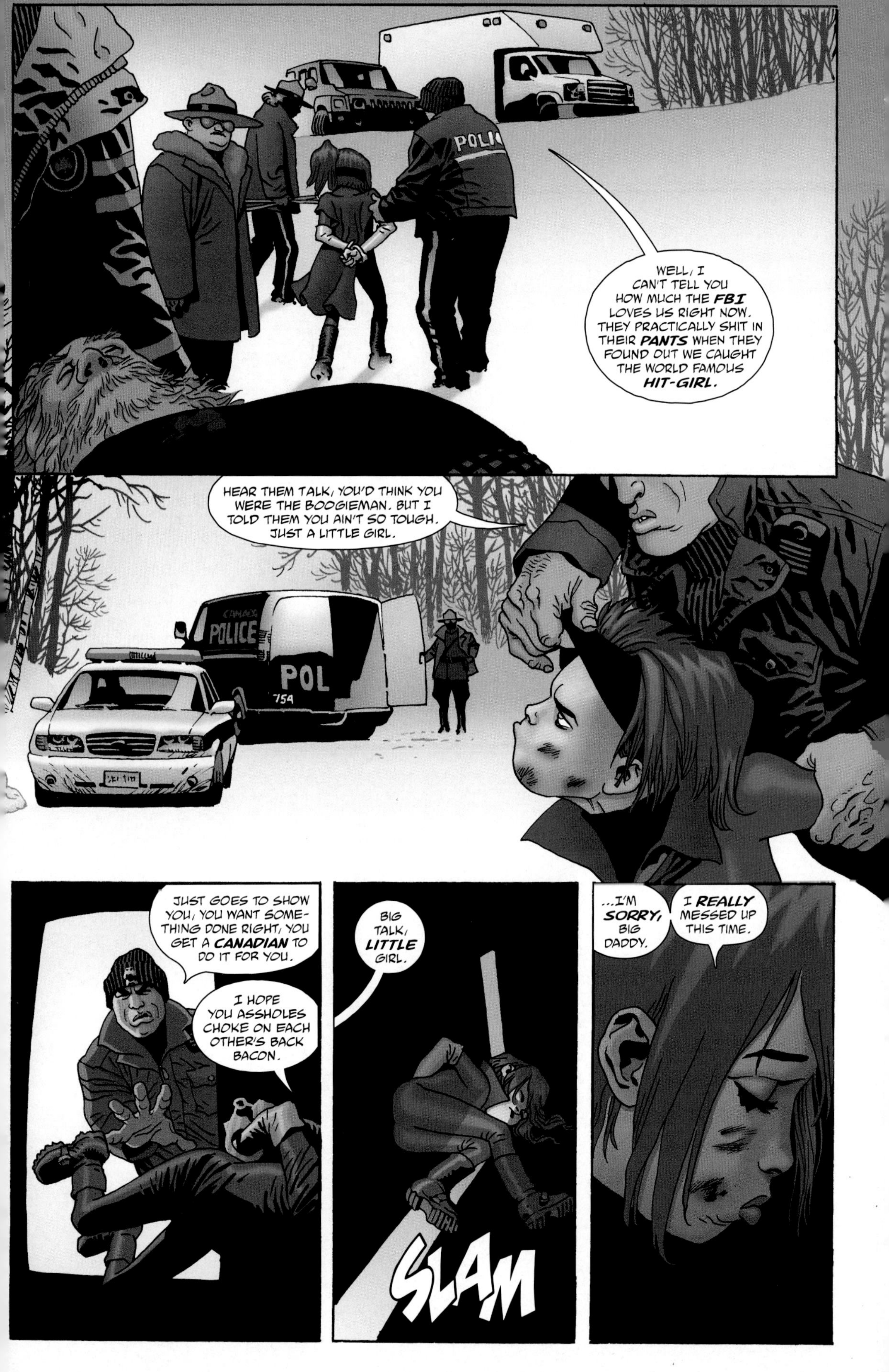
POLIC
WELL, I CAN'T TELL YOU HOW MUCH THE FBI LOVES US RIGHT NOW. THEY PRACTICALLY SHIT IN THEIR PANTS WHEN THEY FOUND OUT WE CAUGHT THE WORLD FAMOUS HIT-GIRL.
HEAR THEM TALK, YOU'D THINK YOU WERE THE BOOGIEMAN. BUT I TOLD THEM YOU AIN'T SO TOUGH. JUST A LITTLE GIRL.
POLICE
POL
754
JUST GOES TO SHOW YOU, YOU WANT SOMETHING DONE RIGHT, YOU GET A CANADIAN TO DO IT FOR YOU.
I HOPE YOU ASSHOLES CHOKE ON EACH OTHER'S BACK BACON.
BIG TALK, LITTLE GIRL.
SLAM
...I'M SORRY, BIG DADDY.
I REALLY MESSED UP THIS TIME.

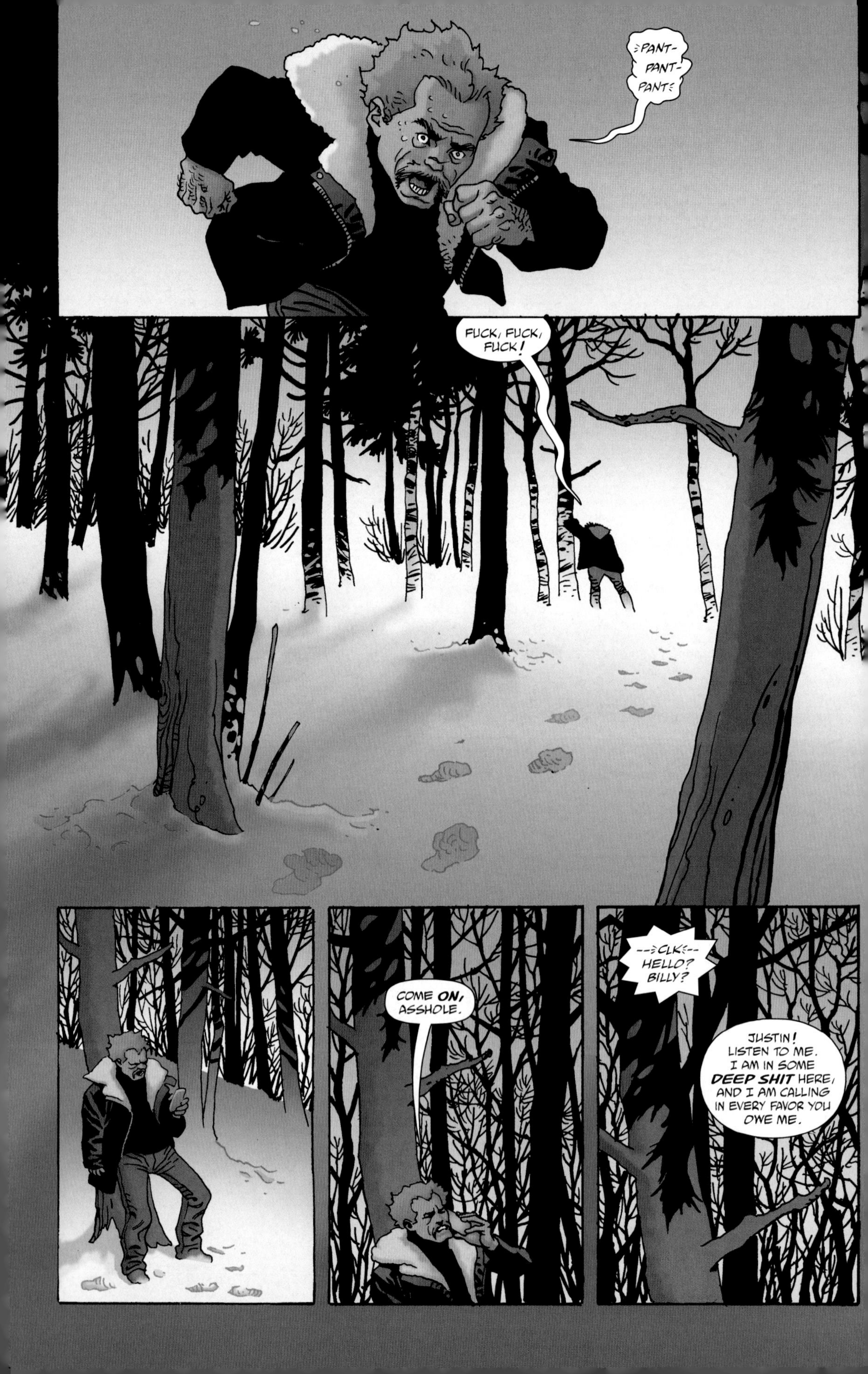
PANT-
PANT-
PANT
FUCK, FUCK, FUCK!
COME ON, ASSHOLE.
CLK
HELLO? BILLY?
JUSTIN! LISTEN TO ME. I AM IN SOME DEEP SHIT HERE, AND I AM CALLING IN EVERY FAVOR YOU OWE ME.

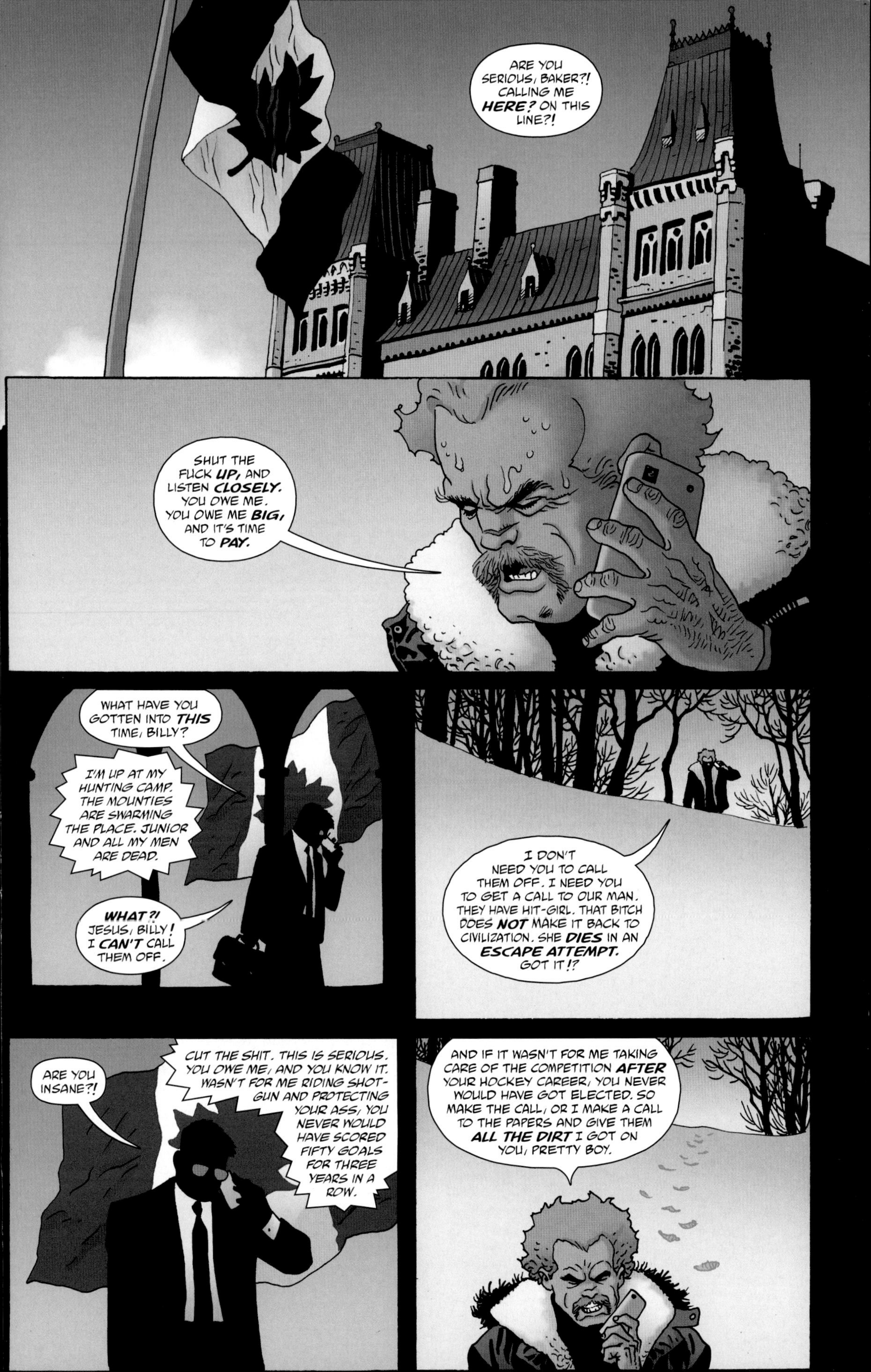

ARE YOU SERIOUS, BAKER?! CALLING ME HERE? ON THIS LINE?!
SHUT THE FUCK UP, AND LISTEN CLOSELY. YOU OWE ME. YOU OWE ME BIG, AND IT'S TIME TO PAY.
WHAT HAVE YOU GOTTEN INTO THIS TIME, BILLY?
I'M UP AT MY HUNTING CAMP. THE MOUNTIES ARE SWARMING THE PLACE. JUNIOR AND ALL MY MEN ARE DEAD.
WHAT?! JESUS, BILLY! I CAN'T CALL THEM OFF.
I DON'T NEED YOU TO CALL THEM OFF. I NEED YOU TO GET A CALL TO OUR MAN. THEY HAVE HIT-GIRL. THAT BITCH DOES NOT MAKE IT BACK TO CIVILIZATION. SHE DIES IN AN ESCAPE ATTEMPT. GOT IT!?
ARE YOU INSANE?!
CUT THE SHIT. THIS IS SERIOUS. YOU OWE ME, AND YOU KNOW IT. WASN'T FOR ME RIDING SHOT-GUN AND PROTECTING YOUR ASS, YOU NEVER WOULD HAVE SCORED FIFTY GOALS FOR THREE YEARS IN A ROW.
AND IF IT WASN'T FOR ME TAKING CARE OF THE COMPETITION AFTER YOUR HOCKEY CAREER, YOU NEVER WOULD HAVE GOT ELECTED. SO MAKE THE CALL, OR I MAKE A CALL TO THE PAPERS AND GIVE THEM ALL THE DIRT I GOT ON YOU, PRETTY BOY.

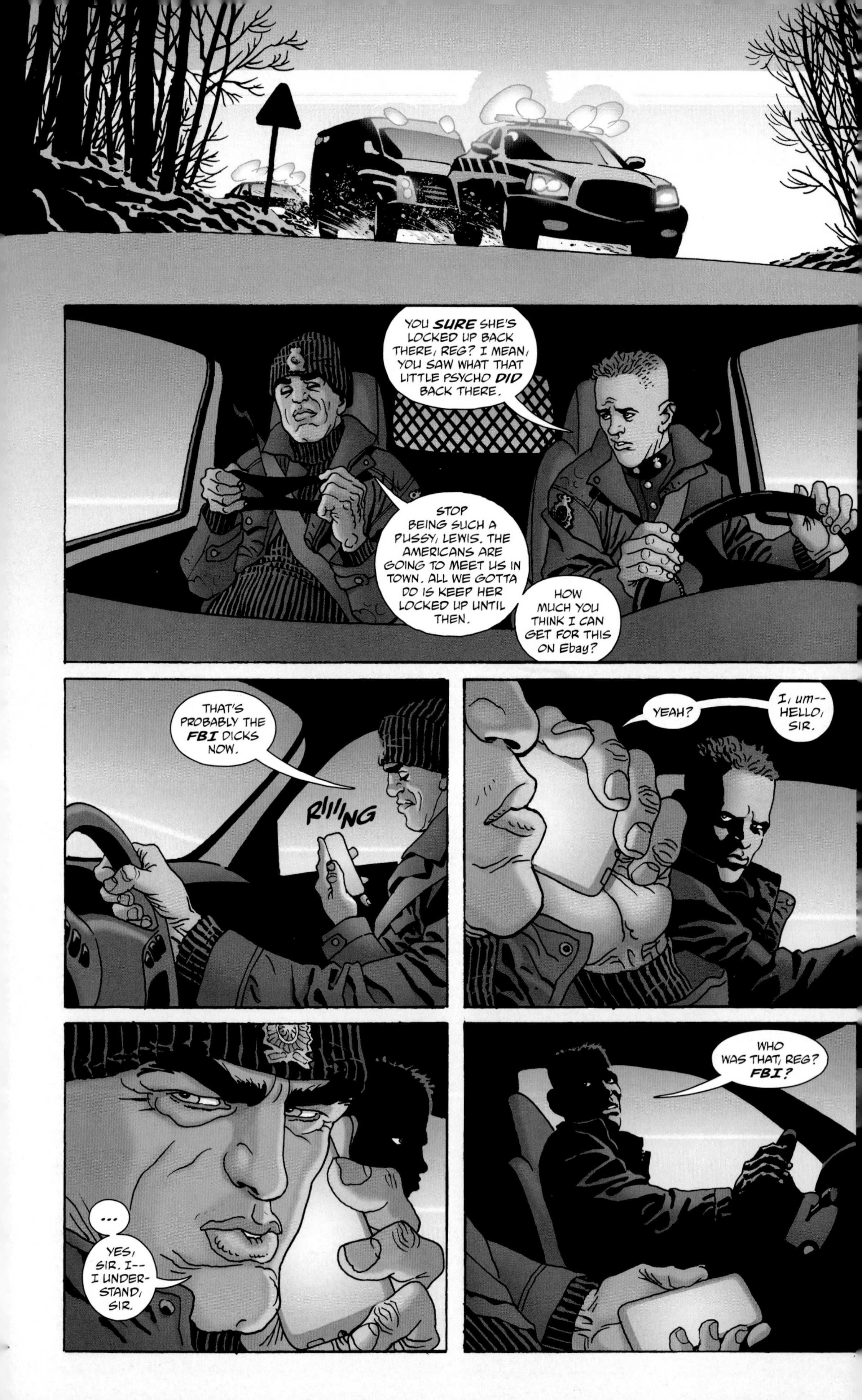
YOU **SURE** SHE'S LOCKED UP BACK THERE, REG? I MEAN, YOU SAW WHAT THAT LITTLE PSYCHO **DID** BACK THERE.
STOP BEING SUCH A PUSSY, LEWIS. THE AMERICANS ARE GOING TO MEET US IN TOWN. ALL WE GOTTA DO IS KEEP HER LOCKED UP UNTIL THEN.
HOW MUCH YOU THINK I CAN GET FOR THIS ON Ebay?
THAT'S PROBABLY THE **FBI** DICKS NOW.
RIIIING
YEAH?
I, um-- HELLO, SIR.
...
YES, SIR. I-- I UNDERSTAND, SIR.
WHO WAS THAT, REG? **FBI?**

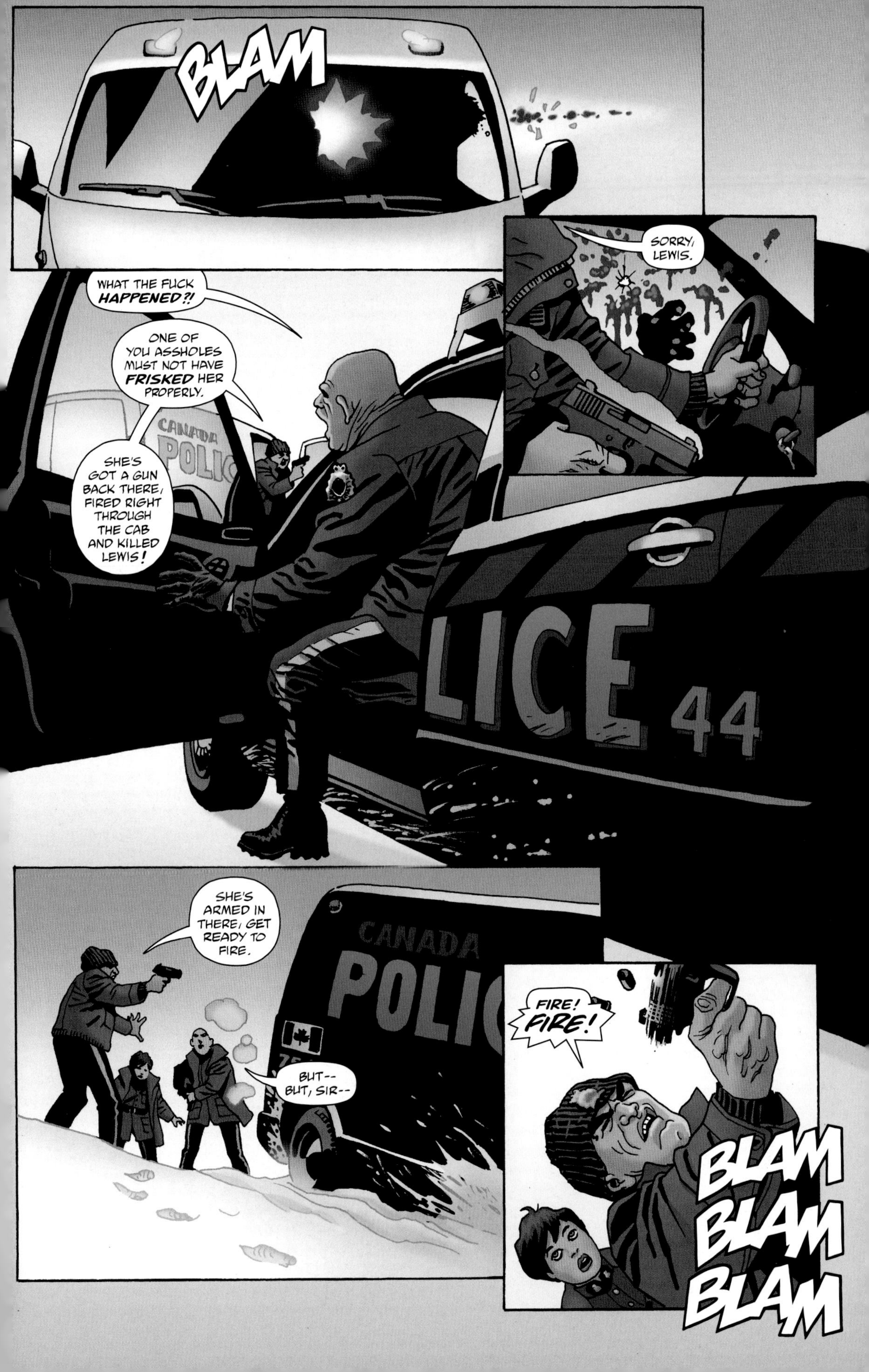
BLAM
SORRY, LEWIS.
WHAT THE FUCK HAPPENED?!
ONE OF YOU ASSHOLES MUST NOT HAVE FRISKED HER PROPERLY.
SHE'S GOT A GUN BACK THERE, FIRED RIGHT THROUGH THE CAB AND KILLED LEWIS!
CANADA POLIC
LICE 44
SHE'S ARMED IN THERE, GET READY TO FIRE.
BUT-- BUT, SIR--
CANADA POLIC
FIRE! FIRE!
BLAM BLAM BLAM

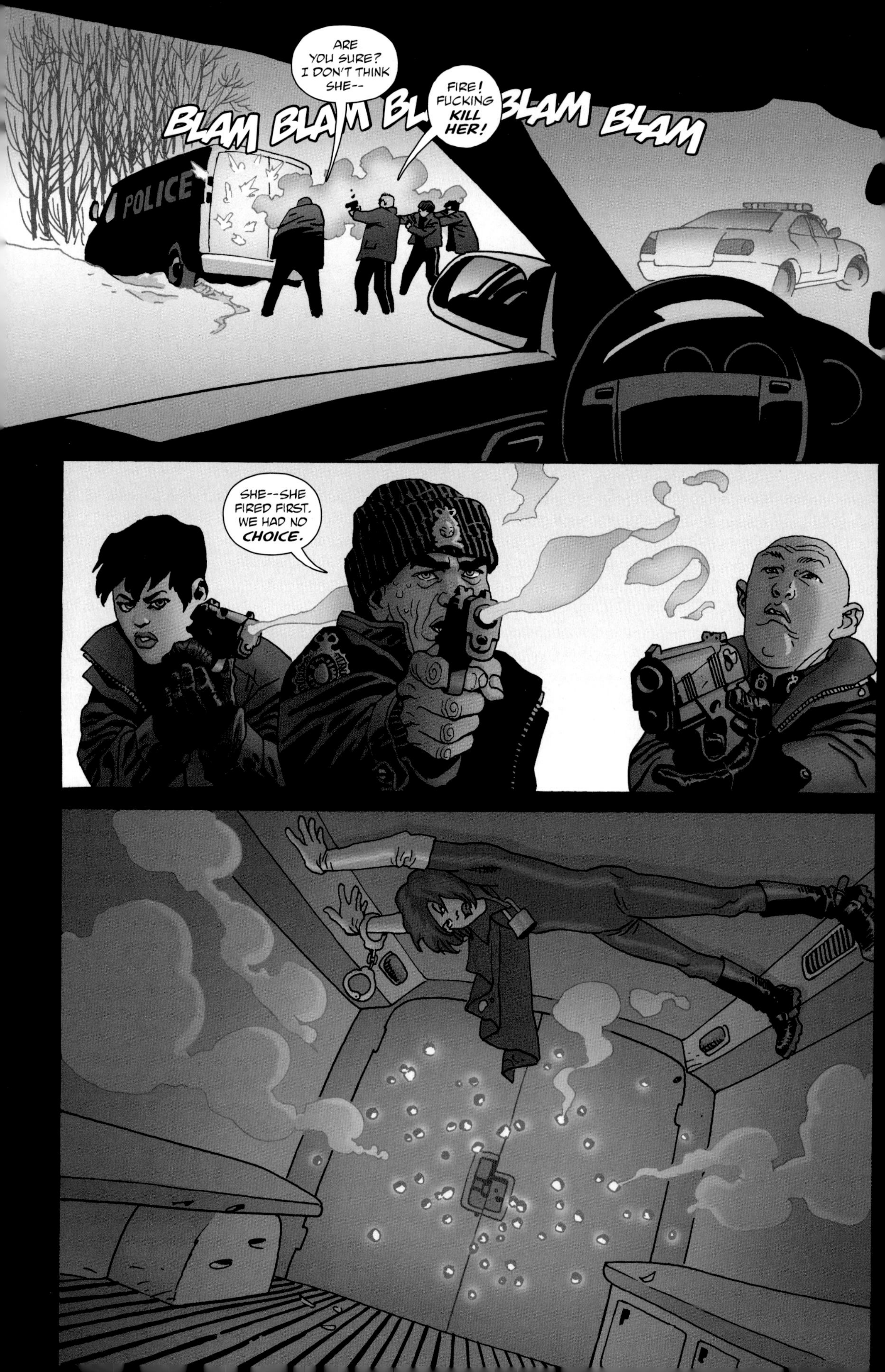
ARE YOU SURE? I DON'T THINK SHE--
BLAM BLAM BLAM BL
FIRE! FUCKING KILL HER!
BLAM BLAM
SHE--SHE FIRED FIRST. WE HAD NO CHOICE.

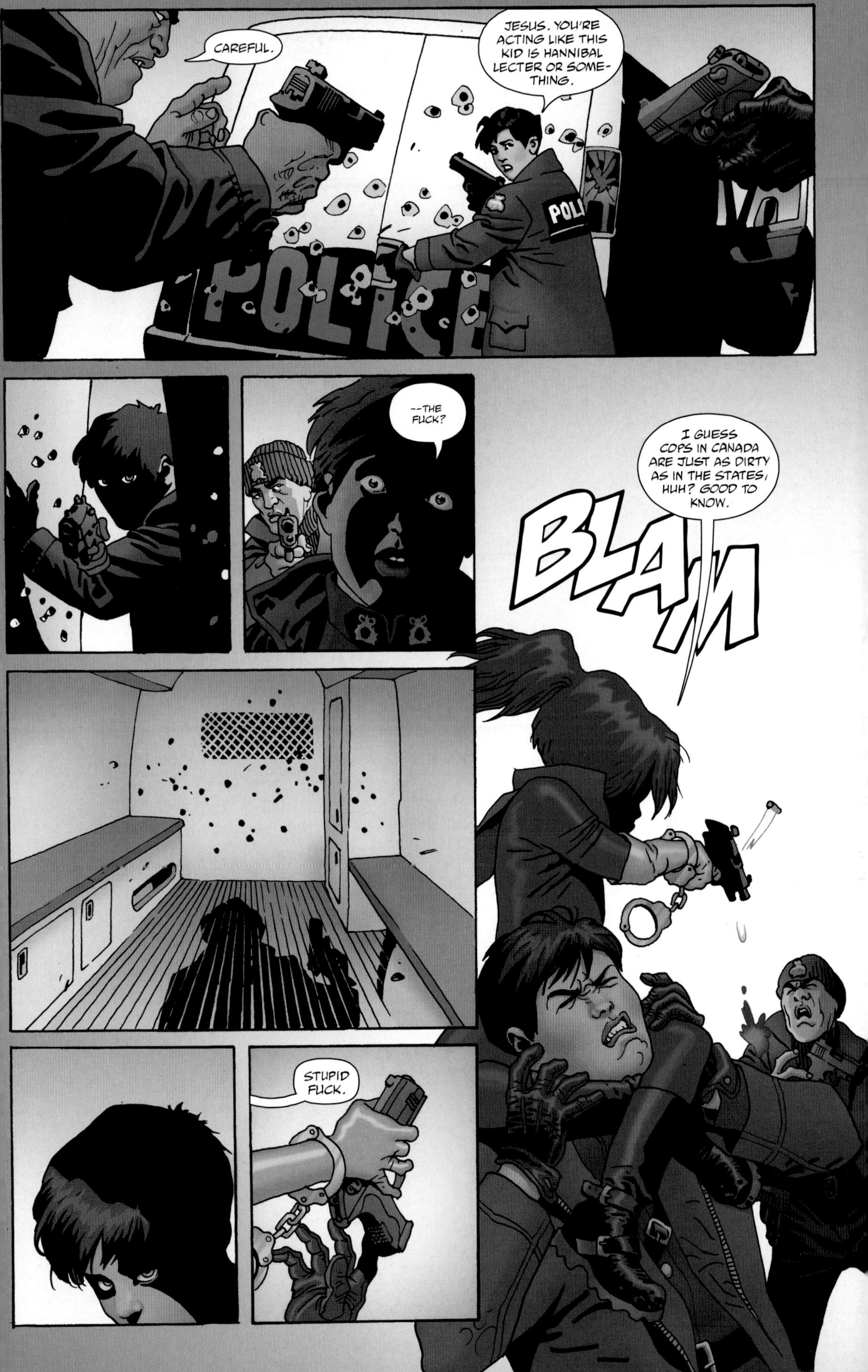
CAREFUL.
JESUS. YOU'RE ACTING LIKE THIS KID IS HANNIBAL LECTER OR SOME-THING.
--THE FUCK?
I GUESS COPS IN CANADA ARE JUST AS DIRTY AS IN THE STATES, HUH? GOOD TO KNOW.
BLAM
STUPID FUCK.

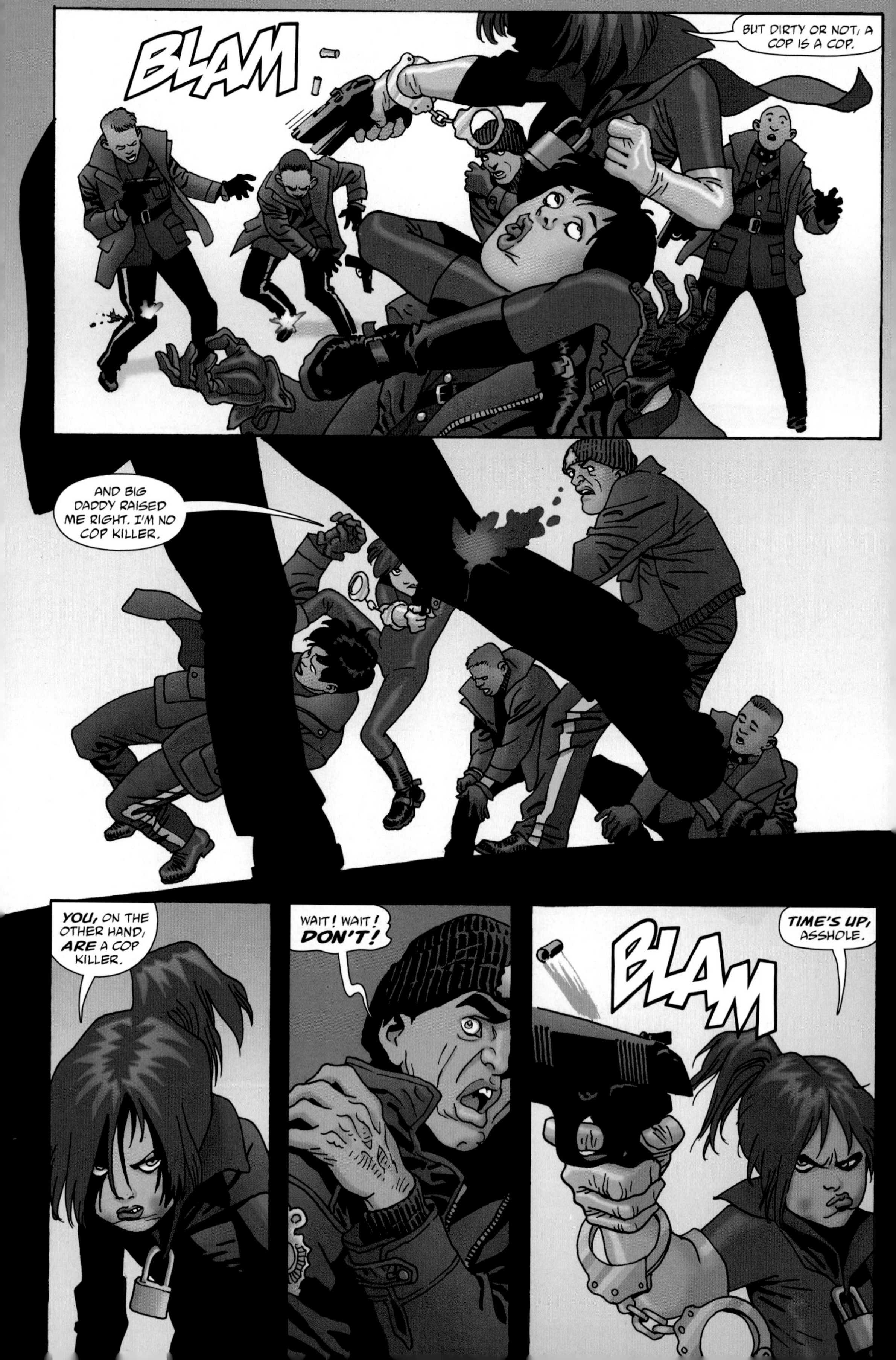
BLAM
BUT DIRTY OR NOT, A COP IS A COP.
AND BIG DADDY RAISED ME RIGHT. I'M NO COP KILLER.
YOU, ON THE OTHER HAND, ARE A COP KILLER.
WAIT! WAIT! DON'T!
BLAM
TIME'S UP, ASSHOLE.

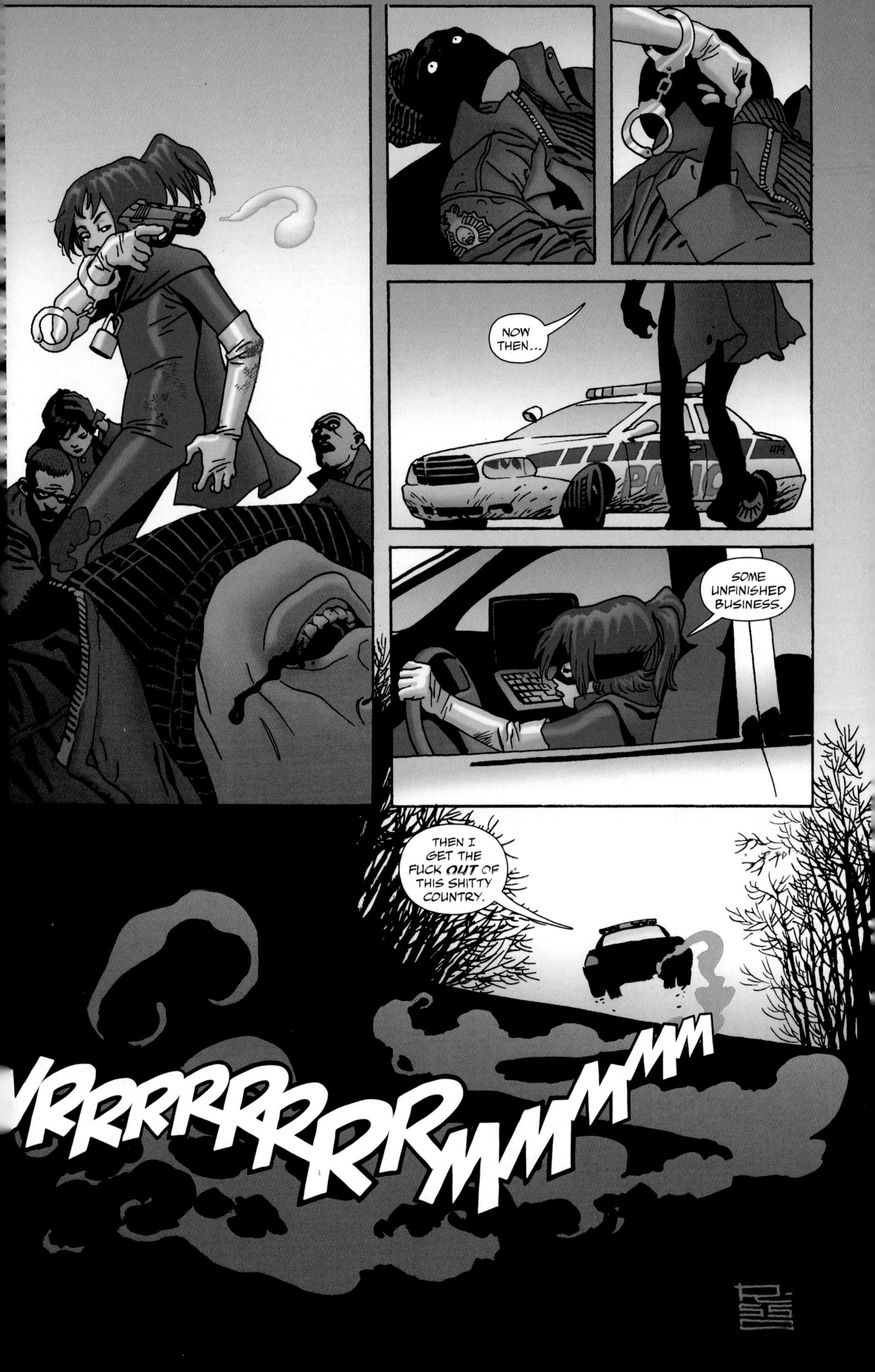
NOW THEN...
SOME UNFINISHED BUSINESS.
THEN I GET THE FUCK OUT OF THIS SHITTY COUNTRY.
VRRRRRRRRRMMMMMM

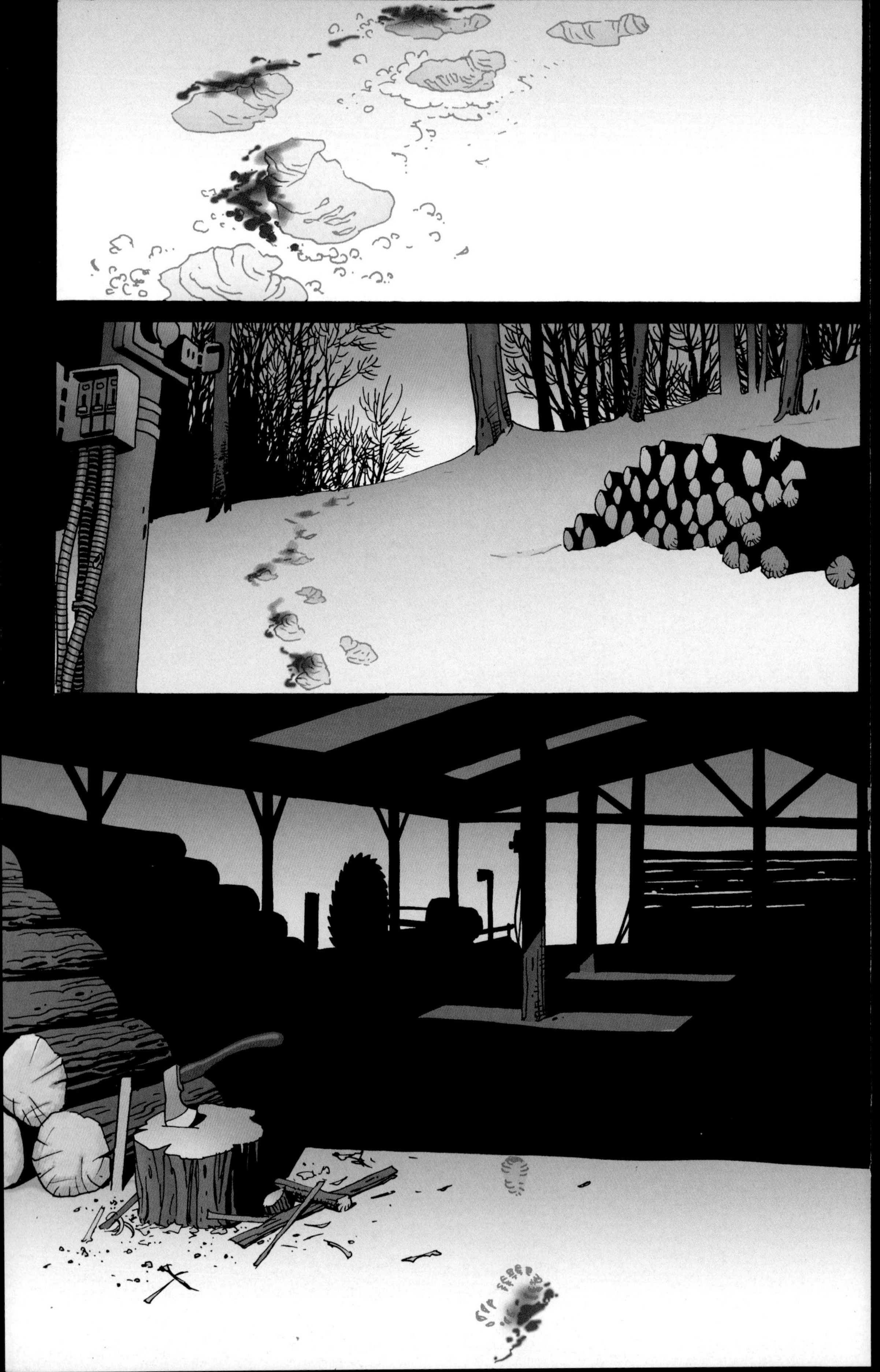

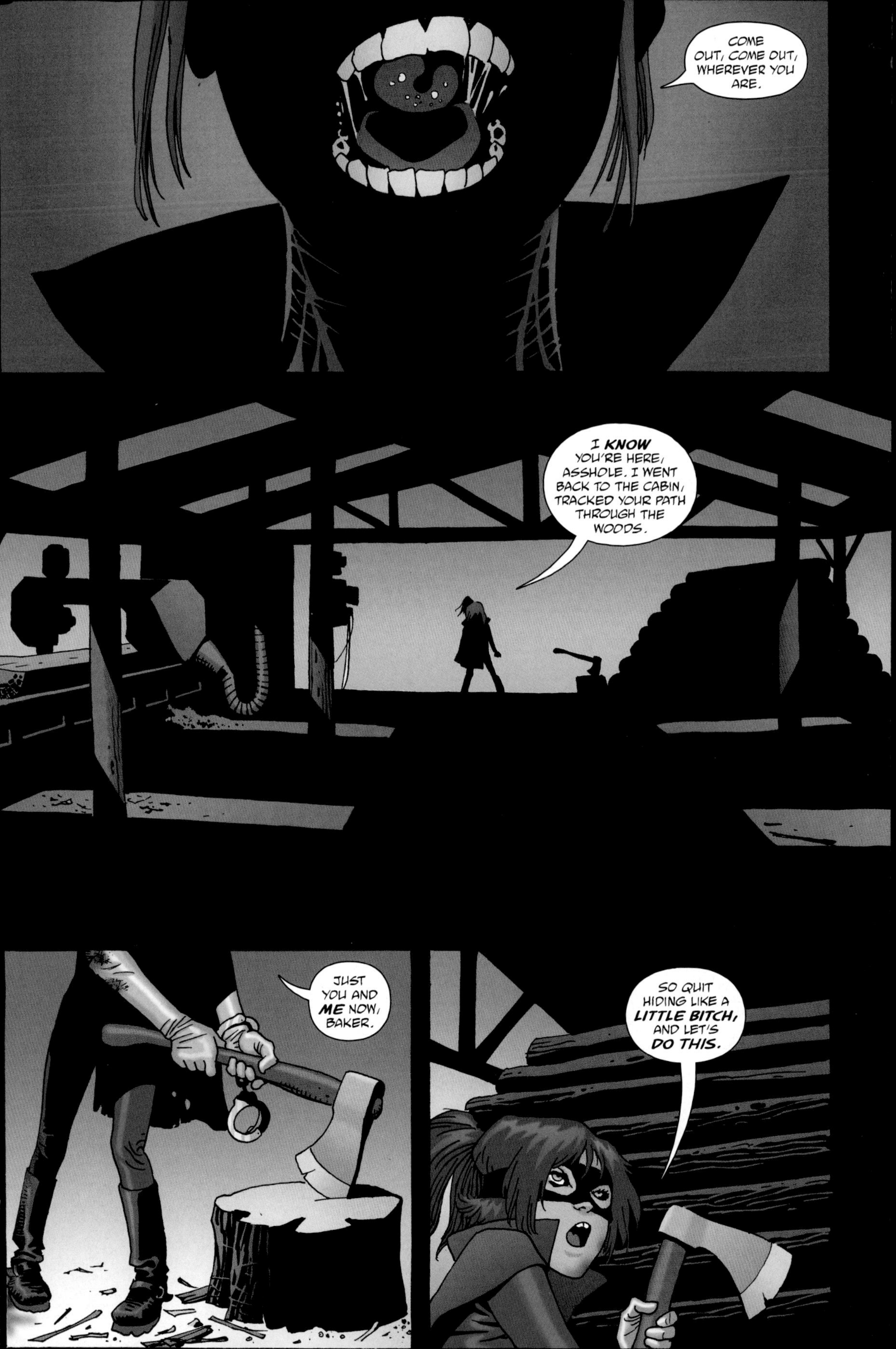
COME OUT, COME OUT, WHEREVER YOU ARE.
I KNOW YOU'RE HERE, ASSHOLE. I WENT BACK TO THE CABIN, TRACKED YOUR PATH THROUGH THE WOODS.
JUST YOU AND ME NOW, BAKER.
SO QUIT HIDING LIKE A LITTLE BITCH, AND LET'S DO THIS.

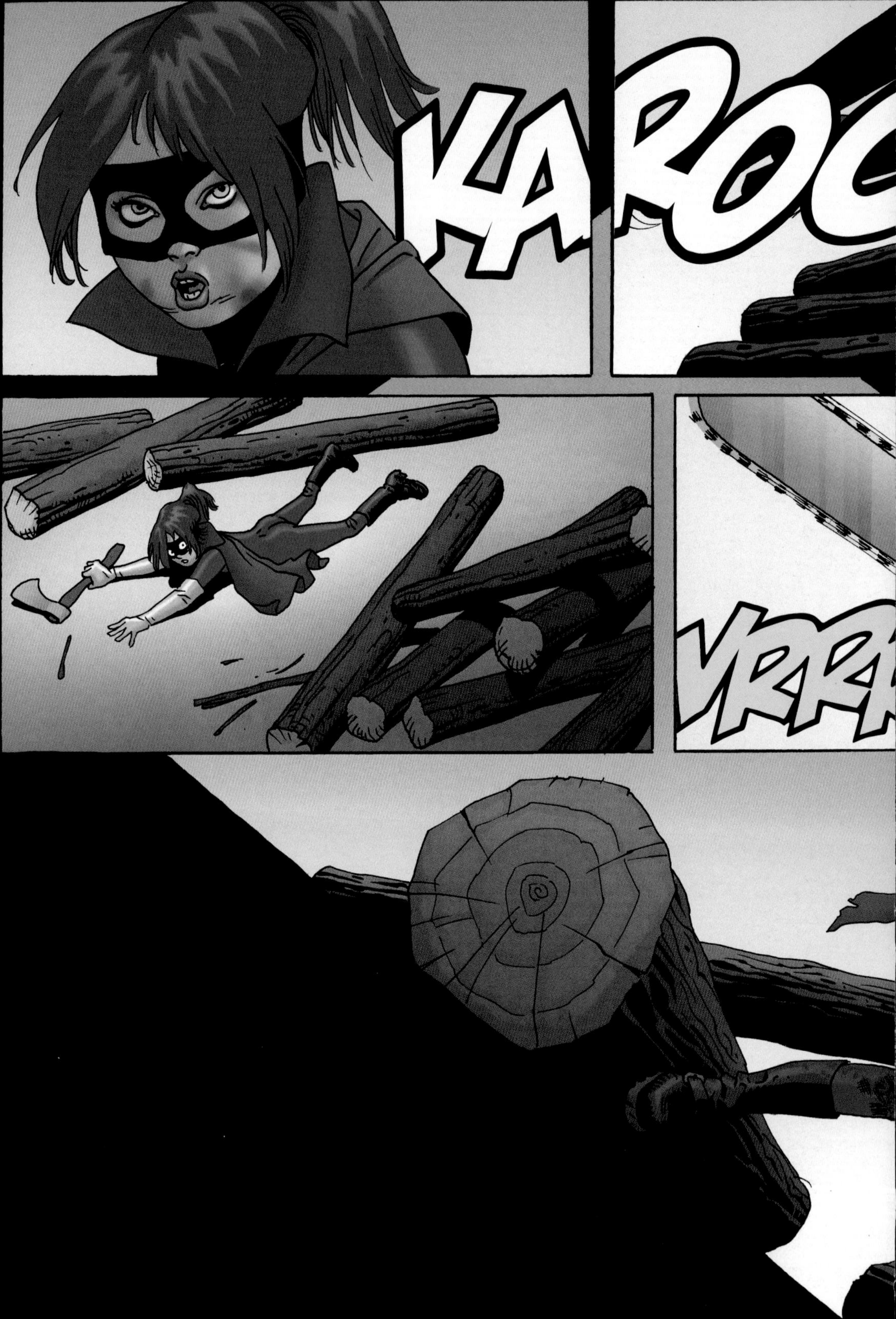
KAROO
VRRR

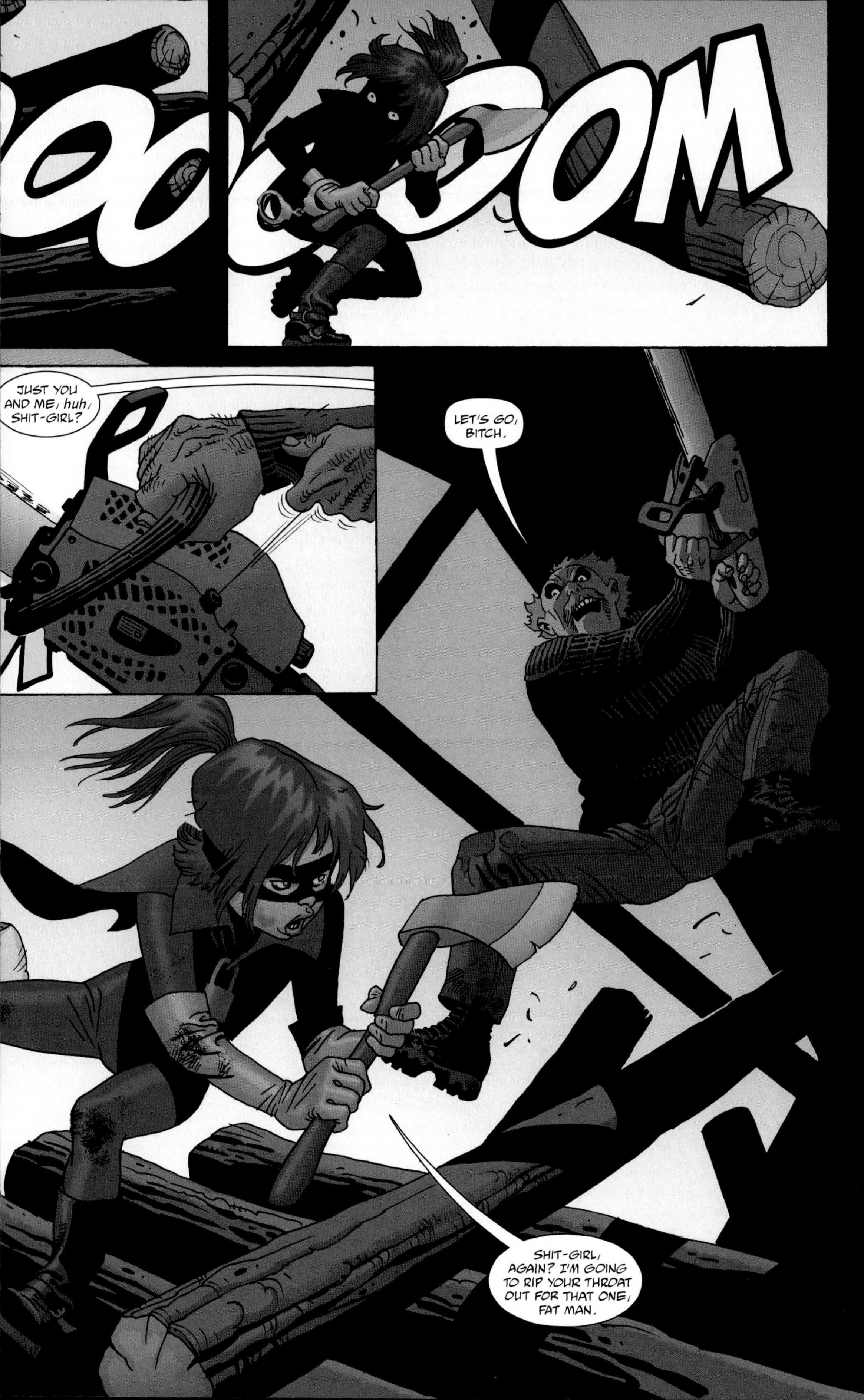
OOOOOM
JUST YOU AND ME, huh, SHIT-GIRL?
LET'S GO, BITCH.
SHIT-GIRL, AGAIN? I'M GOING TO RIP YOUR THROAT OUT FOR THAT ONE, FAT MAN.

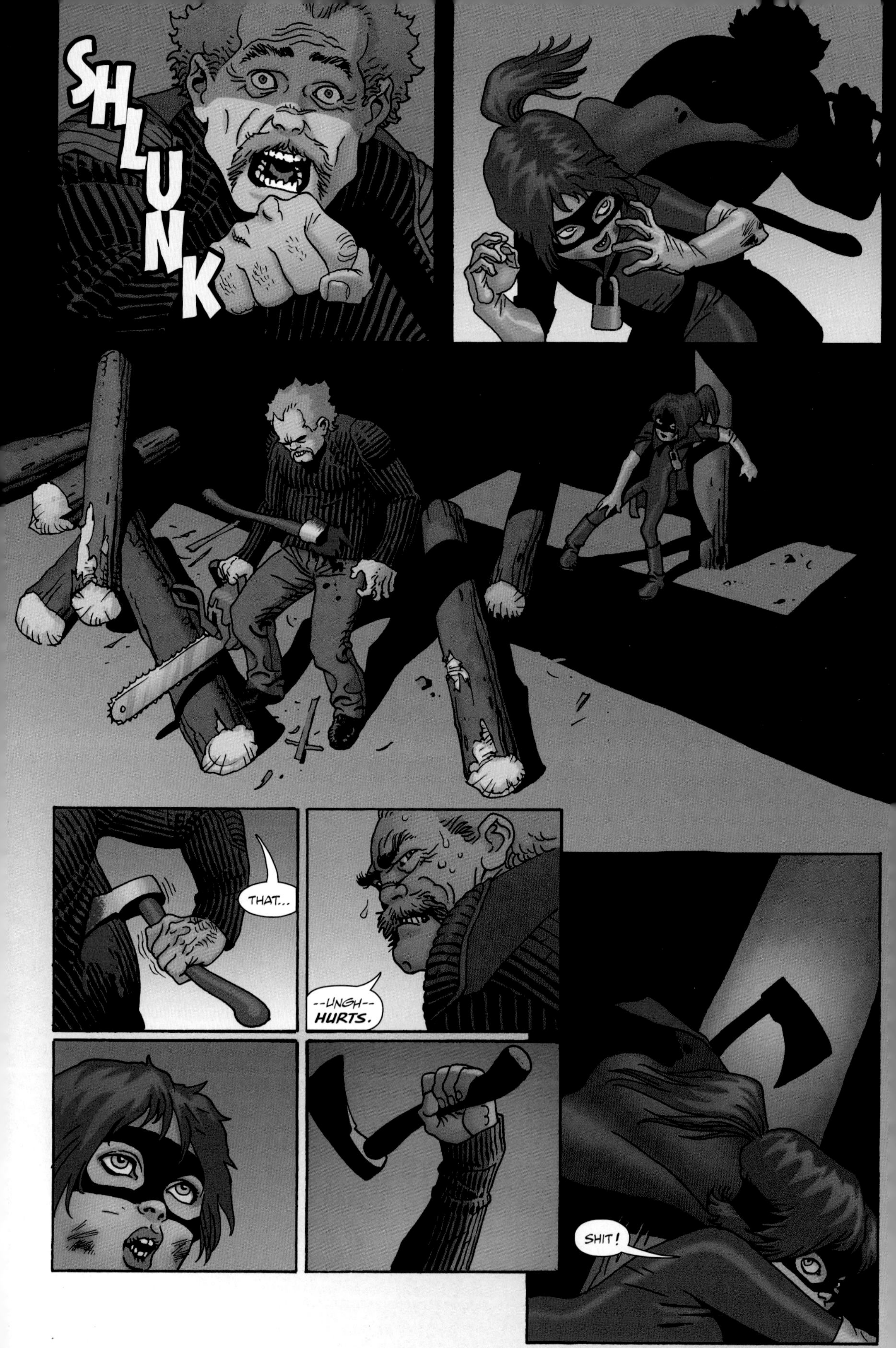
SHLUNK
THAT...
--UNGH--
HURTS.
SHIT!

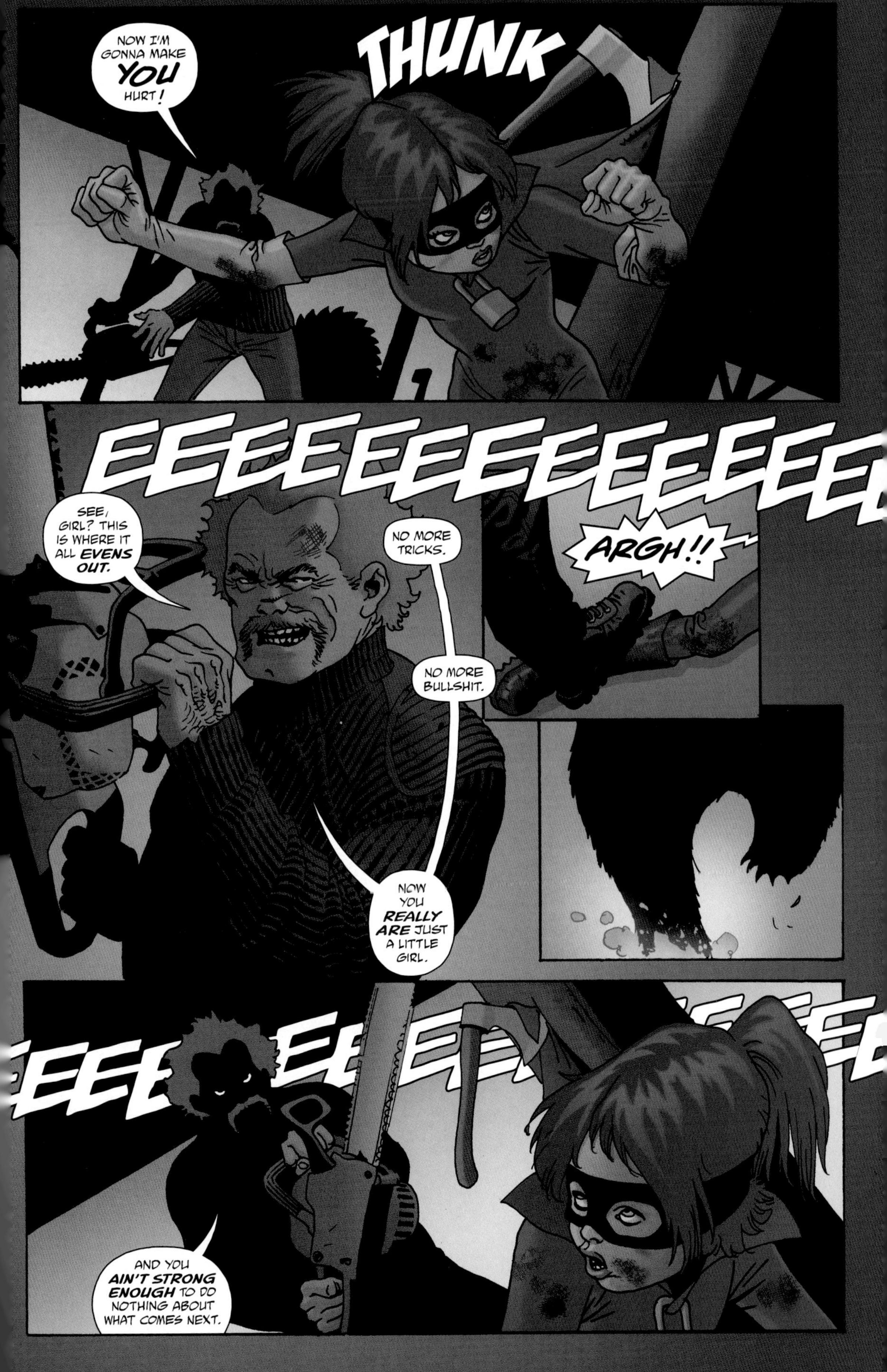
NOW I'M GONNA MAKE YOU HURT!
THUNK
EEEEEEEEEEEEEEEE
SEE, GIRL? THIS IS WHERE IT ALL EVENS OUT.
NO MORE TRICKS.
NO MORE BULLSHIT.
NOW YOU REALLY ARE JUST A LITTLE GIRL.
ARGH!!
EEEEEEEEEEE
AND YOU AIN'T STRONG ENOUGH TO DO NOTHING ABOUT WHAT COMES NEXT.

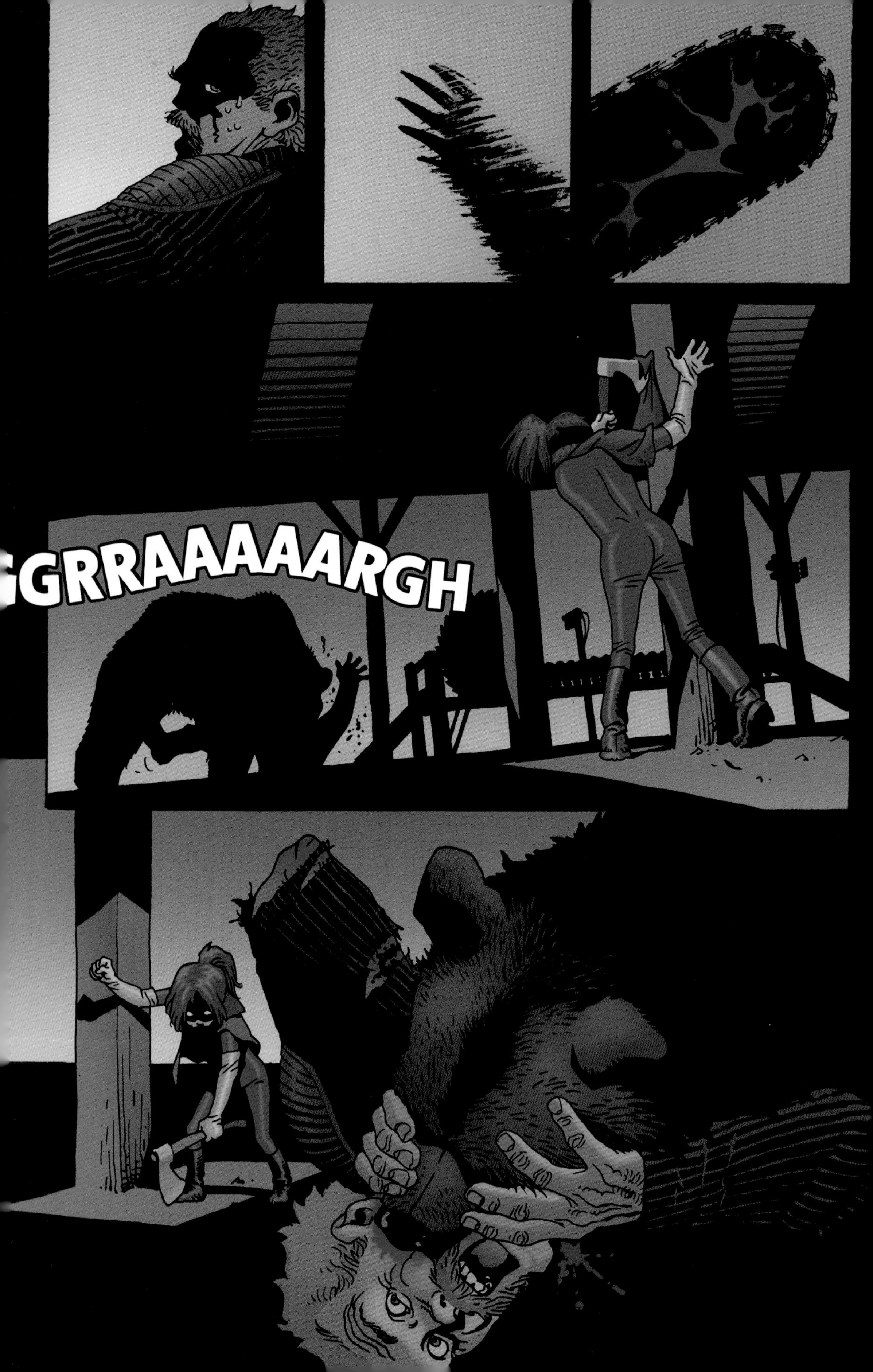
GRRAAAAAARGH

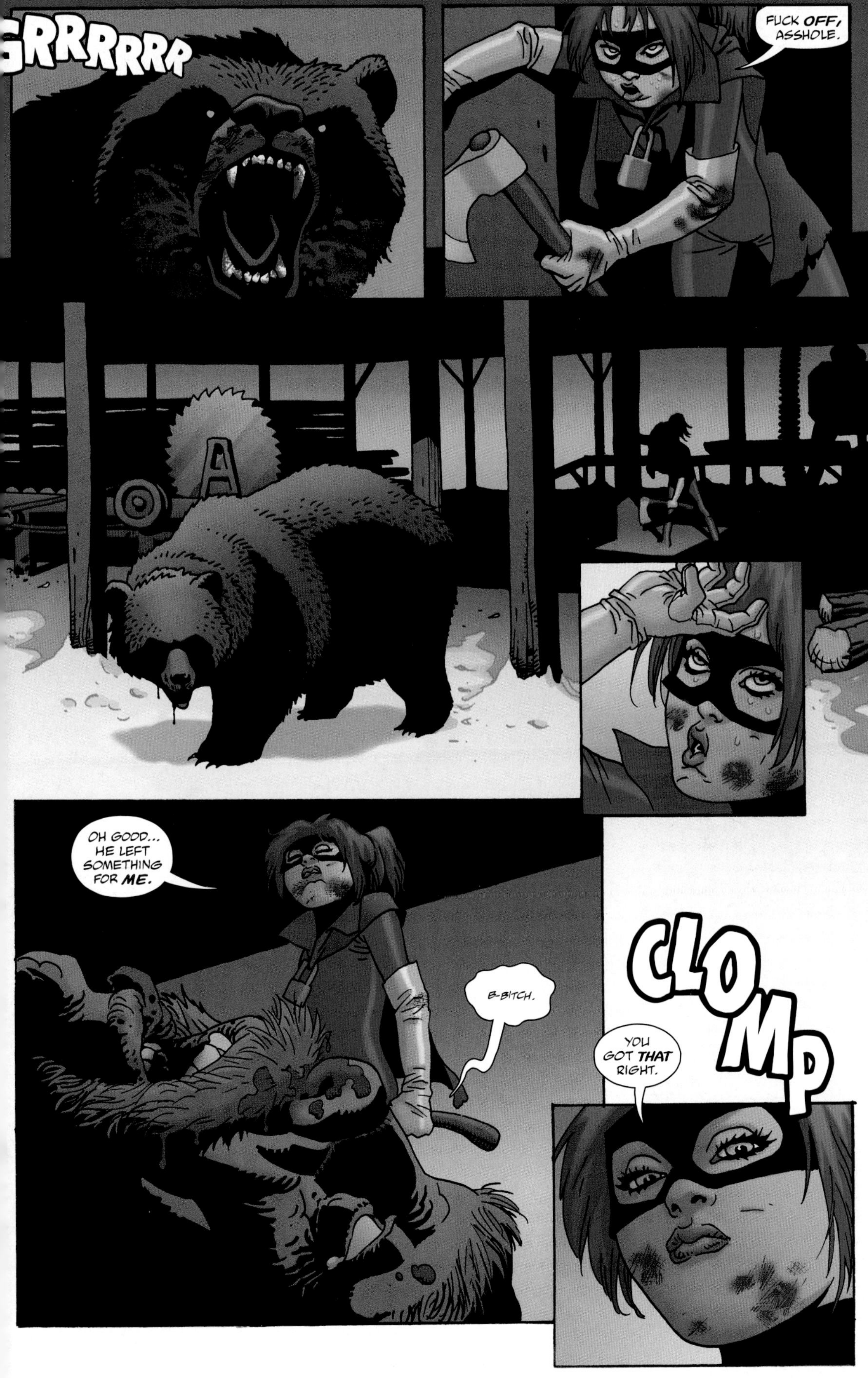
GRRRRRR
FUCK OFF, ASSHOLE.
OH GOOD... HE LEFT SOMETHING FOR ME.
B-BITCH.
CLOMP
YOU GOT THAT RIGHT.

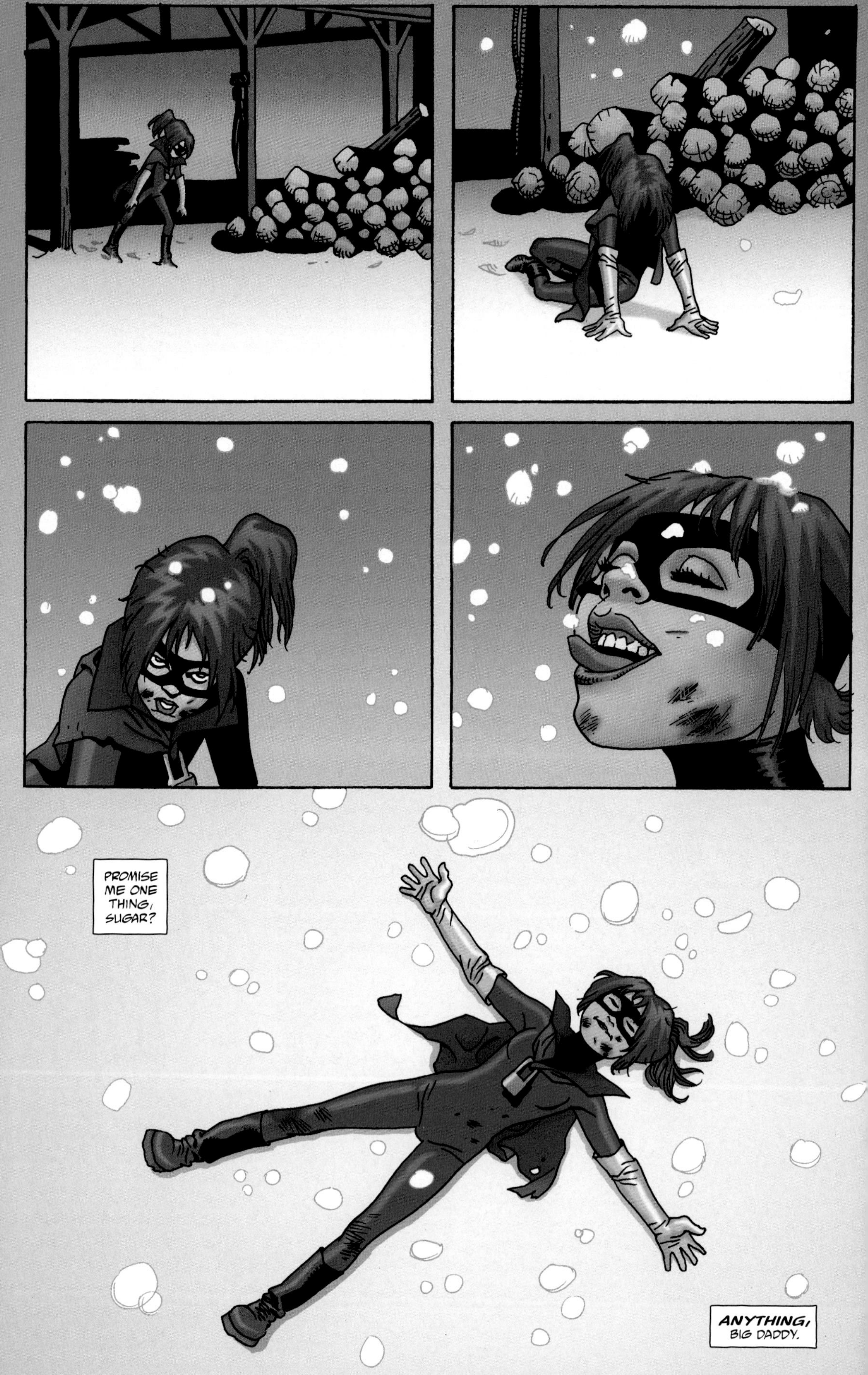
PROMISE ME ONE THING, SUGAR?
ANYTHING, BIG DADDY.

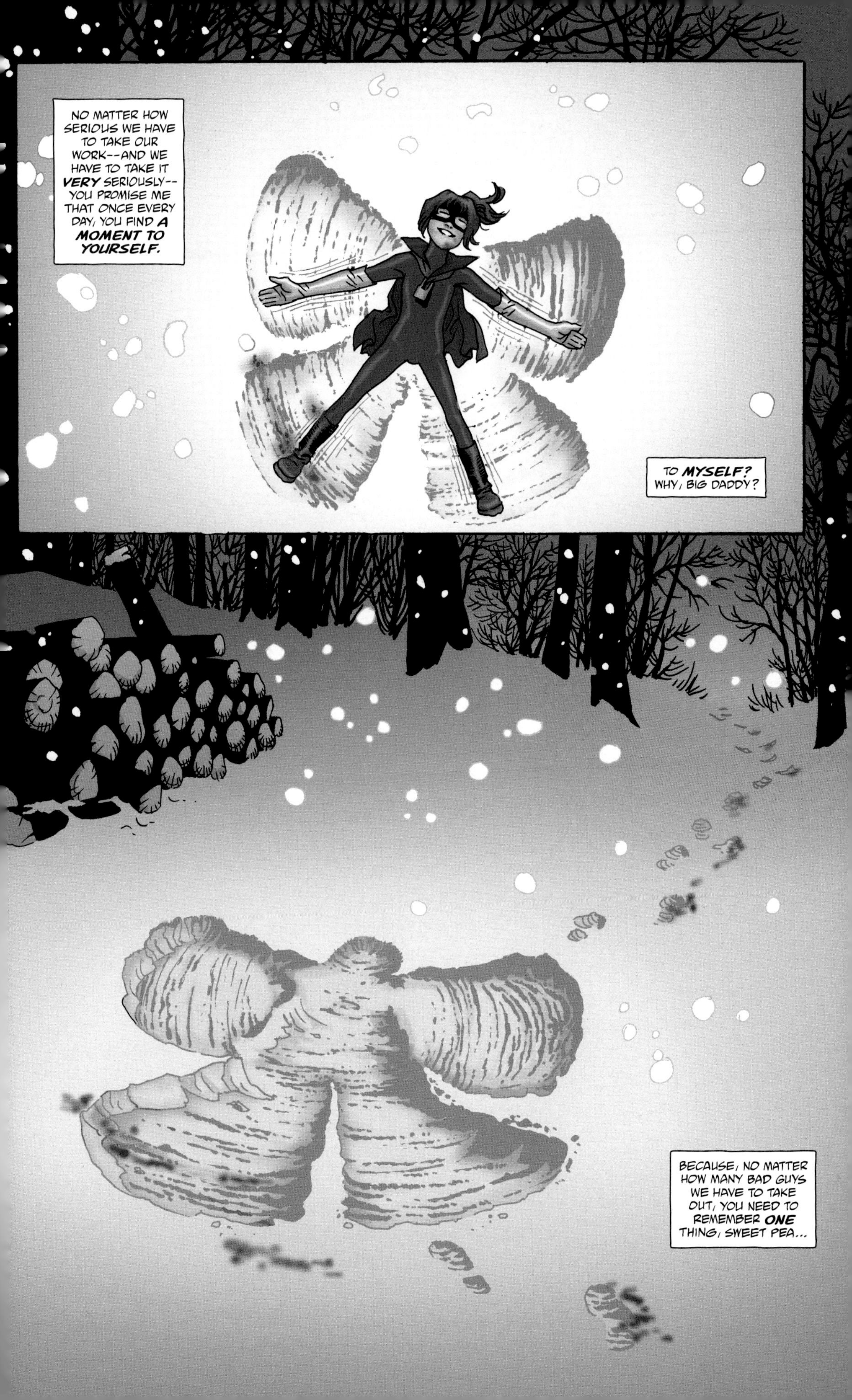
NO MATTER HOW SERIOUS WE HAVE TO TAKE OUR WORK--AND WE HAVE TO TAKE IT VERY SERIOUSLY--YOU PROMISE ME THAT ONCE EVERY DAY, YOU FIND A MOMENT TO YOURSELF.
TO MYSELF? WHY, BIG DADDY?
BECAUSE, NO MATTER HOW MANY BAD GUYS WE HAVE TO TAKE OUT, YOU NEED TO REMEMBER ONE THING, SWEET PEA...

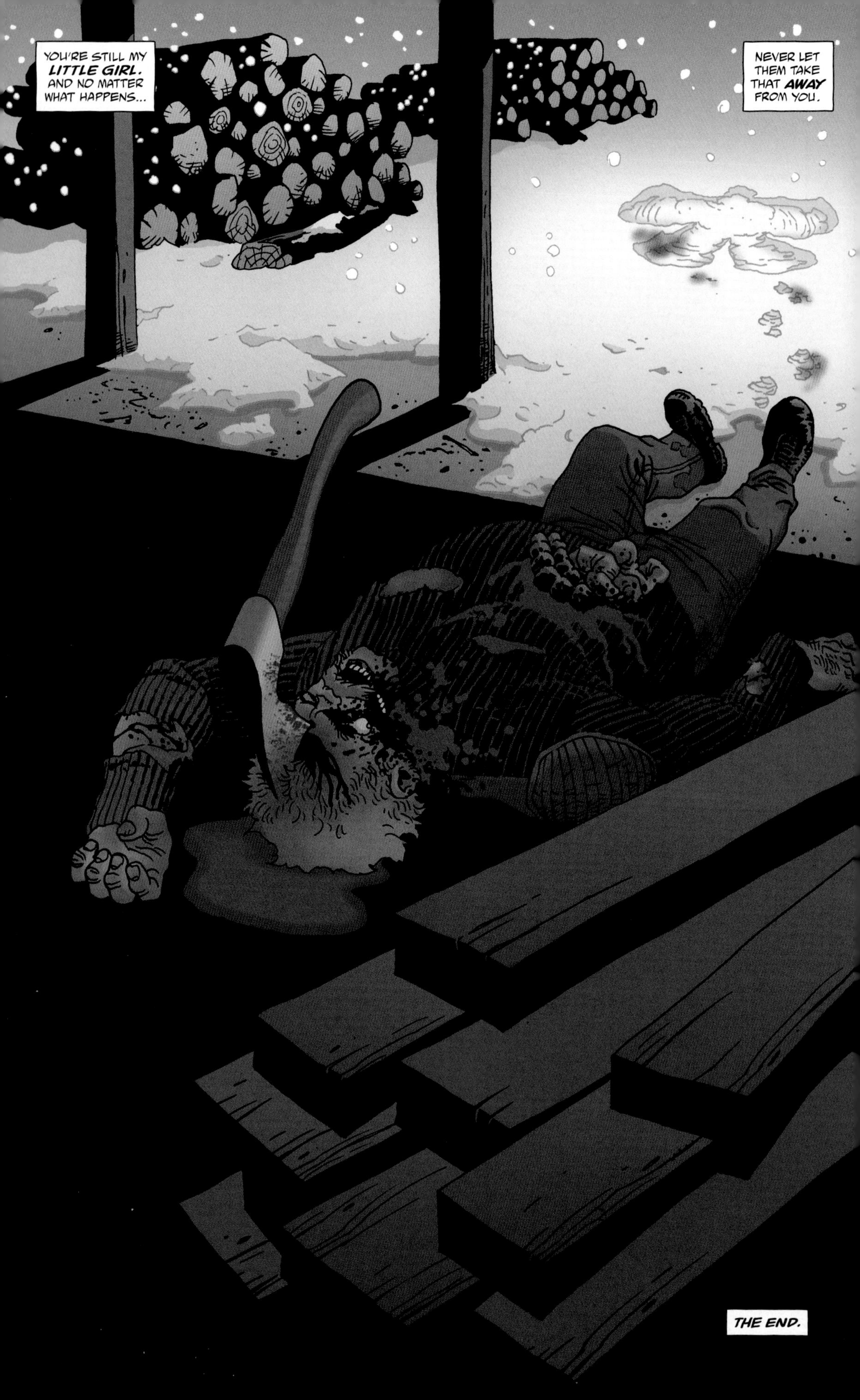
YOU'RE STILL MY LITTLE GIRL. AND NO MATTER WHAT HAPPENS...
NEVER LET THEM TAKE THAT AWAY FROM YOU.
THE END.

EDUARDO RISSO

CHARACTER DESIGNS

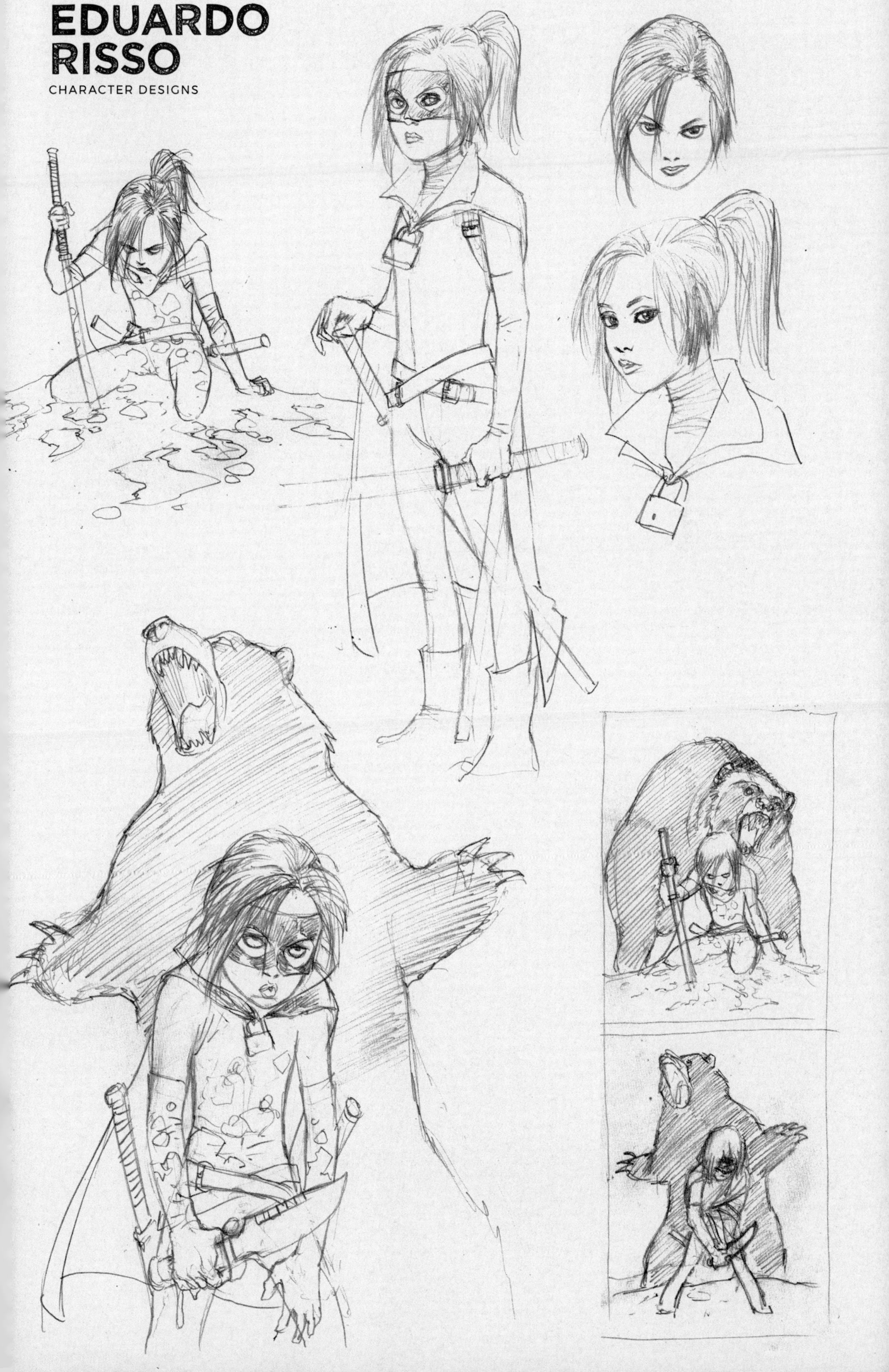

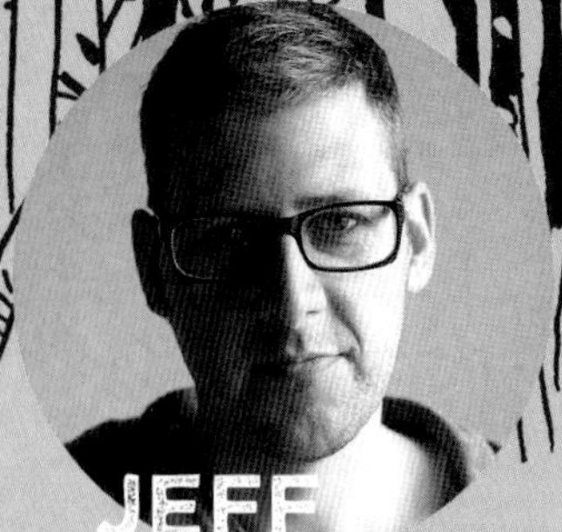

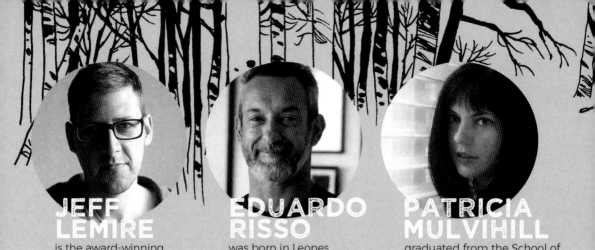

JEFF LEMIRE

is the award-winning, *New York Times* bestselling author of such graphic novels as **ESSEX COUNTY**, **SWEET TOOTH**, **UNDERWATER WELDER** and **ROUGHNECK**, as well as being co-creator of **DESCENDER** with Dustin Nguyen, **BLACK HAMMER** with Dean Ormston, **PLUTONA** with Emi Lenox and **AD: AFTER DEATH** with Scott Snyder.

He also collaborated with celebrated musician Gord Downie on the graphic novel and album **THE SECRET PATH**, which was made into an animated film in 2016. Jeff has won numerous awards, including an Eisner Award and Juno Award in 2017. Jeff has also written extensively for both Marvel and DC Comics.

Many of his books are currently in development for film and television, including both **DESCENDER** and **A.D. AFTER DEATH** at Sony Pictures, **ESSEX COUNTY** at the CBC and **PLUTONA** at Waypoint Entertainment, for which Lemire is writing the screenplay.

He lives in Toronto, Canada with his wife and son and their troublesome pug, Lola.

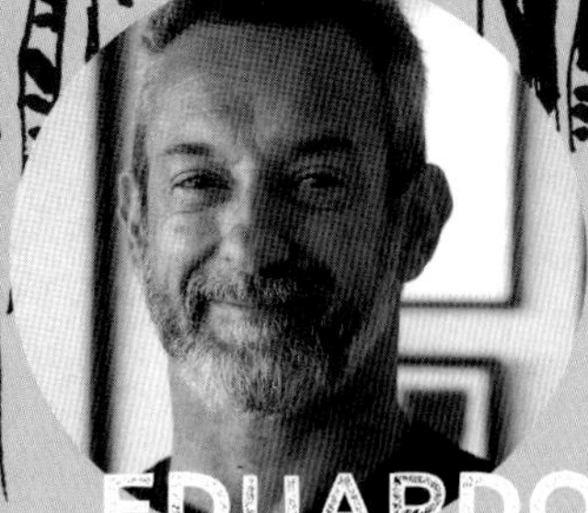

EDUARDO RISSO

was born in Leones, Argentina, in 1959. Some of his best-known works include **CAÍN** and **PARQUE CHAS** with Ricardo Barreiro, and **JONNY DOUBLE**, **100 BULLETS**, **SPACEMAN**, **BROTHER LONO**, **BATMAN: BLACK & WHITE**, **BROKEN CITY**, and **KNIGHT OF VENGEANCE** with Brian Azzarello.

With Carlos Trillo, he has created: **FULÚ**, **SIMÓN**, **VIDEO NOIR**, **BORDERLINE**, **BOY VAMPIRO**, **LUAN ROJA**, **CHICANOS**, and **TALES OF TERROR**. He also worked with Paul Dini on **DARK NIGHT: A TRUE BATMAN STORY**.

He is currently working on **MOONSHINE** with Brian Azzarello and **TORPEDO 1972** with Enrique Sanchez Abulí. He has won several industry awards over the years, including three Eisners and three Harveys.

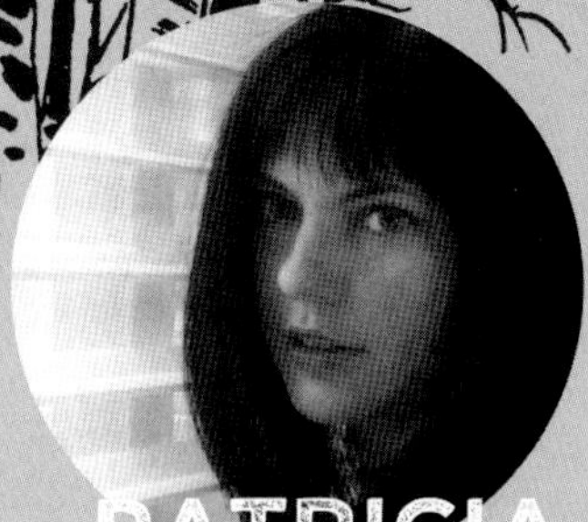

PATRICIA MULVIHILL

graduated from the School of Visual Arts in New York City as an Illustration major, and spent several years painting book jackets and working for the American Ballet Theatre.

Her career detoured after she visited DC Comics, which was — at the time — located next to her apartment building. Her first and longest run as a colorist was on **WONDER WOMAN**, and over the years she has contributed to numerous titles, including **100 BULLETS**, **JOKER**, **WEDNESDAY COMICS** and **100 BULLETS: BROTHER LONO**.

After spending a decade as a family caregiver in Westchester, NY, she is currently preparing to move back to NYC and immerse herself in the city's creativity.

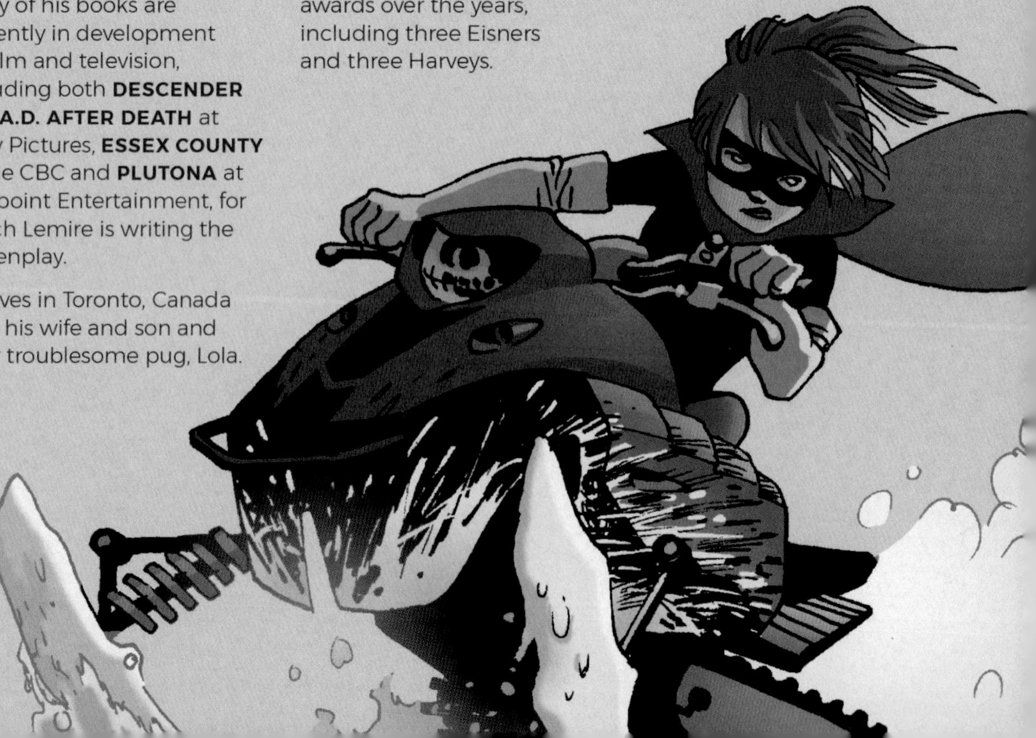

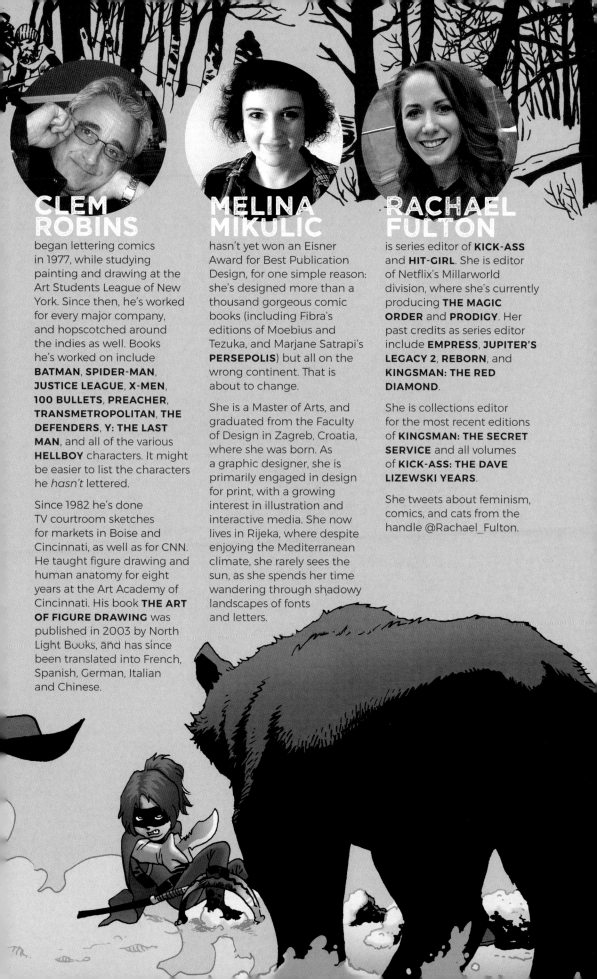

CLEM ROBINS

began lettering comics in 1977, while studying painting and drawing at the Art Students League of New York. Since then, he's worked for every major company, and hopscotched around the indies as well. Books he's worked on include **BATMAN**, **SPIDER-MAN**, **JUSTICE LEAGUE**, **X-MEN**, **100 BULLETS**, **PREACHER**, **TRANSMETROPOLITAN**, **THE DEFENDERS**, **Y: THE LAST MAN**, and all of the various **HELLBOY** characters. It might be easier to list the characters he *hasn't* lettered.

Since 1982 he's done TV courtroom sketches for markets in Boise and Cincinnati, as well as for CNN. He taught figure drawing and human anatomy for eight years at the Art Academy of Cincinnati. His book **THE ART OF FIGURE DRAWING** was published in 2003 by North Light Books, and has since been translated into French, Spanish, German, Italian and Chinese.

MELINA MIKULIC

hasn't yet won an Eisner Award for Best Publication Design, for one simple reason: she's designed more than a thousand gorgeous comic books (including Fibra's editions of Moebius and Tezuka, and Marjane Satrapi's **PERSEPOLIS**) but all on the wrong continent. That is about to change.

She is a Master of Arts, and graduated from the Faculty of Design in Zagreb, Croatia, where she was born. As a graphic designer, she is primarily engaged in design for print, with a growing interest in illustration and interactive media. She now lives in Rijeka, where despite enjoying the Mediterranean climate, she rarely sees the sun, as she spends her time wandering through shadowy landscapes of fonts and letters.

RACHAEL FULTON

is series editor of **KICK-ASS** and **HIT-GIRL**. She is editor of Netflix's Millarworld division, where she's currently producing **THE MAGIC ORDER** and **PRODIGY**. Her past credits as series editor include **EMPRESS**, **JUPITER'S LEGACY 2**, **REBORN**, and **KINGSMAN: THE RED DIAMOND**.

She is collections editor for the most recent editions of **KINGSMAN: THE SECRET SERVICE** and all volumes of **KICK-ASS: THE DAVE LIZEWSKI YEARS**.

She tweets about feminism, comics, and cats from the handle @Rachael_Fulton.

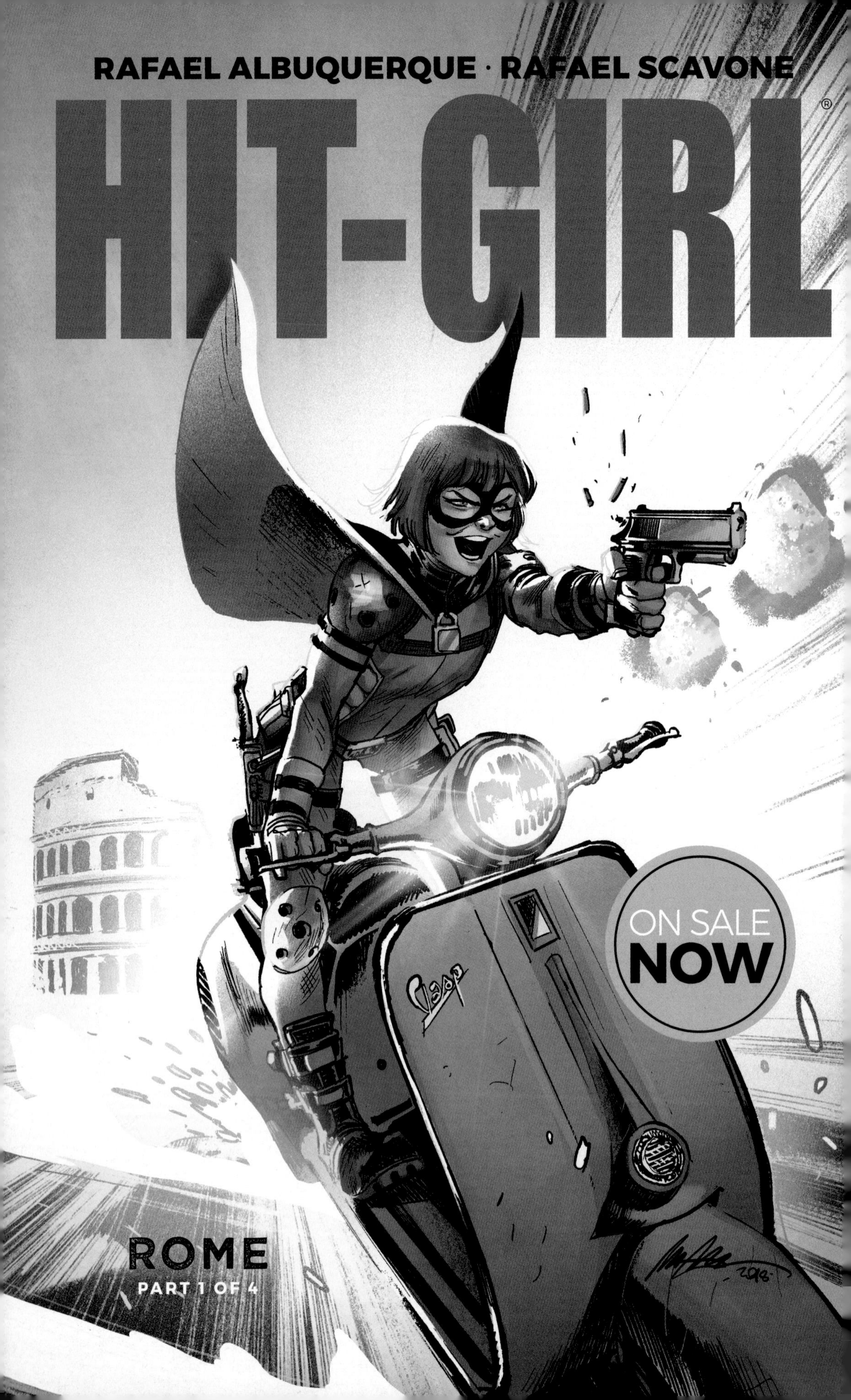
RAFAEL ALBUQUERQUE · RAFAEL SCAVONE
HIT-GIRL®
ON SALE NOW
ROME
PART 1 OF 4

The COMPLETE KICK-ASS and HIT-GIRL

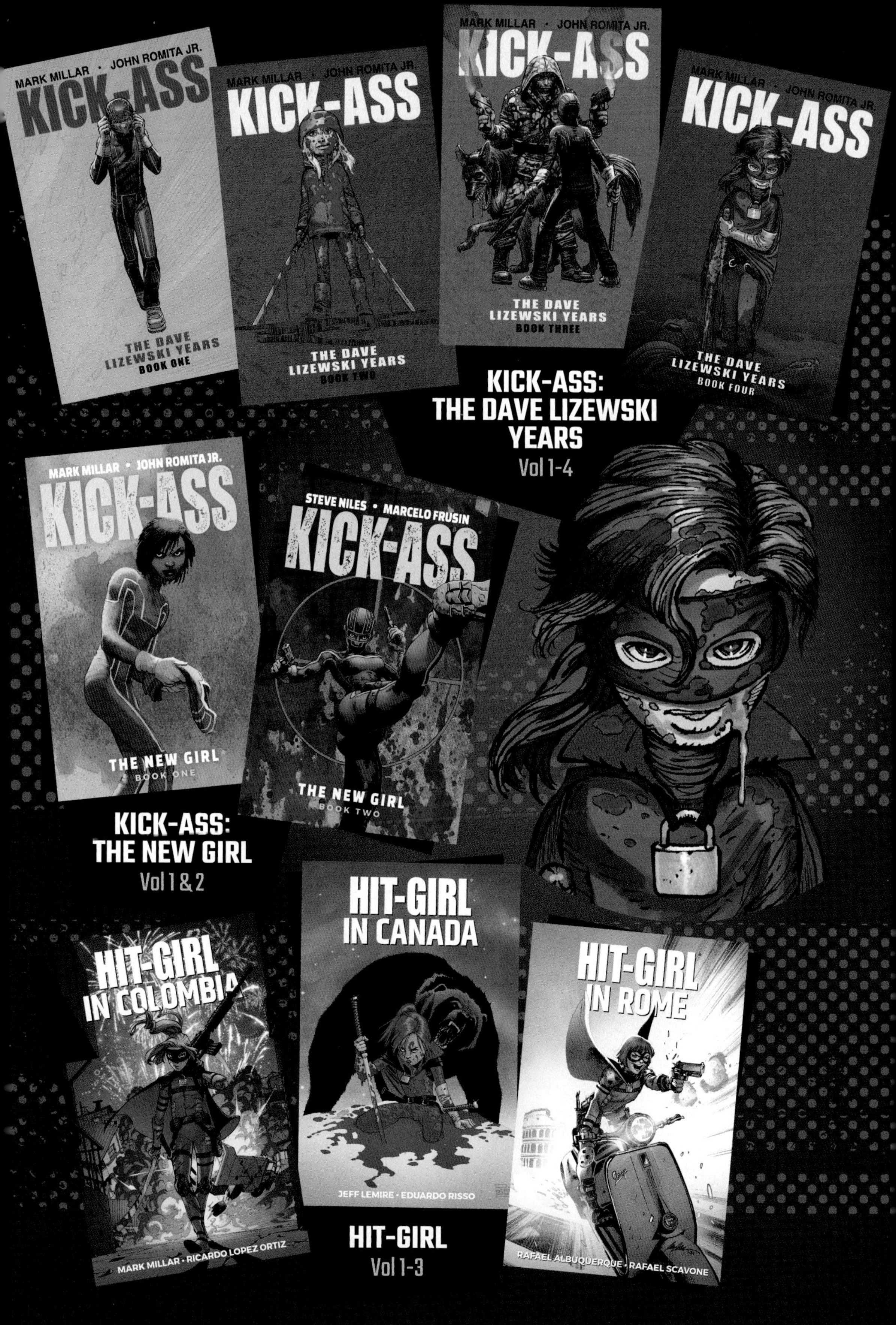
MARK MILLAR · JOHN ROMITA JR.
KICK-ASS
THE DAVE LIZEWSKI YEARS
BOOK ONE
MARK MILLAR · JOHN ROMITA JR.
KICK-ASS
THE DAVE LIZEWSKI YEARS
BOOK TWO
MARK MILLAR · JOHN ROMITA JR.
KICK-ASS
THE DAVE LIZEWSKI YEARS
BOOK THREE
MARK MILLAR · JOHN ROMITA JR.
KICK-ASS
THE DAVE LIZEWSKI YEARS
BOOK FOUR
MARK MILLAR · JOHN ROMITA JR.
KICK-ASS
THE NEW GIRL
BOOK ONE
STEVE NILES · MARCELO FRUSIN
KICK-ASS
THE NEW GIRL
BOOK TWO
HIT-GIRL
IN COLOMBIA
MARK MILLAR · RICARDO LOPEZ ORTIZ
HIT-GIRL
IN CANADA
JEFF LEMIRE · EDUARDO RISSO
HIT-GIRL
IN ROME
RAFAEL ALBUQUERQUE · RAFAEL SCAVONE

KICK-ASS: THE DAVE LIZEWSKI YEARS
Vol 1-4

KICK-ASS: THE NEW GIRL
Vol 1 & 2

HIT-GIRL
Vol 1-3

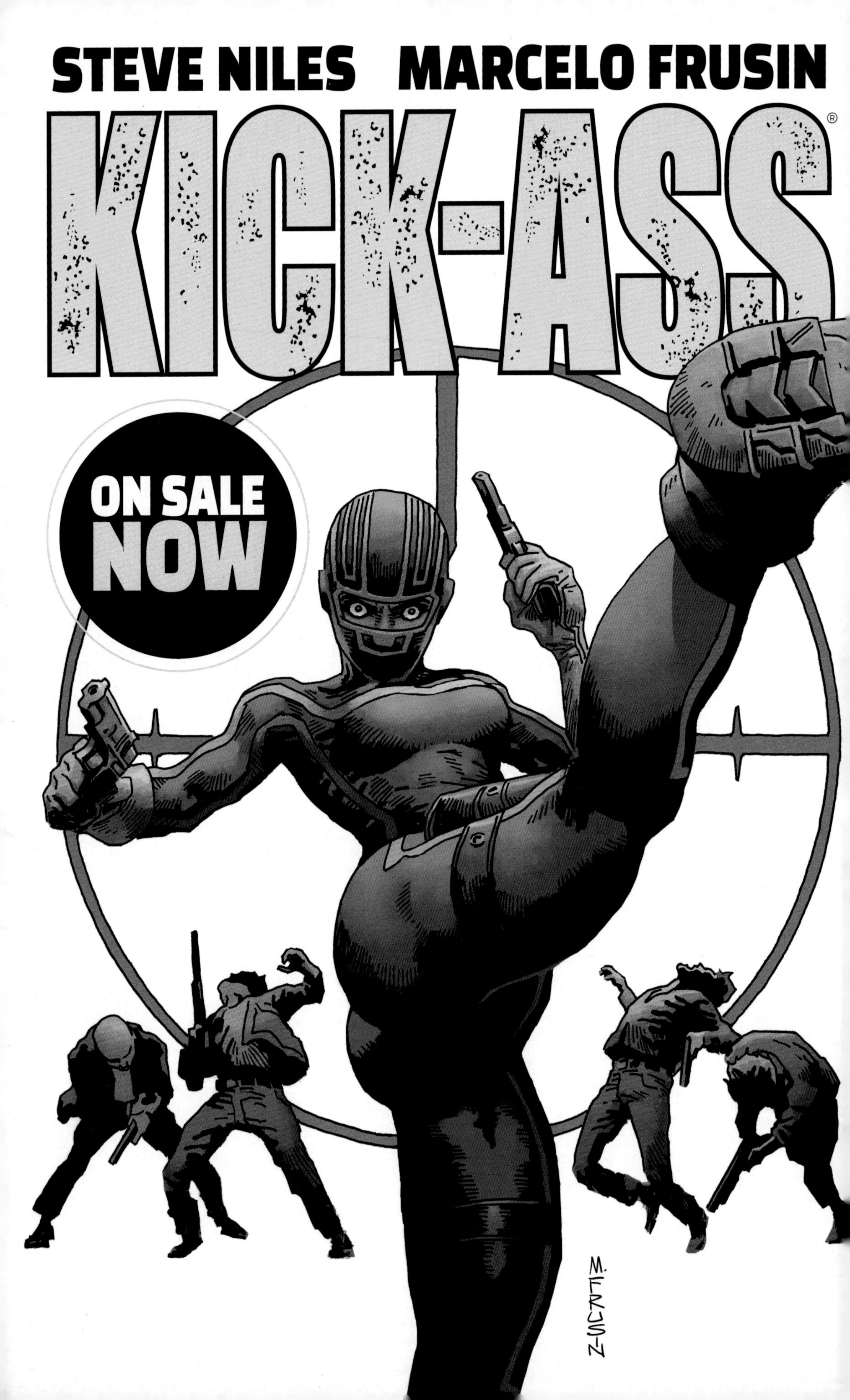
STEVE NILES
MARCELO FRUSIN
KICK-ASS®
ON SALE NOW
M. FRUSIN

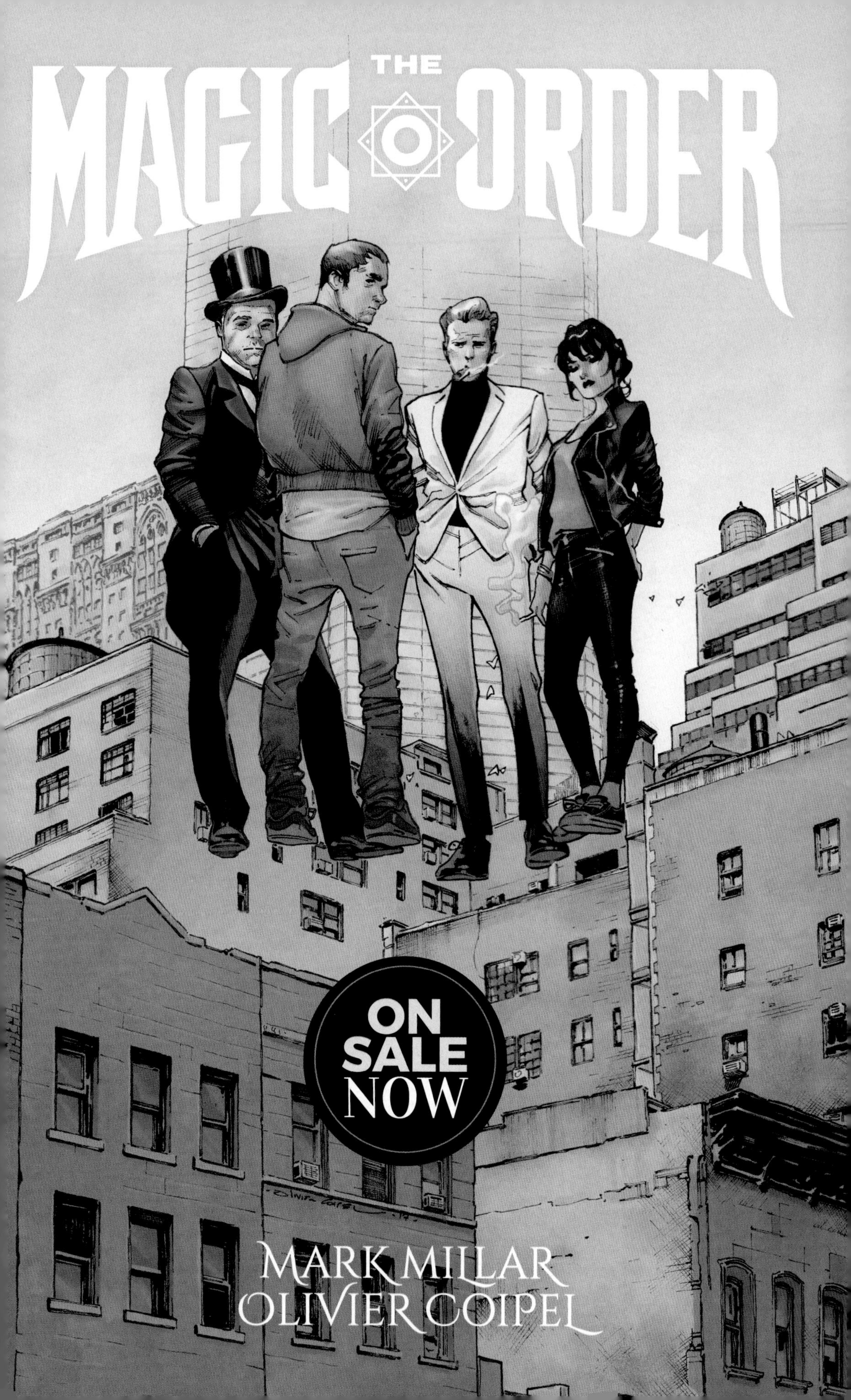
THE MAGIC ORDER
ON SALE NOW
MARK MILLAR
OLIVIER COIPEL

MILLARWORLD

THE COLLECTION CHECKLIST

✓

EMPRESS
Art by Stuart Immonen

HUCK
Art by Rafael Albuquerque

CHRONONAUTS
Art by Sean Gordon Murphy

MPH
Art by Duncan Fegredo

STARLIGHT
Art by Goran Parlov

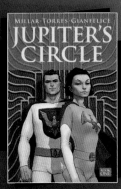

JUPITER'S CIRCLE 1 & 2
Art by Wilfredo Torres

JUPITER'S LEGACY
Art by Frank Quitely

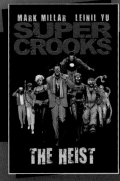

SUPER CROOKS
Art by Leinil Yu

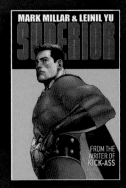

SUPERIOR
Art by Leinil Yu

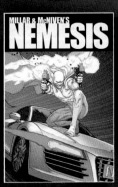

NEMESIS
Art by Steve McNiven

REBORN
Art by Greg Capullo

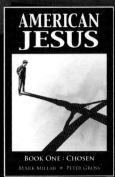

AMERICAN JESUS
Art by Peter Gross